DATE DUE

MY 02			

DEMCO 38-296

THE NATURAL HISTORY OF
CHINA

THE NATURAL HISTORY OF

CHINA

Zhao Ji, General Editor
Zheng Guangmei, Wang Huadong, Xu Jialin

Foreword by Christopher Elliott

McGraw-Hill Publishing Company
New York · St Louis
San Francisco · Toronto

Copyright © 1990 Swallow Publishing Limited
First US publication in 1989 by
McGraw-Hill Book Company

Swallow Books would like to emphasize that
the opinions expressed in the Foreword are those of
Christopher Elliott, and not those of the authors.

Art Director Elaine Partington
Designer Mick Keates
Project Editor Carolyn Pyrah
Editor Jonathan Elphick
Production Manager Siân Jones
Cartographers Swanston Graphics
Picture Researcher Liz Eddison
Typeset by Bournetype

Library of Congress Cataloging-in-Publication Data

The Natural History of China / by Zhao Ji, general editor,
Zheng Guangmei, Wang Huadong, Xu Jialin.
    p.   cm.
Includes bibliographical references.
ISBN 0–07–010752–1
1. Natural history –– China.   I. Zhao Ji.
QH 181.N37   1990   '89–13746
508.51––dc20   CIP

Colour origination and printing
in Hong Kong for Imago

Page 1: Black-faced Spoonbill (Zhang Cizu)
Page 2: Jiuzhaigou Nature Reserve (People's
Pictorial)
Pages 4–5: Tiger (Zhang Cizu)
Page 6: Mount Yujun, Hunan Province (Zhao Ji)

CONTENTS

Authors' Acknowledgments

Many people have contributed to writing and editing *The Natural History of China*. We would like to express our gratitude to Mr Stephen Adamson, Editorial Director, for his help in initiating the project. We would also like to thank Professor Zhang Lansheng, and Ms Millie Yung, China Programme Advisor of the World Wide Fund for Nature, for their help and encouragement while we were writing the book. Sincere thanks to our colleagues and friends Jiang Hong, Qin Wei, Sun Yuehua, Han Chanyu, Liu Feng, Liu Huipeng, Wang Jian, Liu Junping, Zhuang Weile and Peng Qingxiang, who participated in translation, researched information and offered valuable assistance in many ways. We are grateful to Mr Zhang Cizu and many other scientists who have allowed us to use their photographs.

FOREWORD

The variety of China's landscapes is greater than that of any other country. The landscapes range from the deserts of the north-west to the tropical forests in Yunnan, from the peak of Mount Qomolangma (Mount Everest) at almost 9000 metres (29,250 ft), to the Turfan Depression at 154 metres (505 ft) below sea level.

China is also rich in both cultural and biological diversity. The country has 56 minority nationalities, over 400 species of mammals, and over 24,000 plant species.

The country is the centre of the longest continuous civilization that the world has known. Written documents over 3000 years old survive to this day. While the Babylonians and Assyrians mismanaged their water resources, deforested their river catchment areas and turned their croplands to desert, the Chinese have cultivated the same fields in some areas for over forty centuries. The longevity of Chinese civilization must be attributed in part to sound environmental practices in agriculture and water conservancy. Wildlife management also has a long tradition in China.

Unfortunately, despite cultural traditions that stress harmony between man and nature, over the millenia China's natural heritage has become seriously depleted, a process which has accelerated in recent times. Species such as Przewalski's Horse, rhinoceroses and tapirs have become extinct and others such as the South China Tiger, the Giant Panda and the Crested Ibis are critically endangered.

Deforestation was chronicled as long ago as 500 BC by the philosopher Mencius: 'The Bull Mountain was covered by lovely trees. But it is near the capital of a great state. People came with their axes and choppers; they cut the woods down, and the mountain lost its beauty. Yet, even so, the day air and the night air came to it, and rain and dew moistened it till here and there fresh shoots began to grow. But soon cattle and sheep came along and grazed on them, and in the end the mountain became gaunt and bare as it is now; and seeing it thus gaunt and bare, people imagine that it was woodless from the start.'

Nowadays, despite sophisticated agricultural practices which have allowed the same fields to be cultivated for thousands of years, pesticides and soil erosion are causing increasing problems. In the 1950s, following Mao Zedong's dictum 'make grain the key link', large areas of natural habitat were put under the plough to grow crops, in answer to the pressing need to feed China's growing population. However, many of these areas were unsuitable for agriculture and yielded little. Important natural habitats were destroyed in the process; for example, Cao Hai Lake in Guizhou Province, which is a major breeding ground for the rare Black-necked Cranes, was drained and shrank from 45 square kilometres (18 square miles) to 4 square kilometres (1.6 square miles), causing the birds to abandon the area. The population increase also resulted in the growth of towns, road construction and the spread of industry, which encroached on wildlife habitats and increased the level of pollution. More recently the area of land used for agricultural purposes has declined due to industrial expansion, and this poses its own problems for the population.

Also in the 1950s, a war against the four pests (rats, mosquitoes, houseflies and sparrows) was declared, leading to a massive reduction in bird populations for whom the pests provide food. Even today, visitors to China are often surprised by the lack of birds in both the cities and the countryside.

The Cultural Revolution followed from 1966 to 1976, during which time the conservation activities which had begun in the 1950s came to a virtual halt, and large parts of the education system reached a standstill. The resulting lack of trained personnel, and consequent difficulties in many spheres of activity, including conservation, is still felt to this day.

Despite these policies and their consequences, there is hope for nature in China. In recent times, some policies have been changed and new laws protecting wildlife and regulating industry to reduce pollution have been drafted. Cao Hai Lake has now re-emerged and is over 30 square kilometres (12 square miles) wide, and hundreds of Black-necked Cranes have returned. Public awareness about conservation is growing fast and has meant that a controversial project to build the world's largest dam in the Yangtze Gorges region has been shelved.

The problems are still severe, however: China's forest resources are severely depleted and can no longer meet the country's timber needs. The air and water in many of China's cities are polluted, and there are difficulties in implementing many of the new wildlife laws. In recent years China has begun to collaborate with conservation organizations, governments and United Nations agencies to improve natural resource management. Such collaboration will be particularly important in relation to air pollution, which not only affects China but also contributes to the 'greenhouse effect' worldwide.

Outside China most of us have until now had only a sketchy idea of the wealth of China's natural resources, and thus the importance of conserving them. The authors, from one of China's leading universities, have collated a wide range of previously unpublished information, about some of which there has been conflicting evidence in the past (largely due to difficulty in accessing information). Here the information is presented in a clear and concise manner, and I hope this will help create awareness of the beauty and extent of China's natural world.

Christopher Elliott
China Programme Co-ordinator
WWF – World Wide Fund for Nature

INTRODUCTION 导言

China is a vast country. From east to west it covers 60 degrees of longitude – a sixth of the world's circumference – while from north to south it encompasses 50 degrees of latitude. Its climate ranges from cool-temperate in the north to tropical in the south, with humidity levels rising from those of arid desert to tropical rain forest. The world's highest peak, Mount Qomolangma (Everest) at 8848 metres (29,028 ft), and second lowest land, around Aydingkol Lake at −154 metres (−505 ft), are located in China. The country has a wide variety of forests, grasslands and deserts; as well as huge mountains it has vast plateaux; it also has many extensive rivers and lakes. All these natural features combine to create a wide diversity of environments suitable for a dazzling array of plants and animals, many of which have become familiar throughout the world as a result of their introductions to other countries.

Location

China occupies much of the eastern part of Asia. The northernmost point is located in the middle of the Heilong River, to the north of Mohe, Heilongjiang Province, at a latitude of 53° 31′N. The southernmost point is Zengmu Shoal in the Nansha Islands at a latitude of about 4°N. Most of the territory lies in the temperate and subtropical zones where there are distinct seasons, but a small part of southern China is in the tropical zone and experiences high temperatures and heavy rainfall throughout the year. This means that in early spring, when Heilongjiang in the north is covered with ice and snow, the people of Hainan Dao Island off the southern coast of the mainland are busy planting their crops, and the islanders in the South China Sea are baking under the tropical sun.

The westernmost point of China is the western tip of Xinjiang Autonomous Region in the Tien mountain range, at a longitude of roughly 73°E. The easternmost point is the confluence of the Wusuli River and the Heilong River, at longitude 135° 5′E. From east to west the time difference is more than four hours: when the sun rises in the morning on the Wusuli River, the stars are still bright in the night sky above the Tien Mountains.

Area

The total land area in China is approximately 9,600,000 square kilometres (about 3,750,000 square miles). This constitutes one fifteenth of the total land surface worldwide and one quarter of the total area of Asia. China is the third largest country in the world, after the USSR and Canada.

Besides the mainland territories there are more than 5000 islands scattered along the coast, the southernmost of these being some 1800 kilometres (1118 miles) from the mainland. About nine out of ten of these islands are in the East China Sea and the South China Sea; the rest are in the Bo Hai Sea and the Yellow Sea, north of Shanghai. Taiwan Island is the largest island in China with an area of 36,000 square kilometres (13,900 square miles), and Hainan Dao Island is the second largest with an area of 34,000 square kilometres (13,127 square miles). The Zhoushan Islands along the coast of Zhejiang Province form the largest archipelago. Some of the islands are made up of coral reefs; these include the Xisha Islands, the Zhongshan Islands and the Nansha Islands, all in the South China Sea.

For administration purposes, China is divided into 23 provinces, five autonomous regions and three municipalities. The municipalities are Beijing, the nearby Tianjin, and Shanghai, which come directly under the Central Government.

PREVIOUS PAGE: this man harrowing in a rice field reflects a typical Western image of rural China and demonstrates just one way in which man influences the environment.

Population

Autumn colours seen from the Great Wall of China give an impression of the great diversity of trees and forests in China.

Of all the countries in the world, China has the largest population. In 1989 there were 1,100,000,000 Chinese, which amounts to as much as 22 per cent of the population of the planet. As elsewhere, population growth has been accelerating tremendously in recent years. During the Western Han Dynasty (206BC to AD24), the population numbered approximately 60 million people, and during the ensuing 1700 years, from the Western Han Dynasty to the early Qing Dynasty, the population remained stable at between 60 and 70 million. By 1741, though, the population had increased to more than 100 million. This was the start of an upward trend, and when the People's Republic of China was founded in 1949, a mere 208 years later, the population had reached 540 million people. Forty years on the population has more than doubled again.

CHINA'S ADMINISTRATIVE REGIONS

1 Beijing Municipality
2 Tianjin Municipality
3 Shanghai Municipality
4 Ningxia Autonomous Region

Large as China is, it cannot comfortably accommodate such a huge number of people. The population density is 114 people per square kilometre (296 per square mile), which is about three times the world's average density. Owing to environmental conditions, the historical development of the country and the social economy, the distribution of people is also very uneven. A line drawn on the map from Mohe in Heilongjiang Province to Tengchong in Yunnan Province defines two contrasting areas. The south-eastern part accounts for about 43 per cent of the total area of the country, yet 94 per cent of the population live there. The average density in the south-east is 236 people per square kilometre (611 per square mile). However, the north-western part, 57 per cent of the total land area, supports only six per cent of the people: a density of 10.6 per square kilometre (27.4 per square mile).

In recent decades, people have been encouraged to migrate from the coastal areas to the sparsely populated west, as part of a scheme to develop the latter area. Over the last 30 years, about 25 to 30 million people have made the move. As well as favouring re-location, the Chinese government has been encouraging family planning as a means of controlling the population increase in the south-east.

It should be mentioned here that some desert oases in the north-western area have a population density that approaches that of the south-east. For example, in Urümqi and Kashi in the Xinjiang Autonomous Region, the density is about 200 people per square kilometre (518 per square mile). Naturally, the distribution of people has a considerable effect on the pattern of wildlife and vegetation.

Most of China's population is rural. It was even more so in 1949, when less than 11 per cent of Chinese lived in towns, than today. However, the development of industry, transport and commerce brought about a rapid increase in the urban population, and by the end of 1985 the urban population had grown to 36.5 per cent of the total.

Nationalities

China is a country of many nationalities. Altogether there are 56, but of these the largest by far is the Han: people of Han nationality make up more than 93 per cent of the total population. The other 55 'minority nationalities' account for only 6.7 per cent of the whole, but 6.7 per cent of the Chinese population is a lot of people – some 73 million, in fact. So in absolute terms the populations of some of the 'minority nationalities' are quite large. For example, the Zhuang nationality of the Guangxi Autonomous Region consists of 13,380,000 people. The smallest nationalities include the Luoba, who live in Tibet and number a mere 2100, while the Hezhe of Heilongjiang Province consist of only 1500 people.

Originally each nationality occupied its own area, but this is no longer so. Various migrations through history, changes of dynasty and past policies of moving garrisons or encouraging peasants to cultivate former wildernesses have gradually led to mixed nationalities across the country. This mix, however, is not uniform, as there remain many areas where, paradoxically, the minority nationalities are in the majority.

The main regions where minority nationalities live in sizeable contained communities are Inner Mongolian Autonomous Region in the north, the Xinjiang Uygur Autonomous Region and Ningxia Hui Autonomous Region in the north-west, the Tibet Autonomous Region in the south-west and Guangxi Zhuang Autonomous Region in the south. There are many such communities in the provinces of Yunnan, Guizhou, Qinghai, Sichuan and Gansu; in particular there are more than 20 minority nationalities living in Yunnan Province in the south (see chart, right).

Most of these areas are mountainous and sparsely populated. Although the minority nationalities are small, in many cases they make up a large proportion of the local population and are a major influence on the local way of life. The degree of intermarriage varies from nationality to nationality.

MINORITY NATIONALITIES WITH POPULATIONS OF MORE THAN ONE MILLION	
Nationality	Population
Zhuang	13,380,000
Hui	7,220,000
Uygur	5,960,000
Yi	5,450,000
Man	4,300,000
Zang (Tibetan)	3,870,000
Mongolian	3,410,000
Tujia	2,830,000
Buyi	2,120,000
Korean	1,760,000
Dong	1,430,000
Yao	1,400,000
Bai	1,130,000
Hani	1,060,000

Climate

Two major factors determine the nature and distribution of animals and plants in any part of the world – climate and landforms. Being situated in the south-

Originally different nationalities occupied their own areas of China, but now nationalities are mixed across the country.

eastern part of Eurasia and bordering on the Pacific Ocean, much of China is subject to a monsoon climate which is induced by the temperature difference between the land and the sea.

Winter chill

In winter, cold, dry air sinks over the Asian landmass to create a high pressure system. Pushed down by the pressure above, the cold air spills south and east: a biting wind blows southward and the temperature plummets. This normally occurs at intervals of seven to ten days. When the north-westerly wind blows in Beijing the temperature normally drops about 10°C (18°F) in a day. The wind is so strong that it is hard to walk against it.

Less dramatic southward movements of relatively light, cold air occur even more frequently, and the two in combination exert such an influence that the greater part of China is generally cold and dry throughout the winter. On average, towns in China are colder than those in other countries on the same latitude. For example, the latitude of Huma in Heilongjiang Province is almost the same as that of London, but whereas the average January temperature in London is about 4°C (39°F), in Huma it is −29°C (−20°F).

Monsoon rains

The summer monsoon originates over the Pacific Ocean and the Indian Ocean, bringing heavy rain. Basically the winter weather system goes into reverse: the warm air over the sunbaked land rises, and moisture-laden air rushes in from the oceans to take its place. As the moist air rises in turn the water condenses and falls as near-continuous rain. The amount of rainfall in any area is closely related to the movement of this monsoon weather system. If the movement is irregular, then large areas suffer either drought or flooding.

On the plains the onset of the rainy season is gradual, but in mountainous areas it begins with a sudden warm cloudburst. Over most of China the rainy season starts in May and lasts until September. Generally speaking, the front fringe of the south-eastern monsoon hits southern China in mid-May. It arrives at the middle and lower reaches of the Yangtze (Chang) River in mid-June, introducing a season of intermittent drizzle. In Chinese this is known as the 'plum rainy season', so-called for two reasons: because it coincides with the ripening of the plums, and also because of a pun on the Chinese word for plum and that for the mould that invariably spreads everywhere in the damp weather.

By the middle of July the monsoon has moved north of the Huai River, bringing the rains to northern China. When the front fringe of the summer monsoon retreats southward in late August the rains in the eastern part of China retreat with it, from north to south.

In the area to the west of longitude 105 to 110°E, the south-western monsoon originating in the Indian Ocean dominates the summer weather. In late May it pushes quickly northward, bringing increasingly heavy rain to Yunnan Province and the southern part of Sichuan Province. The rainy season does not end until the south-western monsoon retreats in October. The end of the monsoon is as abrupt as its beginning, which makes for a clear distinction between the dry and wet seasons in this area.

North and south

The difference in climate between the north and south is pronounced in winter, when the scenery is icebound throughout the northern half of the country.

In northern Heilongjiang the mean January temperature is −30°C (−22°F). By contrast the mean January temperature in southern China, such as in Guangdong, Guangxi and the southern parts of Fujian Province, is

COMPARATIVE MEAN TEMPERATURES IN EASTERN CITIES		
	January	*July*
Harbin (46°N)	−19°C (−2°F)	22.8°C (73°F)
Beijing (40°N)	−4.7°C (23.5°F)	26°C (78.8°F)
Shanghai (32°N)	3.2°C (38.7°F)	27.9°C (82.2°F)
Guangzhou (23° 30′N)	13.4°C (56°F)	28.2°C (82.8°F)

above 10°C (50°F) and the trees and grass remain green all year round. On Hainan Dao Island, southern Taiwan and in southern Yunnan Province the mean January temperature is above 15°C (68°F) and tropical rubber trees and coconut palms thrive. Even hotter than this are the islands of the South China Sea where the temperature of the coldest month ranges between 22°C (72°F) and 26°C (79°F).

Between these extremes the mean January temperatures of the cities of eastern China show the way the winter climate varies progressively according to latitude. In summer, however, the temperature is comparatively high all over China and there is little difference between north and south. In much of southern China the mean temperature in July is about 28°C (82°F). The July temperature over most of Heilongjiang Province in the north may be above 20°C (68°F). The mean temperature difference between Harbin and Guangzhou is only 5.4°C (9.7°F) in July, but 32.5°C (58.5°F) in January (see chart opposite).

This pine (*Pinus*) on Huang Mountain in Anhui Province has gradually been distorted by strong winds.

East and west

The climate of China varies considerably from east to west. One reason for this is the immense distances between these areas – some 5000 kilometres (over 3000 miles) overall. Another reason is that many mountain ranges lie between the sea and the interior. These force the moisture-laden air masses to rise repeatedly and deposit their water content on the mountains below. As a result the precipitation gradually decreases from the south-east to the north-west.

If one takes 500 mm (20 in.) annual rainfall as the boundary between humid and arid climates, China falls into two fairly equal halves. East of this line there is abundant rainfall, which nourishes dense forests and a flourishing agriculture. West of the line, with the exception of the windward mountain slopes where the precipitation is somewhat higher, the climate is dry. The landscape consists of extensive plains of grass with few trees, and deserts. Some low basins in the mountains of the north-west have an annual precipitation of less than 50 mm (2 in.).

In the east the rainfall is not, of course, evenly distributed. The north-eastern region receives 400 to 1000 mm (16 to 40 in.) of rain, the North China Plain and the Loess Plateau in northern central China experience 400 to 800 mm (16 to 32 in.) and the area stretching from the Yangtze (Chang) River to the Yunnan-Guizhou Plateau receives about 1000 mm (40 in.). The mean annual rainfall is about 2000 mm (80 in.) on the south-eastern coast, Taiwan and Hainan Dao Island, and in Huoshao Liao in Taiwan the annual rainfall may be as high as 6576 mm (259 in.). To put this in perspective, the annual precipitation is less than 200 mm (8 in.) in the Qinghai-Tibet Plateau and in the north-west.

Another feature of the rainfall that affects vegetation is the large variation in annual precipitation in any one place. For example, the mean annual precipitation in Beijing is 682.9 mm (26.9 in.), but this more than doubled to 1408 mm (55.4 in.) in the record year of 1958. Conversely, less than a quarter of this amount, 168.5 mm (6.6 in.), fell in 1891. The reason for this is the unreliability of the monsoon, which can vary considerably from year to year and frequently causes disastrous flooding or drought. As a measure of this, about 26 million hectares (64 million acres) of cultivated land are hit by some sort of natural calamity each year. Not surprisingly, water conservancy is a major Chinese priority.

Rhododendrons (*Rhododendron*) proliferate in the Wolong Nature Reserve, Sichuan, photographed here in spring.

Plant and animal life

The geographical and climatic variety of China has created a wide diversity of natural environments and a correspondingly rich natural history. In the case of angiosperms (the higher plants which incorporate ducts for transporting water and nutrients), China can boast 27,150 species – representatives of 353 families or more than half the total number of families in the world. When it comes to terrestrial vertebrates, China has more than 2100 species belonging to 156 families – about 40 per cent of the families found worldwide. There are approximately 1500 species of fish in the coastal waters and 700 species of freshwater fish in the lakes and rivers, plus a comparable variety of marine and freshwater invertebrates.

Seed-bearing plants

Of the angiosperms, 24,490 are seed-bearing plants, grouped into 2980 genera and 301 families. Among these, there are more than 2800 species of trees, over 1000 of which have commercial uses. The trees include representatives of every family of conifer and conifer-related trees (gymnosperms) with the exception of the Araucariaceae family, and as a result the forests of

China are characterized by a great variety of tree types. For example, there are more than 1400 species of trees in Hainan Dao Island alone. Southern China is internationally famous for its groves of bamboo – tall, tree-like grasses found throughout south-east Asia. Of the 1000 or so species that occur worldwide, 300 are found in China.

China also has some of the largest tracts of grassland in the world, with a total area of some five million square kilometres (two million square miles). These grasslands support more than 3600 species of seed-bearing plants, while 1000 or so species occur on the plains of the arid lands.

Because of its particular geological history, especially its having escaped the worst effects of the last ice age, China has a large number of plants that are found here and nowhere else. Among these are the bretschneidera family (Bretschneideraceae), the Dove Tree family (Davidiaceae), and the eucommia family (Eucommiaceae), all of which are trees. A particularly well-known example of these endemic plants is the Dawn Redwood (*Metasequoia glyptostroboides*), a tall, cypress-like tree which now grows wild only in eastern Sichuan, south-western Hubei, and north-western Hunan, but which flourished across much of the globe in the Tertiary period 70 million years ago. Other 'prehistoric' plants that still thrive include the Chinese Golden Larch (*Pseudolarix keaempferi*) and the Whitearil Yew (*Pseudotaxus chienii*).

Azaleas (*Rhododendron*) and maples (*Acer*) grow among water-worn rocks in Lu Yuan, Shanghai.

Plant exploitation

Of the 1200 species of cultivated plants (excluding ornamental plants) grown worldwide, more than 200 species originated in China, including highland barley (grown in Tibet and Qinghai), millet, buckwheat, soya beans, oilseed rape and sesame. The main contribution to the world's larders is probably rice, which has been grown in China for about 6700 years.

Kumquat, pomelo (large, grapefruit-like fruit) and orange all originated in China along with over 190 other species of citrus fruit, and lychee and loquat can still be seen growing wild in Guangdong Province and in the southern part of Yunnan Province. Tea, mulberry, radish, Chinese cabbage, chilli and garlic all seem to have come from China as well. A non-edible crop of worldwide significance is jute.

China has proved a rich source of ornamental plants. The Dawn Redwood and ginkgo *Ginkgo biloba* are only two of the endemic Chinese trees that are now grown in parks and gardens throughout the world, and the glorious blossoms of many rhododendrons, azaleas, roses and camellias were first seen in the mountains of China.

Wild harvest

Agriculture apart, China has a flourishing tradition of using wild plants as sources of food, fibre, chemicals and medicines. Altogether there are some 1800 species of oil-bearing plants, fibre plants, fruit-bearing plants, starch plants and tanning-material plants and 7000 species of wild medicinal plants. The southern province of Sichuan is especially rich in medicinal plants, with more than 3000 species.

The edible plants can be divided into starch plants, oil-bearing plants and fruit-bearing plants. There are more than 300 species of wild starch plants belonging to the yam family (Dioscoreaceae), palm family (Palmaceae), beech family (Fagaceae), and others. The starch contained in the stems, stem tubers or seeds of these plants may account for up to 50 per cent of their weight. Wild fruit trees are even more abundant. They include Chinese Bay Berry (*Myrica rubra*), Lychee (*Litchi chinensis*), Longan (*Dimocarpus longan*) and Kiwi Fruit or Chinese Gooseberry (*Actinidia chinensis*) in the subtropical zone, and Chinese Date (*Zizyphus jujuba*), Sea Buckthorn (*Hippophae rhamnoides*) and Sievers's Apple (*Malus sieversii*) in the temperate zone. All these are still found in the wild, although to a greater or lesser degree they are also cultivated.

From the beginning of recorded history the Chinese have been employing plants for medicinal purposes, to the extent that today 500 species are in common use. Ginseng (*Panax ginseng*) is the most famous but Ural Liquorice (*Glycyrrhiza uralensis*), Chinese Wolfberry (*Lycium chinense*) and Tall Gastrodia (*Gastrodia elata*) are just as commonly used in China, as cures for coughs, dizziness and lumbago, and headaches respectively.

There are about 600 species of plants that have industrial uses. Of these, 400 are fibre-yielding plants. Several members of the grass family (Gramineae), palm family (Palmaceae) and mulberry family (Moraceae) are used as the raw material for papermaking, boardmaking and weaving. Many species of bamboo are used in the same way. Fragrant oil-containing plants include Wild Mint (*Mentha arvensis*) and Rugose (Rugosa) Rose (*Rosa rugosa*), both from northern China. Turpentine, rosin (colophony) and lacquer are produced from the Masson Pine (*Pinus massoniana*) and from the True Lacquertree (*Rhus verniciflua*) amongst others.

Animal life

The variety of plant life across China is reflected in the wealth of animals, with over 400 mammal species, 1186 bird species, 380 reptile species and 220 amphibians. Some of these are unique to the area, the most celebrated

Chinese Golden Larch (*Pseudolarix kaempferi*) is a rare species which can be found in areas of the middle and lower reaches of the Yangtze (Chang) River.

being the Giant Panda (*Ailuropoda melanoleuca*) which is found in the cool bamboo forests mainly in the Hengduan and Qin Ling mountains in southwestern China. The country harbours the few remaining specimens of Przewalski's Horse (*Equus przewalskii*), and most of the few remaining Bactrian Camels (*Camelus bactrianus*), which are found in the Qaidam and Tarim Basins of the Gobi Desert. Other unique or rare mammals include the Golden Monkey (*Pygathrix roxellanae*), Chiru (*Pantholops hodgsoni*), Takin (*Budorcas taxicolor*), Tufted Deer (*Elaphodus cephalophus*) and Sika Deer (*Cervus nippon*).

Of the five species of freshwater whale in the world, one, the Chinese River Dolphin (*Lipotes vexillifer*), is found in the lower reaches of the Yangtze (Chang) River. The Chinese Alligator (*Alligator sinensis*) found in the middle and lower reaches of the Yangtze is one of only two species of alligator which occur outside the tropical or subtropical zones (the other is found in the Mississippi delta) while the Chinese Giant Salamander (*Andrias davidianus*) is one of the largest amphibians in the world.

Many species of birds are also unique or mainly confined to China, including the Japanese Crane (*Grus japonensis*), Brown Eared-Pheasant (*Crossoptilon mantchuricum*), Golden Pheasant (*Chrysolophus pictus*), Mandarin Duck (*Aix galericulata*) and Japanese Ibis (*Nipponia nippon*).

FAR LEFT: the endemic Reeve's Muntjac (*Muntiacus reevesi*) can be seen in the lower mountain regions of southern China and is extremely rare.
BELOW: Sika or Japanese Deer (*Cervus nippon*) are common in the mountain forests of eastern China.

Man's impact on the environment

China has a large population and a long history, so the effect of human activity on the natural environment has been considerable. The evidence suggests that agriculture has been practised for 7000 years, and the consequent reclamation and cultivation of land has completely destroyed the natural vegetation in many areas.

Animal husbandry was introduced even earlier than agriculture, and some animals, such as dogs, were domesticated here during the Old Stone Age more than 30,000 years ago. Pigs, sheep, cattle, horses, chickens, ducks, yaks and camels have been widely reared since the New Stone Age.

Wild animals have been hunted since man first appeared on the planet, but recent years have seen a more long-sighted approach to their exploitation. Some, such as Sika Deer (*Cervus nippon*) and Sable (*Martes zibellina*), have been artificially raised for commercial purposes, while others such as the Elk or Moose (*Alces alces*), Tiger (*Panthera tigris*) and Japanese Crane (*Grus japonensis*) have been given special protection because of their rarity. Conversely, several species have been declared undesirable and treated accordingly as part of a pest control policy.

Inevitably, there has been a great decline in the numbers of both animals and plants as a result of human activity. Much of this is a consequence of habitat destruction. In the course of several thousand years many forests, grasslands and even some cultivated lands have been destroyed by excessive tree felling, land cultivation and over-grazing. The resulting denudation has led to serious water loss and soil erosion, particularly on the Loess Plateau where Chinese agriculture originated.

In the arid and semi-arid areas, this type of imprudent land use has caused desertification. For example, the Mu Us Desert, near the Great Wall on the Ordos Plateau in Inner Mongolia, has been suffering increasing desertification for about 1000 years, and the dunes have been gradually spreading from the north-west towards the south-east. Dunes to the immediate north-west of the Great Wall developed during the period from the ninth to the fifteenth centuries, and in the last 300 years they have moved to the other side of the Great Wall of China and are located as well on the south-eastern side. There is now a desert strip 100 kilometres (62 miles) wide in an area which 1000 years ago was grassland.

The wild animals which inhabit the north-western arid regions and the Qinghai-Tibet Plateau, such as the Mongolian Gazelle (*Procapra gutturosa*), Asiatic Wild Ass (*Equus hemionus*) and Bactrian Camel (*Camelus bactrianus*), have been seriously affected by hunting and the deterioration of their habitat caused by over-grazing. Consequently, the numbers of these animals have declined dramatically during the last 100 years. Some wild animals have

BELOW: replanting with Prince Rupprecht's Larch (*Larix principis-rupprechtii*) on Sumu Mountain has replaced the natural vegetation.
BOTTOM LEFT: the Slavonian (Horned) Grebe (*Podiceps auritus*) breeds in the Zhalong Nature Reserve in Xinjiang.
RIGHT: north- and south-facing slopes of the Loess Plateau, west of the North China Plain, show how climate and aspect affect the extent of soil erosion. The drier south-facing slopes are not able to support the kind of vegetation that holds soil in place on north-facing slopes (on the right in the picture).
BELOW RIGHT: Père David's Deer (*Elephurus davidianus*) disappeared from China at the end of the nineteenth century but were reintroduced in 1986.

almost disappeared entirely because vast areas of their original habitats no longer exist. For example, the areas inhabited by the Giant Panda (*Ailuropoda melanoleuca*) and the Golden Monkey (*Pygathrix roxellanae*) became much smaller as the forests were felled either for their timber, or in order to free the land for cultivation.

Mankind has also been directly responsible for the near disappearance of several animals. For example, Père David's Deer (*Elaphurus davidianus*) used to roam widely across the North China Plain and along the middle and lower reaches of the Yangtze River, but excessive hunting reduced numbers until by 1894 there was only one small group left, in Nanyuan, Beijing. These were then captured and transported to Europe, where their descendants are to be found in zoos and parks. Some of these deer were reintroduced to China in 1986, almost a century after their removal.

Of course, China is not unique in facing a decline in the natural environment, as this is a worldwide phenomenon. In the last 40 years various conservation measures have been taken to halt, and hopefully reverse, the decline. Measures cannot be applied blindly, but have to take into consideration human needs and demands. The nature of these conservation policies, and the degree to which they have succeeded, will be discussed in the final chapter on Conservation.

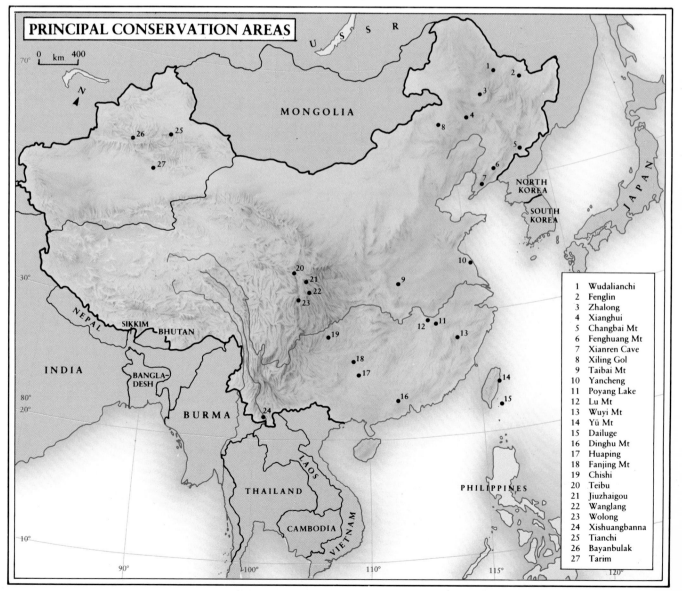

THE GEOGRAPHY OF CHINA

地理概况

地
理
概
况

The area of modern China is bordered on one side by mountains, on another by the sea and on another by desert. It is a geographical entity, with distinct regions and differing environments created by the geological upheavals of millions of years ago that shaped the landmasses of the planet as it is today.

Geological evolution

In terms of plate tectonics, most of China lies on the Eurasian Plate which adjoins the Indo-Australian Plate in the south and the Pacific Plate in the east. It is the thrust of these adjoining plates towards the Eurasian Plate that has created the basic shape and the geography of China.

Between 2500 and 1000 million years ago, during the pre-Cambrian era, land was being formed in what is now northern, north-eastern and north-western China. At this time much of present-day China was covered by sea, but during the ensuing Paleozoic era, which lasted from about 590 to 250 million years ago, the area of sea gradually shrank and the land area increased. After the great Caledonian and Hercynian upheavals, which ended some 400 and 300 million years ago respectively, this trend became even more obvious, and during the late Paleozoic period the seawater retreated to the south and west to form the Tethys, the large prehistoric ocean, leaving a broad area of dry land in eastern and northern China.

The next important event in the formation of China was the Indosinian mountain-building movement of the early Mesozoic era, some 200 million years ago, which unified the present territory of China into a continuous landmass with the Tethys Ocean to the south-west.

The late part of the Mesozoic era, between 150 and 100 million years ago, was significant in that it generated the foundations of the present-day landscape. Numerous faults and folds occurred in the eastern part of the country, leading to the formation of block mountains and basins running from north-east to south-west. This was accompanied by a great deal of volcanic activity, in which molten rock was forced into the fissures in the folded sediments. By the end of the Mesozoic era, some 65 million years ago, China was beginning to look as it does today – with the exception of the Himalayas, which were yet to be formed, and the fact that Taiwan and the south-western part of the Tarim Basin (in western China south of the Tien Mountains) were still covered by sea.

Early plants and animals

During the Mesozoic era the overall climate of the earth was warm. This is indicated by the wide distribution of red sandstones of that age, which were formed under warm conditions, as well as the widespread sedimentation of gypsum and rock salts which occurs only in arid areas. In China these conditions were caused by the increase in land area, which resulted in a dry continental climate.

The warm conditions were reflected by changes in the biological sphere. In the course of the early Mesozoic period, plants with seeds borne on open scales of cones, known as gymnosperms, flourished. The most familiar of these are the conifers. Until the end of the Jurassic period, some 144 million years ago, the most common terrestrial plants – which can still be found in China today – were cycads, pines, cypresses and ginkgos. The cycad *Cycas revoluta* was particularly successful and is widespread in fossil-bearing deposits of the Jurassic era.

Towards the end of the Jurassic period the dominance of the gymno-

PREVIOUS PAGE: West Mountains, seen from Fubo (Whirlpool) Hill, Guilin. Major geological movements over the ages have resulted in some dramatic land formations.

26

sperms was challenged by the appearance of new types of plants which had seeds enclosed in ovaries – these were the flowering plants. Known as angiosperms, they rapidly adapted to the changing climatic conditions to evolve into herbs, shrubs and trees, and by the end of the Mesozoic era, about 65 million years ago, they were beginning to dominate the vegetation of the earth.

The success of the angiosperms was closely linked with the development of insects, for in most cases flowers are simply mechanisms to attract insects which in turn pollinate the plant and ensure its reproductive success. Insects had, in fact, appeared in the Paleozoic era, some 400 million years ago. By the end of the Paleozoic they were sharing the land with the early reptiles, and the ensuing Mesozoic era saw a tremendous increase in the number of reptiles, and this became known as the age of dinosaurs.

Dinosaurs have caught the imagination of us all, mainly because of their immense size and assumed ferocity. Particularly rich finds of fossil remains have been made in the Chinese provinces of Sichuan and Yunnan, including *Yangchuanosaurus*, which was a large carnivore, stegosaurs, which were swamp-dwelling herbivores, and *Ichthyosaurus*, which was a dolphin-like reptile adapted to life in the sea.

For some reason that is still not known, the dinosaurs disappeared from the world at the end of the Mesozoic era, 65 million years ago. Suddenly the mammals and birds, which had been slowly evolving over the preceding 150 million years, predominated. The succeeding era, the Cenozoic (which we are still in now), saw a massive increase in the number and diversity of these animals, and has become known as the age of mammals.

ABOVE LEFT: the Japanese Crane (*Grus japonensis*) can be found in the north, chiefly in the Zhalong Nature Reserve, Heilongjiang Province.
ABOVE TOP: *Deracantha onos* is distributed in northern China.
ABOVE CENTRE: *Orthetrum albistylum* is widespread in China.
ABOVE: The hoverfly *Metagyrphus nitens*. Insects aided the evolution of angiosperms by pollinating them.

Nanjia Bawa Peak in the Himalayas,
formed about 40 million years ago. The
Himalayas constitute the highest mountain
range in the world.

The origins of the Himalayas

In the early Cenozoic era the geological formation of the land was comparatively slow, and the surface of the globe was eroded and smoothed into a
series of relatively flat and low landforms. The climate was warm then, and a
thick red weathering crust developed and spread across the area of modern
China. At that time, because of the greater global warmth, the northern
boundary of the subtropical zone was 7 to 10° north of the present boundary.
This meant that the north-eastern region and the northern part of Inner
Mongolia, which today are quite cold, were in the warm-temperate zone.
The North China Plain and the southern part of Inner Mongolia were in the
subtropical zone, and the Yangtze (Chang) River basin was in the trade-wind
zone. The southern part of China was in the tropical zone.

This period of geological calm was followed by an event that was to have a
profound effect on the landscape of western China. About 40 million years
ago the northern boundary of the Indian subcontinent collided with Asia, and
was carried beneath the Eurasian continental crust by the continuing
northward movement of the Indo-Australian Plate. The two layers of thick
continental crust buckled and folded to create a combined area of crust 70

kilometres (43 miles) thick, surmounted by the highest mountain range in the world – the Himalayas.

At the same time, the Pacific Plate was being thrust under the Eurasian Plate, in what is known as the Taiwan Movement. But because the ocean crust of the Pacific Plate is relatively thin it slipped beneath the Eurasian Plate with relative ease, and the landforms created in eastern China by the Taiwan Movement were quite modest compared with those in the west.

The rise of the Qinghai-Tibet Plateau, which lies some 4000 metres (13,000 ft) above sea level, and its associated mountain peaks had a dramatic effect on the Chinese environment. The Tethys Ocean retreated, shrinking to become the Mediterranean, and the lands of China joined up to form a continuous landmass. The elevation of the Qinghai-Tibet Plateau also changed the structure of the trade-wind zone at low level, and strengthened the eastern Asian monsoon circulation. It created a dominant weather pattern whereby continental low pressure prevailed in summer – previously there had been subtropical high pressure. This in turn resulted in the penetration of the moist oceanic air masses – the monsoons – into inland China during the summer, and so the eastern part of China became more humid. In winter, a strong continental high-pressure system became the norm, producing the cold, dry winds that blow over most of eastern China during the winter months today.

The Qinghai-Tibet Plateau itself, although situated in comparatively low latitudes, has the generally cold climate typical of mountain ranges.

Changes in plant and animal life

Changes in the natural environment were echoed by changes in the plant and animal life. In the early Tertiary period, 60 million years ago, woody plants such as trees dominated the landscape. These included various ferns and gymnosperms (conifers and their allies), including the ginkgos (*Ginkgo*), cycads (*Cycas*), Plum Yew (*Cephalotaxus fortunei*) and Dawn Redwood (*Metasequoia glyptostroboides*). The deciduous Swamp Cypress (*Taxodium*) thrived then but is now extinct in China.

However, many herbaceous angiosperms were beginning to appear, such as plants of the dock family (Polygonaceae), carrot family (Umbelliferae), daisy family (Compositae), mint family (Labiatae), pink family (Caryophyllaceae) and, perhaps most significantly, the grasses (Gramineae). By 25 million years ago, in the late Tertiary period, these herbaceous plants began to increase enormously. Plants of the goosefoot family (Chenopodiaceae), carrot family and daisy family were flourishing, and the grasses began to take over the great open plains. Meanwhile, the more primitive plants declined in importance and range, and retreated to the warmer areas. By this time many of the individual species of plants were identical with those that exist today.

In the temperate parts of the eastern monsoon region, north of the Qin Ling Mountains, mixed forests of deciduous trees such as oak (*Quercus*) and coniferous trees such as pine (*Pinus*) took hold and spread. The area to the south of the Qin Ling Mountains and north of the Nan Ling Mountains was then subtropical and tropical, and here evergreen species of the beech family (Fagaceae) predominated, interspersed with members of the witchhazel family (Hamamelidaceae), magnolia family (Magnoliaceae), and laurel family (Lauraceae). The area to the south of the Nan Ling Mountains was tropical and covered with great forests of evergreens, of which plants of the laurel family, the beech family and the pea family (Leguminosae) were the most abundant.

It was during this period that the characteristic montane flora developed on the Qinghai-Tibet Plateau. Fossils have been found of Alpine Oak (*Quercus*

Pillars formed from earth deposits left after land erosion in the Tertiary period.

semicarpifolia), Indian Azalea (*Rhododendron simsii*) and spruces (*Picea*), all typical species of mountain environments.

During the early Tertiary era (65 to 38 million years ago) the mammals developed very rapidly in the void left by dinosaurs. The appearance of the grasslands in the late Tertiary period gave them another tremendous boost as species evolved to take advantage of this abundant food source. The ancestors of familiar grazing mammals appeared, together with the carnivores that preyed on them. These animals were abundant in the northern part of China, which was then in the subtropical to temperate zones, with widely distributed steppe and forest-steppe. They included modern types such as the Goitered Gazelle (*Gazella subgutturosa*), horses (*Equus*) and rhinoceroses (*Rhinoceros*). Forest-dwelling mammals predominated in the southern tropical area where there was little grassland.

During the great ice ages of the Quaternary period, which began two million years ago, most of China was not directly affected by the continental glaciers. However, the colder overall climate in the northern hemisphere led to the formation of glaciers in the high mountains of the western part of the country. Small-scale glaciers also formed on the higher mountains of eastern China, but generally southern China remained warm. As such it acted as a haven for the animals and plants that had previously thrived in the temperate and subtropical zones of pre-Ice-Age northern and central China. Many of these species have survived to this day, such as the Giant Panda (*Ailuropoda melanoleuca*) and the ginkgo *Ginkgo biloba*. Simultaneously, quite a number of new arctic-alpine animals and plants that were adapted to cold conditions became established on the high mountains as well as on the Qinghai-Tibet Plateau. Another consequence of the area's relative warmth during the ice ages is that the landscape of most of central and southern China does not bear the marks of glaciation.

LEFT: Yak (*Bos grunniens*) grazing in front of Mount Gungar in north-western China. As grasses began to flourish in the vast plains in the late Tertiary period, species of grazing mammals evolved to take advantage of the new habitat. These first appeared in northern China, which was then in the subtropical to temperate zones, but during the ice ages of the Quaternary period they either adapted to the colder conditions or moved to the warmer south.

ABOVE: the Asiatic Wild Ass (*Equus hemionus*) is found in Qinghai and Gansu, living in semi-desert grassland. It can run surprisingly fast, at speeds of over 60 km (38 miles) per hour, and can withstand extremes of heat and cold. This may account for its existence in northern China after the Quaternary ice ages, when many other mammals less well adapted had been forced to seek the warmth of southern China in order to survive.

31

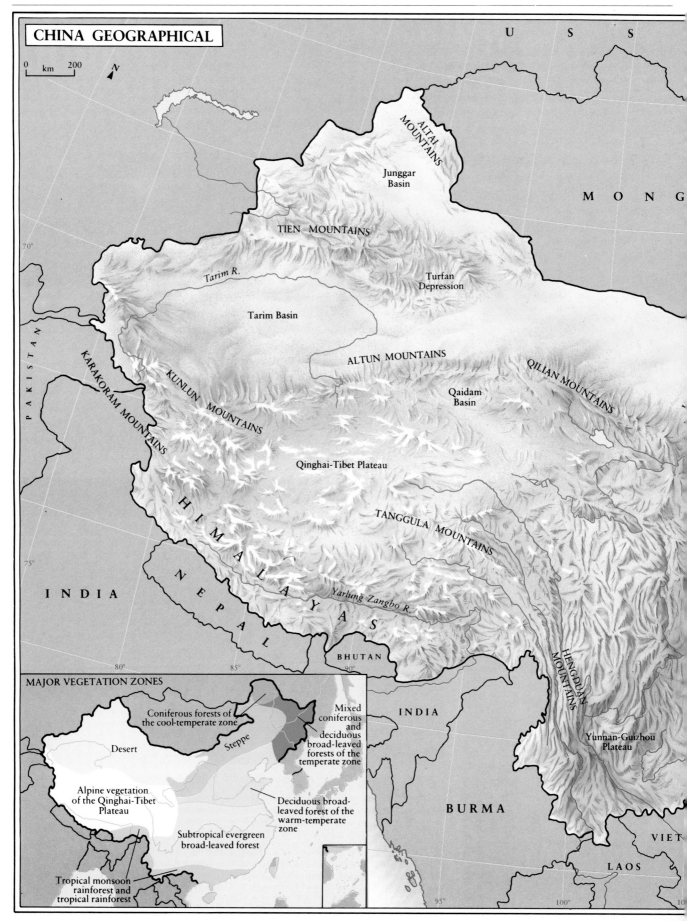

CHINA GEOGRAPHICAL

0   km   200

N

U S S S

ALTAI MOUNTAINS

Junggar Basin

M O N G

TIEN MOUNTAINS

Tarim R.

Turfan Depression

Tarim Basin

ALTUN MOUNTAINS

QILIAN MOUNTAINS

PAKISTAN

KARAKORAM MOUNTAINS

KUNLUN MOUNTAINS

Qaidam Basin

Qinghai-Tibet Plateau

TANGGULA MOUNTAINS

70°

75°

H I M A L A Y A S

INDIA

NEPAL

Yarlung Zangbo R.

HENGDUAN MOUNTAINS

80°   85°   90°

BHUTAN

INDIA

Yunnan-Guizhou Plateau

MAJOR VEGETATION ZONES

Coniferous forests of the cool-temperate zone

Desert

Steppe

Mixed coniferous and deciduous broad-leaved forests of the temperate zone

Alpine vegetation of the Qinghai-Tibet Plateau

Deciduous broad-leaved forest of the warm-temperate zone

Subtropical evergreen broad-leaved forest

Tropical monsoon rainforest and tropical rainforest

BURMA

VIET

LAOS

95°   100°   10

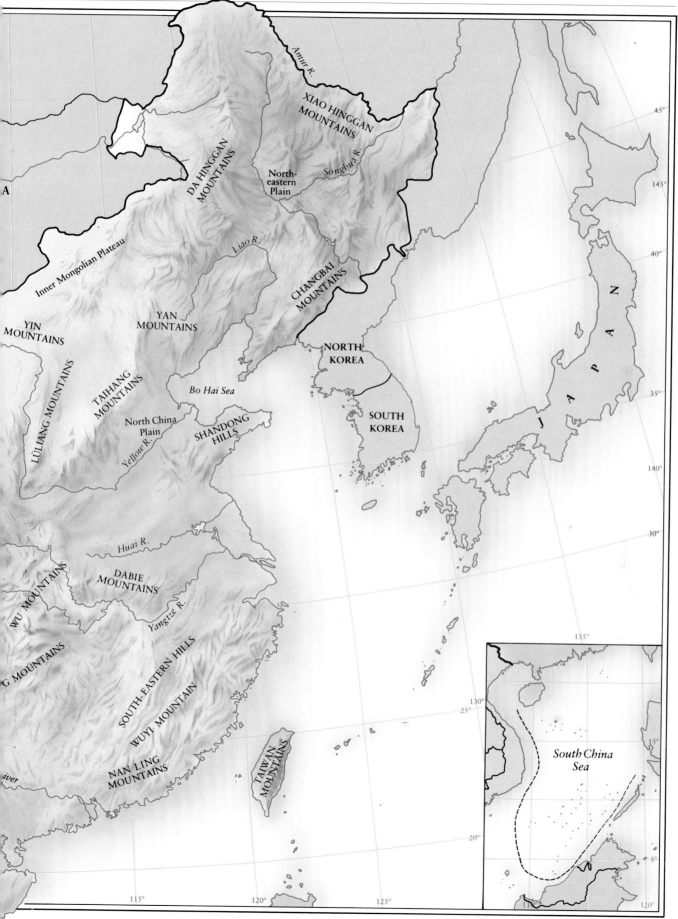

Amur R.

XIAO HINGGAN
MOUNTAINS

DA HINGGAN
MOUNTAINS

North-
eastern
Plain

Songhua R.

Inner Mongolian Plateau

Liao R.

CHANGBAI
MOUNTAINS

YIN
MOUNTAINS

YAN
MOUNTAINS

NORTH
KOREA

TAIHANG
MOUNTAINS

Bo Hai Sea

LÜLIANG MOUNTAINS

North China
Plain

SHANDONG
HILLS

SOUTH
KOREA

Yellow R.

J A P A N

Huai R.

DABIE
MOUNTAINS

WU MOUNTAINS

Yangtze R.

G MOUNTAINS

SOUTH-EASTERN HILLS

WUYI MOUNTAIN

NAN LING
MOUNTAINS

River

TAIWAN
MOUNTAINS

45°

145°

40°

35°

140°

30°

135°

130°

25°

South China
Sea

15°

20°

5°

115°   120°   125°

110°   120°

Mount Qomolangma (Everest) in the Himalayas, which tower over the Qinghai-Tibet Plateau (nicknamed 'The Roof of the World'). Qomolangma is the highest mountain on earth, and marks the border between China and Nepal.

Outline of present-day geography

China can be divided into three major physical geographical regions: the Eastern Monsoon Region, the North-western Arid Region and the Qinghai-Tibet Plateau Region.

The Eastern Monsoon Region is the largest, covering 47 per cent of the country. Most of the land surface is less than 1000 metres (3280 ft) above sea level, and much of the eastern part is even lower than 500 metres (1640 ft), with many low-lying alluvial plains. The oceanic monsoon in summer has a very significant impact on the region, which experiences considerable changes in wind direction and precipitation from season to season.

The area also has fertile soils which, combined with the low altitude and high summer rainfall, means that the area is well suited to agriculture. As a result some 94 per cent of the human population lives there. Man has had a very significant impact on the region, with intensive use of the land for agriculture and habitation. Accordingly, there is little natural vegetation remaining. What is left is mainly forest, because forest was the predominant vegetation before the landscape was settled by man. The remainder is mostly forest-steppe. Despite the fact that there are few large areas of natural vegetation left the plants and animals are comparatively varied, largely because this area escaped the worst of the Quaternary ice ages.

The North-western Arid Region covers about 30 per cent of the whole area of China. It is a region of mountain ranges and plateaux separated by basins, and most of the rivers drain inland into the basins. Since the oceanic monsoon has little influence the climate is largely arid, with strong, dry winds. As a result there are large areas of stony and sandy desert. There are high levels of lime and mineral salts in the soils and the organic matter content is comparatively low, so the soils are not very fertile. The variety of wild species is much poorer than in the Eastern Monsoon Region. Only 4.5 per cent of the Chinese population lives there so, not surprisingly, the impact of human activity on the natural environment is much less significant than in the densely populated Eastern Monsoon Region. Livestock farming is the main activity, although there is some agricultural use of land on fertile oases, which can be irrigated.

The Qinghai-Tibet Plateau covers 23 per cent of China. It is an extremely high plateau with an elevation of over 4000 metres (13,120 ft) above sea level, and its southern boundaries are formed by the highest mountains in the world, the Himalayas.

On the Qinghai-Tibet Plateau the air is thin, the average temperature is low and there are glaciers. The soil is permanently frozen over a large area. The soils that are not frozen are thin and rather poor, and most of the vegetation consists of steppe, alpine grassland and mountain scrub, with small areas of cold desert. Forests are few and far between. The human population is very small – a mere 0.5 per cent of the Chinese people lives there and most of the region remains a wilderness.

The pattern of China's landforms

The vast area covered by these three regions includes a great variety of landscapes: ranges of high mountains, undulating plateaux, rolling hills, broad basins and plains. But although the three regions are quite distinct there is a pattern to the land formations that unite them.

The higher mountains, plateaux and large-scale inland basins occur mainly in the west of the country, while comparatively low mountains, hills and plains are found in the east. The difference between the high and steep west and the low and flat east is pronounced, but it is not a sudden transition. The height decreases from west to east in phases, forming the 'three steps' which are the main physical features of China.

The Qinghai-Tibet Plateau is the highest step of the geographic staircase. It is also the highest plateau on earth and is often called 'the roof of the world'. A series of mountains running east to west tower over the plateau. Most of the mountains rise to 5000 to 6000 metres (16,400 to 19,700 ft) above sea level, with a number of high peaks reaching well over 7000 metres (23,000 ft). The highest are the Himalayas, which lie along the southern fringes of the plateau. They have an average elevation of 6220 metres (20,400 ft) and include the highest mountain on earth, Mount Qomolangma (Everest), situated on the border between China and Nepal with its peak at 8848 metres (29,028 ft) above sea level.

North and east of the Qinghai-Tibet Plateau, the average height of the land above sea level decreases strikingly. The terrain consists of a series of plateaux and basins with an elevation of 1000 to 2000 metres (3300 to 6600 ft). They include the Junggar Basin and the Tarim Basin in north-western China, the Inner Mongolian Plateau and the Loess Plateau in northern China, and the Sichuan Basin and Yunnan-Guizhou Plateau in south-western China. Together these form the second step of the great west-to-east staircase.

The mountain ranges running from the north-east down towards central southern China – the Da Hinggan Mountains in the north-east, the Taihang Mountains in the north and Xuefeng Mountain further south – form the

BELOW: the Bar-headed Goose (*Anser indicus*) breeds on the Qinghai-Tibet Plateau.
BOTTOM: the Crested Honey Buzzard (*Pernis ptilorhynchus*) inhabits the mountains of the north-east and south-west.

boundary with the third and lowest step of the staircase. In general, the land in this part of China is less than 500 metres (1600 ft) above sea level. It consists of the great plains of the north and north-east, and the alluvial flats bordering the middle and lower reaches of the Yellow (Huang) and Yangtze (Chang) rivers, and their fringes of low mountains and hills.

The low coastal 'step' in the Chinese landscape favours the inland penetration of the warm, humid monsoon air current from the south-eastern ocean, which then exerts a significant influence on the climate, soil and vegetation of eastern China. The 'three-step' pattern also affects the major rivers, creating a series of fast-flowing stretches that are being harnessed for power generation.

From this it must be clear that despite the average Westerner's image of China as a land of green hills and plains, it is actually a country with a great many mountains. As already stated, the Qinghai-Tibet Plateau covers 23 per cent of the country, but altogether mountains, plateaux and hills account for about 69 per cent of the total land area. Much of the remaining area is also quite high, for only 25.2 per cent of the whole country is less than 500 metres (1600 ft) above sea level. An even more startling statistic is that 25.9 per cent of the country is above 3000 metres (9800 ft).

The mountains of China are classified according to a simple system. Mountains that rise to 5000 metres (16,400 ft) above sea level are classed as 'extremely high mountains'; these tower above the present snow-line. Mountains that are 3500 to 5000 metres (11,480 to 16,400 ft) high are generally termed 'high mountains'; these rise above the tree line, and like their higher neighbours most of them have been affected by recent glaciation and frost weathering. The mountains that reach 1000 to 3500 metres (3280 to 11,480 ft) and 500 to 1000 metres (1640 to 3280 ft) are termed 'medium mountains' and 'low mountains' respectively. Both are strongly affected by water erosion, and the low mountains are characterized by comparatively gentle slopes and shattered landforms.

The pattern of the three steps is fairly rigid: nearly all the extremely high and high mountains are distributed on the highest step, and most of the medium mountains are found on the second step – although a few are scattered on the third step among the low mountains and plains. The mountains make up 33 per cent of the total area of the country, the plateaux 26 per cent and hills 10 per cent. Of the rest, basins and plains occupy 19 per cent and 11 per cent of the total area respectively.

AREA OF LAND OCCUPIED BY MOUNTAINS

Elevation above sea level in metres (ft)	Area in 1000 sq km (1000 sq miles)	% of total land area
Less than 500 (1640)	2,417 (933)	25.2
500–1000 (1640–3280)	1,625 (627)	16.9
1000–1500 (3280–4920)	1,746 (674)	18.2
1500–2000 (4920–6560)	653 (252)	6.8
2000–3000 (6560–9840)	676 (261)	7.0
Over 3000 (Over 9840)	2,483 (959)	25.9

The geographical areas of China

The three basic landforms described above subdivide into smaller areas according to soil type, climate, vegetation and other natural conditions. Geographers normally divide China into 19 major units, each with distinctive characteristics. They are as follows.

The Qinghai-Tibet Plateau

Tibet, the neighbouring Qinghai and the western part of Sichuan form a huge plateau of bleak vistas. Apart from the mountains at the edges most of it is flat, producing wide open landscapes where little grows. Although direct sunshine can raise the surface temperature, the prevailing conditions are cold, and snow flurries in the middle of summer are not uncommon. Even in July the ground is frozen in the early morning, so what plants exist are tiny. Parts of the plateau are like arctic tundra, with the soil frozen to a depth of a hundred metres or more. There are no trees to soften the stony landscape, or to break the force of the wind which howls across the open plateau for much of the time.

Not surprisingly, not many people live there, and it is possible to travel for days without seeing anyone; some areas are not visited at all, except by intrepid adventurers. In fact, the air is so thin that it is difficult to breathe, and visitors commonly suffer from mountain sickness. The pressure is so low that water boils at only 80°C (176°F). The few inhabitants are mostly nomadic and live in tents, although there are permanent settlements at the warmer southern edge and in the few fertile green valleys.

The total area of this massive region is 2.2 million square kilometres (850,000 square miles), which is about four times the size of France, and the average height of the plateau is an impressive 4000 metres (13,120 ft). It is surrounded by and includes a number of high mountains, notably the Himalayas in the south, the Kunlun and Qilian mountains in the north, and the Karakoram Mountains in the west. The high peaks of these mountains are always covered by snow and glaciers. In the interior of the plateau there are many basins and lakes, including Qinghai Lake, which is the largest in China, covering 4456 square kilometres (1720 square miles) and situated at an altitude of 3175 metres (10,417 ft), and the Nam Lake which extends for 2000 square kilometres (772 square miles) with an elevation of 4600 metres (15,090 ft). There are large areas of semi-arid steppe with good grassland around the lakes where horses and sheep graze.

Although the overall climate on the plateau is cold, it does vary significantly from south to north. The south-eastern Tibetan valley benefits from the south-western monsoon, and the climate here is warm and humid. The annual mean temperature is about 10°C (50°F) and in many places the annual precipitation may reach 1000 mm (39 in.). Forest trees grow well and agriculture has been successfully developed here, and the combination of green, wooded and grassy slopes and snow-capped peaks makes for mountain views as spectacular as anywhere in the world.

In the cold northern and central parts of Tibet, the annual precipitation is less than 200 mm (8 in.). The sun can be powerful in the thin mountain air with a daily variation of shade temperature as large as 20°C (68°F). Indeed the temperature can be so changeable that when a Tibetan goes out he normally puts only one arm into a sleeve of his coat, just pulling the coat over the other shoulder. This enables him to slip the coat off quickly when he enters a patch of hot sunshine. Among the plants of the highland meadow, Kobresia (*Kobresia* spp.) predominates; the Purpleflowered Needle Grass or Feather Grass (*Stipa purpurea*) is typical of the plants of the highland steppe.

Zabuye (salt) Lake in Tibet. Deposits of calcium carbonate have been formed by precipitating mineral waters from the island in the centre of the lake.

Despite the height and the climate the plateau is home to a large number of vertebrate animals, including 191 species of mammals, 532 species of birds, 49 species of reptiles and 24 species of amphibians, all of which have become well adapted to the highland conditions. Relatively common mammals found in the wild include Yak (*Bos grunniens*), which is found in herds of over a hundred, Blue Sheep (*Pseudois nayaur*), Tibetan Gazelle or Goa (*Procapra picticaudata*), Chiru or Tibetan Antelope (*Pantholops hodgsoni*), Himalayan Marmot (*Marmota himalayana*), and Asiatic Wild Ass (*Equus hemionus*), the latter also found in herds of over a hundred. The reclusive and rare Snow Leopard or Ounce (*Panthera uncia*) is found in China only in Tibet.

The Chiru or Tibetan Antelope is particularly well adapted to the highland environment, with a nasal cavity that is enlarged to draw in more of the thin air and high-crowned teeth to deal with the tough highland vegetation. These adaptations enable the Chirus to thrive on this extremely high plateau where there are few competitors for their food supply.

Birds include the Tibetan Snowcock (*Tetraogallus tibetanus*), Black-necked Crane (*Grus nigricollis*), and snow finches (*Montifringilla* spp.).

The Qaidam Basin

To the north of the Qinghai-Tibet Plateau the bottom of the Qaidam Basin is 2500 to 3000 metres (8200 to 9840 ft) above sea level, and the surrounding high mountains and plateaux rise to over 4000 metres (13,120 ft). The climate is dry with an annual precipitation of less than 100 mm (4 in.).

'Qaidam' is the Mongolian word for salt, and the area is aptly named. Most of the basin was once a salt lake which has almost completely evaporated, leaving a vast, flat, salty desert stretching as far as the eye can see in any direction. Nothing grows on it. In places the salt crust is as thick as 15 metres (49 ft), and is the dominant mineral – even the homes of people who temporarily work there have been constructed of salt. The only break in the otherwise featureless scenery is provided by a number of small salt lakes in the centre of the basin, which are all that is left of the original large expanse of water.

In welcome contrast, parts of the edge of the basin have been successfully cultivated. There is plenty of sunshine, so melting snow from the surrounding mountains makes up for the shortfall in precipitation.

In the western part of the basin there is a lot of wind erosion, and in the eastern part there are sand dunes and deposits of wind-blown dust, or loess. Short, scrubby plants like Przewalski's Ephedra (*Ephedra przewalskii*), Reaumuria (*Reaumuria*), Russian Thistle (*Salsola abrolanoides*) and other plants adapted for arid conditions survive on the uncultivated edges away from the salt flats. Few animals live here; in general the wildlife resembles that of the Qinghai-Tibet Plateau, with a number of desert species such as camels, rodents and lizards.

The Tarim Basin

This is an inland basin covering an area of 500,000 square kilometres (193,000 square miles) of which 330,000 square kilometres (127,400 square miles) is desert, on average about 1000 metres (3280 ft) above sea level. The character of the landscape is formed in rings: stony desert forms an outer ring at the fringe of the basin, sandy desert covers the centre (and the largest area), and soil-covered plain with occasional oases forms another ring between the stony and sandy desert areas.

The climate is extremely dry: the annual precipitation is less than 80 mm (3 in.) and in many places it is even less than 10 mm (⅜ in.). As a result plants are sparse. The extreme dryness means that sand covers 85 per cent of the total area and forms dunes normally 100 to 200 metres (330 to 660 ft) high, that shift about like vast, slow waves in the wind.

The sandy part of the desert, or Taklimakan Desert, is the largest desert in China and is extremely inhospitable. It is very hot: sand temperatures of 84°C (183°F) have been recorded, which is hot enough to cook an egg. Sometimes rainclouds gather and it starts to rain, but the water does not reach the ground because it evaporates first. The surrounding mountains retain the heat at night so it never gets cold.

On clear days it is quite common to see eight or ten tornadoes from the same viewpoint, reaching several kilometres into the sky. But on windy days, especially in April and May, the wind whips up sandstorms that darken the sky as if it were night. When this happens the wild asses and camels, which are the only large animals that can cross the desert, lie down and turn their backs to the wind.

Soil types include brown desert soils, polygonal fissure soils and saline soils, and the vegetation is limited to plants such as Przewalski's Ephedra (*Ephedra przewalskii*) and Nitraria (*Nitraria sphaercarpas*) which can withstand the arid conditions.

In the local Uygur language, the word 'tarim' means the converging of the rivers, and various rivers cross the basin. The water supply has encouraged a richer vegetation and the formation of fertile soils along the banks of the rivers, and forests of the poplar *Populus diversifolia* form a striking contrast with the surrounding yellow sand. The Tarim River itself is the longest inland river in China, and flows through the central Taklimakan Desert before it finally disappears in the Lop lowland in the east of the Tarim Basin. In the past the river flowed into the Lop Nur Lake, but in 1970, owing to the diversion of water for irrigation, the lake dried up.

The desert mammals are mainly rodents and hoofed mammals, such as wild asses and camels. Reptiles are well suited to the desert environment and lizards in particular thrive there.

Sand dunes on the edge of the Taklimakan Desert, Xinjiang Province, where sand temperatures are sometimes hot enough to cook an egg. When it rains, the water evaporates before it even reaches the ground.

The Tien Mountains

The Tien Mountains, or Tien Shan, lie between the Tarim and the Junggar basins and consist of more than 20 parallel ranges and valleys running in an east-west direction. Most of the ridges are more than 3000 to 4000 metres (9840 to 13,120 ft) above sea level, towering over the deserts to the north and south. On the windward slopes, which are on the north side, the average annual precipitation may be as high as 400 to 500 mm (16 to 20 in.). More than 200 rivers, some quite long, originate in the Tien Mountains.

The mountains make a splendid sight, especially from the northern fertile side. At their foot is the desert, and they display a full range of vegetation belts, starting with scrubby steppe grasslands at the lowest level, then a line of forest followed by mountain pastures. Higher still there is bare rock and finally snow-capped peaks, many of which have associated glaciers.

The people who live in the mountains move up and down these zones according to season. In summer the upper grasslands are very green, so they take themselves, their animals, their villages and schools up into the meadows. In the spring and autumn they settle on the steppe, and in winter, when the mountains become very cold, they move the whole community down to the desert.

Because of the availability of water the vegetation is much richer on the mountains than on the plains, and more than 2000 species of trees, shrubs and grasses can be seen in this area. Rodents such as Long-tailed Marmots (*Marmota caudata*) are common on the mountain steppe. The forests or forest-steppes of the northern slopes harbour hoofed mammals such as Red Deer or Wapiti (*Cervus elphus*) and Roe Deer (*Capreolus capreolus*). The wild sheep called Argalis (*Ovis ammon*) live on the high peaks.

The Junggar Basin

The structure of the Junggar Basin, which, apart from the Altai Mountains, is China's most north-westerly area, is somewhat similar to that of the Tarim Basin, but it does not form such an enclosed environment. A cool north-westerly air current frequently flows into it through a gap at the western end of the basin, and in January the air temperature can drop very low to an average low of −20°C (−4°F).

The north-westerly air current also brings in rain and snow, and the annual precipitation is normally in the range of 100 to 200 mm (4 to 8 in.). Accordingly, even in the central desert area, plants grow better than in the arid Tarim Basin. In the Tarim Basin plants grow several metres apart, but in the Junggar Basin they grow in clusters and cover as much as 25 to 30 per cent of the ground surface. These plants can fix or partially fix the sand dunes, and these stabilized dunes are used as winter pastures. At the northern foot of the Tien Mountains are plains with good quality soil and abundant water which have become quite widely cultivated.

The Altai Mountains

This is one of the major mountain systems of the Eurasian continent, although only the southern slopes of the middle of the range are in China. The western end of the mountains is in the USSR and the eastern end in the People's Republic of Mongolia.

A continuous process of faulting and upheaval has raised several topographical 'steps' in the landscape: the high, middle and low mountain belts. The high mountain belt is primarily influenced by the action of ice and snow, the middle mountain belt is forested, and the low mountain belt is characterized by upland steppe. The summers are very short, and the climate is generally cold and suitable only for cold-adapted plants and animals. Predominant plants in the forest are Siberian Larch (*Larix sibirica*), of which this is the largest concentration in China, and Siberian Fir (*Abies sibirica*). The

Gentians (*Gentiana*) are widespread in China (here in Yunnan Province, south-western China). Many herbaceous and alpine species introduced to China are also common in the West.

animal life is rather restricted: the hoofed animals most commonly seen are Musk Deer (*Moschus moschiferus*) and Roe Deer (*Capreolus capreolus*). Among the rodents, the Red Squirrel (*Sciurus vulgaris*) and Siberian Chipmunk (*Tamias sibiricus*) are common. The representative carnivores are the Red Fox (*Vulpes vulpes*) and Lynx (*Felis lynx*).

The word 'altai' means gold in Mongolian, referring to the gold deposits that have been discovered in the mountains. Quite apart from the actual gold, the connotations of the word are appropriate as these mountains are extremely beautiful. A few of the high peaks have snow cover all year round, and all the slopes are mantled with lush green virgin forests. Glaciation has created many lakes among these forests, producing tranquil scenes of great beauty. In a more accessible part of the world the Altai Mountains would certainly be an important tourist centre.

The Inner Mongolian Plateau

East of the Tien mountain range is the Inner Mongolian Plateau. Having been raised a very long time ago and continuously eroded ever since, the plateau is rather flat with an average elevation of 1000 to 1300 metres (3280 to 4260 ft). In winter it is cold and windy. In summer the area is affected to some extent by the monsoon originating from the Pacific Ocean; this is not as strong by the time it reaches the plateau, so the annual precipitation is low, about 150 to 350 mm (6 to 15 in.). However, there are significant variations from year to year, depending on the force of the monsoon.

In keeping with the semi-arid climate, the predominant vegetation is steppe, with desert-steppe gradually becoming desert in the western part of the plateau. The eastern part is the most fertile, especially in the Hulun Buir and Xilin Gol Highlands where the climate is relatively humid, making the Inner Mongolian Plateau an important region for raising livestock. The wild grasses of the open steppe grow very tall. As an ancient poem has it: 'When the wind blows, the grasses bow down, and groups of cows and sheep can be seen.' The domestic animals share the grasslands with a variety of burrowing rodents and wild grazing animals: swift-footed Mongolian Gazelles (*Procapra gutturosa*) are common, herding in hundreds; when disturbed they run together *en masse* at a speed hard to equal in some automobiles.

The birds of this area are mainly ground-nesters; the Japanese Crane (*Grus japonensis*) found in the occasional meadow swamps is the most famous. Far more common is Pallas's Sandgrouse (*Syrrhaptes paradoxus*), which is a plump creature somewhere between a chicken and a pigeon in size, and which can be seen in flocks of a hundred or more, looking for water.

The Da Hinggan, Xiao Hinggan and Changbai mountains

The Da Hinggan Mountains, Xiao Hinggan Mountains and Changbai Mountains form a semicircle of high land in north-eastern China with an average elevation of 1000 metres (3280 ft) above sea level, although some peaks are twice this height. With the exception of the northern section of the Da Hinggan Mountains, which is in the cool-temperate zone, most of these mountains are in the temperate humid climatic zone.

Trees grow well in this climate, and the dominant vegetation is coniferous forest and mixed conifer/broad-leaved forest which stretches right over the tops of the mountains. The forests are the home of deer, bears and tigers. This is the largest forestry base in China, and is used extensively for commercial timber extraction.

The North-eastern Plain

The semicircle of mountains in the north-east partially surrounds the largest plain in China, covering an area of 350,000 square kilometres (135,000 square miles). It is a low-level alluvial plain, in parts only 50 metres (164 ft) above

Coniferous forests, mainly of larch (*Larix*), in the Da Hinggan Mountains. Trees thrive in the temperate humid climate of this region which is the largest forestry base in China.

41

sea level, formed by the Songhua River system and Liao River system (the plain is also known as the 'Song-Liao Plain'). It is very cold in winter, with four to six months of frost, but in summer the temperature is quite high; the mean temperature in July may exceed 20°C (68°F), which is favourable for plant growth. The plain is also fertile, for it has a thick soil layer with a high level of organic matter, and it is a major component of the 'fertile black soil belt' of China.

These favourable conditions have made the North-eastern Plain an important agricultural area, producing soya beans, maize, sorghum, wheat, beetroot and flax. Rice is grown as well, and the plain is an important source of early-season rice in China. The significance of this region to Chinese food production is such that large-scale land reclamation schemes have been implemented. In the northern part of the North-eastern Plain there were at one time large areas of uncultivated land consisting of marshes and meadow steppes. These were collectively known as the 'Great Northern Uncultivated Land'. In recent years, much of the land has been drained and put under cultivation, and many modern farms have been built; as a result the area is now known as the 'Great Northern Granary'.

Despite this there are still a number of marshes remaining on the plain, and many migratory birds such as the Japanese Crane (*Grus japonensis*), Mandarin Duck (*Aix galericulata*), Mallard (*Anas platyrhynchos*) and Swan Goose (*Anser cygnoides*) fly here to lay their eggs in summer. At this time the cranes can be seen flying to the marshes together in large flocks.

The North China Plain

This is an alluvial plain created by the Yellow (Huang) River, the Huai River and the Hai River. The Yellow River flows through the Loess Plateau in northern China, where it picks up huge amounts of sediment; this is then deposited on the North China Plain in such quantities that from time to time it changes the course of the river. This has led to a series of disastrous floods that seriously hampered the economic development of the region until quite recently. The present-day course dates from 1855, with minor variations, and in the last few decades the river has been regulated and brought under control, almost eliminating the flood problem.

Despite these difficulties the North China Plain has a long history of farming, for it has an ideal combination of flat terrain, fertile soils, high temperatures and abundant precipitation in summer. It has become an important area for producing grain and cotton. Centuries of agriculture have all but destroyed the natural vegetation, and the wild animals are limited to those that are capable of adapting to an environment of temporary secondary shrub or steppe.

The Loess Plateau, west of the North China Plain, has been eroded by run-off water. Terraced fields help minimize the amount of soil erosion.

The Shandong Peninsula

The low mountains and hills to the south of the lower reaches of the Yellow River form a peninsula dividing the Yellow Sea (Huang Hai) and the Bo Hai Sea. The hills are mostly less than 500 metres (1640 ft) above sea level, with a few peaks of 1000 metres (3280 ft) or more such as Tai Mountain and Lao Mountain. These have resisted the erosion that has affected the surrounding hills because they consist of very old, very hard rock. Despite not being very high they have some beautiful mountain scenery, which makes them popular with tourists. The peninsula has a tortuous coastline and several deepwater ports such as Qingdao and Yantai.

Owing to the moderating influence of the sea, the climate is temperate and relatively humid. The annual precipitation is about 600 to 900 mm (24 to 35 in.), the temperature of the coldest month rarely drops below −10°C (14°F), and the frost season is short. The natural vegetation is now relatively sparse for a monsoon area because of clearance for agriculture, housing and industry, but the predominant wild trees are oak (*Quercus*) and pine (*Pinus*), particularly Japanese Red Pine (*Pinus densiflora*). There are many orchards of cultivated fruit trees on the low mountains and hills of Shandong, for it is an important centre of production for apples, pears and other fruits. The plain is also cultivated, mainly for peanuts and cotton.

The Loess Plateau

The Loess Plateau to the west of the North China Plain lies about 1000 to 1500 metres (3280 to 4920 ft) above sea level, and covers 530,000 square kilometres (204,650 square miles).

Loess is essentially a thick deposit of wind-blown dust. About 2 million years ago winds blew this dust from the deserts in the north-west, depositing it here. With exposure to rain it has gradually developed into a yellow-brown soil-like material. In several parts of the plateau the loess is up to 200 metres (656 ft) deep, and when seen from the hills the impression is of an all-yellow landscape carved into dramatic gulleys by streams and rain which have eroded the terrain.

The loess is porous and silty, with comparatively high levels of nitrogen, phosphorus and potassium – the basic components of most fertilizers. This means that the plateau is fertile, and the area has been extensively farmed for a long time. According to historical literature about the area the original vegetation consisted of dense forests and grasslands, but these disappeared long ago, largely because of clearance for agriculture, but also as a result of runaway soil erosion.

Being a loose, fine-grained material, loess is sensitive to erosion and the removal of the original plant cover has left it completely unprotected. When

THE YELLOW EARTH OF THE LOESS PLATEAU

The Loess Plateau of Northern Shaanxi and Gansu is one of the most fertile areas of China, though also one of the most fragile. Ironically, it is the product of desert, as it was created from fine particles of dust blown from the deserts to the north-west of China over a long period of time. Its fertility is not just due to the rich natural components of which it consists, but also because it is moisture-retentive.

This makes it highly suitable for agriculture, livestock and forestry, though nowadays examples of the latter are mainly the product of planned planting as there is almost no original forest left. However, its soft, loose nature means that loess also erodes very easily unless it is carefully controlled. The effects of both wind and rain are immediately apparent.

ABOVE: the soft earth is highly susceptible to erosion by water, which forms streams and gullies in the yellowish landscape.
LEFT: the eroded loess terrain can form landscapes of soft, pointed peaks.

it is dry the wind blows it away, and in summer rainstorms occur frequently so most of the plateau has been seriously eroded by run-off water to create a landform characterized by thousands of gullies. This makes the surface so uneven that it has proved difficult to build railways across it. These gullies can be very spectacular, with deep ravines displaying vertical, pillar-like joints. The loess is sufficiently firm for people to have excavated caves into it and made them their homes.

By developing water and soil preservation projects, planting trees and grasses to protect the slopes from erosion and building terraced fields, the local people have brought soil erosion under control. The problem of water loss has also been minimized by the construction of numerous reservoirs.

The Qin Ling and Dabie mountains

The Qin Ling range is in central China, south of the Loess Plateau. The range runs in an east-west direction with steep northern slopes, and the highest mountain, Taibai Mountain, rises to 3767 metres (12,360 ft). It forms an important physical dividing line, because it is the catchment area between the Yellow (Huang) River and the Yangtze (Chang) River drainage basins. Similarly, the Dabie mountain range to the south-east is the catchment area between the Yangtze and the Huai River drainage basins.

These mountains also serve as the boundary between the subtropical evergreen forest to the south and the warm-temperate deciduous forest to the north. With respect to animal geography, they mark the boundary between the Palaearctic region and the Oriental region, and because of this position, with a foot in each zoogeographic region, the mountains have a wide variety of animals and plants.

Many tropical or subtropical animals are found on the south side of the mountains, including tree frogs (Rhacophoridae), crested porcupines (Hystricidae), and bamboo rats (Rhizomyinae) as well as birds such as jacanas (Jacanidae), bulbuls (Pycnonotidae), and flowerpeckers (Dicaeidae). The animals and birds of the north side are typical species of northern China, such as jumping-mice (Zapodidae), Holarctic tree creepers (Certhiidae), sandgrouse (Pteroclididae) and bustards (Otididae).

The Sichuan Basin

The Qin Ling Mountains form the northern boundary of the Sichuan Basin, an area of 180,000 square kilometres (69,500 square miles), with an elevation of 300 to 500 metres (980 to 1640 ft) above sea level. It is a region of hills and low mountains, with the Chengdu Plain in the west.

The climate is warm and humid in winter, with frequent fogs, and very hot in summer. The area is notable for the striking purple colour of the soil, which is derived from the underlying purple sandstones and shales. This soil is as fertile as it is colourful, with a high content of nitrogen, phosphorus and potassium. The combination of fertile soil and favourable climate has encouraged intensive agriculture, and careful management of the land allows crops to be harvested three times a year. About 100 million people live in the basin and it is commonly known as 'The Land of Plenty'. Inevitably, the intensive land-use has reduced the area of uncultivated ground to a minimum, and there is little wildlife.

The middle and lower reaches of the Yangtze (Chang) River

The middle reach of the Yangtze flows over a plain dotted with numerous lakes, the largest of which are Dongting Lake and Poyang Lake. Both are less than 100 metres (328 ft) above sea level. The lower reach has formed a broad delta plain – the site of Shanghai – less than 10 metres (33 ft) above sea level.

The whole area has the largest concentration of deepwater lakes in China. It is a heavily populated region, and flotillas of tiny fishing boats are a

The Blue-tailed Skink (*Eumeces elegans*) is widely distributed in the mountain forests of central and southern China.

common sight on the lakes. Fishing is a major industry and the lakes hold 250 species of fish including Chinese Sturgeon (*Acipenser sinensis*) and Chinese Paddlefish (*Psephurus gladius*). Lotuses and reeds grow around the edges of the lakes, with cultivated paddy fields behind them, and the plain has become known as 'The Land of Fish and Rice'. Various migratory birds appear annually on the lakes, including the Japanese Crane (*Grus japonensis*) which migrates in thousands to Poyang Lake.

BELOW: fishing is a major industry on the deep-water lakes of the middle and lower reaches of the Yangtze (Chang) River.

The south-eastern hills

The hills and low mountains to the south of the Yangtze River and to the east of the Yunnan-Guizhou Plateau consist mainly of granite, sandstone and shale. Loose red stones that easily erode characterize a number of 'red basins' in the hills. A few of the mountains are as high as 1500 metres (4920 ft). Of these, Lu Mountain, Huang Mountain, Heng Mountain and the Wuyi Mountains are famous for their beautiful scenery.

Because of extensive faulting and folding these mountains have been formed into remarkable shapes, with sheer precipices, overhanging rocks, rapids and waterfalls. In the Zhuang Autonomous Region of Guangxi the hills are characterized by eroded limestone landforms with well-developed stone pillars (hoodoos) along the valleys. These remarkable and beautiful features have earned the scenery around Guilin the reputation of being 'the finest under heaven'.

Owing to the influence of the monsoon the south-eastern hills have abundant rainfall, and this has encouraged a lush growth of vegetation. This is the main area of subtropical evergreen forest in China, and bamboo is also widely distributed. Tea, tung-oil trees and tea-oil trees as well as subtropical fruit trees such as tangerine, pomelo, longan and lychee occur naturally and are now cultivated. Subtropical reptiles including poisonous snakes such as the Asian Cobra (*Naja naja*) are frequently seen.

ABOVE: Sericeous Nealitsea (*Nealitsea sericea*) can be found only in Putuo and Taohua Dao islands, in the Zhoushan Qundao Islands (opposite the mouth of the Yangtze River). It is an extremely rare and endangered plant.

THE LIMESTONE PINNACLES OF GUILIN

ABOVE TOP: sunrise through the mists on the Li River.
ABOVE: Spiny Bamboo (*Bambusa arundinacea*) growing by the Li.

Some of the most spectacular scenery in China, and quite possibly in the world, is found in the region around Guilin in the northern part of Guanxi Autonomous Region in southern China. The mountains for which the region is famous are not particularly high, reaching at most only about 180 metres (600 ft), but it is their shape and their dramatic setting rather than their height that make them remarkable.

The mountains rise precipitously from a flat landscape along the fertile edges of the Li River. Consisting of porous limestone, they are highly susceptible to erosion by the winds and heavy monsoons of this rainy area, and as a result they have been worn into spectacular pinnacles. The prevailing humidity also makes for a misty climate, and this too has contributed to the area's fame as it has made for popular views for generations of Chinese painters.

The Yunnan-Guizhou Plateau

Most of this plateau in the south of China is about 1000 to 2000 metres (3280 to 6560 ft) above sea level. It follows the general topographical trend by descending from the north-west to the south-east, and at the southern and eastern fringes of the plateau the valleys have an elevation of only 500 metres (1640 ft) or so. The heavy summer rains of the monsoon have carved the widely distributed limestones into spectacular shapes: the rock pillars of Lunan in Yunnan Province and the waterfall of Huangguo Shu in Guizhou Province are famous for their natural beauty. There are many lakes on the plateau, most of which are formed in deep faults; examples are the Dianchi and Erhai lakes in Yunnan Province.

The area is in the subtropical zone, and has a remarkably mild climate. The annual mean temperature is about 15°C (59°F), and to the visitor it appears to be spring all year round, with flourishing trees, lush grasses, colourful flowers and green mountains glittering with clear mountain streams. It is possible that the plateau is the origin of the Himalayan flora in China. Yunnan Pine (*Pinus yunnanensis*) and Schottky Oak (*Cyclobalanopsis glaucoides*) are the predominant plant species.

Yunnan is the home of most of the endemic single species plant genera of China. These species are isolated survivors of genera that were once more numerous, but have been all but wiped out by climatic changes. There are 60 such genera in the whole province and about half of them are endemic to Yunnan, such as Funing Parepigynum (*Parepigynum funingense*) of the periwinkle family (Apocynaceae), and Cyphotheca (*Cyphotheca*) of the melastoma family (Melastomataceae). The animals in this area include the extremely rare Biet's Snub-nosed Monkey (*Pygathrix bieti*), the scarcely less rare Brelich's Snub-nosed Monkey (*Pygathrix brelichi*), the tree frog *Hyla annectans* and the viper *Trimeresurus jerdonii*.

ABOVE TOP: Huangguo Shu Falls in Guizhou Province. The falls have been spectacularly shaped by heavy summer monsoon rains.
ABOVE: the rock pillars of Lunan in Yunnan formed by weathering into a stone forest.

LEFT: *Rhododendron yunnanense* growing near Dali in Yunnan at over 3000 metres (16,290 ft).

TOP: Western Heaven Lake in the beautiful Tien Mountains, Xinjiang Province. The Tien have a tremendous variety of vegetation.

ABOVE: mangroves in the nature reserve on Hainan Dao Island. Seedlings are often carried away in the water before being washed up on mud banks where they grow.

The Hengduan Mountains

The western parts of Sichuan and Yunnan provinces consist of several mountain ranges running from north to south. The mountains are higher in the north of the region, reaching some 4000 metres (13,120 ft), while in the south they are less than 3000 metres (9840 ft) high. Several large rivers running through the mountains form a landscape of parallel mountain ridges separated by deep valleys.

The mountains provide an excellent example of the vertical distribution of vegetation, with tropical plants at the foot of the mountains, rising through the subtropical and temperate to alpine at the top. As a result of this vertical zonation the Hengduan Mountains have one of the richest montane floras in the world.

This region is the original home of several popular garden flowers which are now widely grown in the West, including species of rhododendron, primula and gentian. As for the animals, there are representative species from both the southern and northern faunas, as well as survivors from before the Quaternary ice ages such as the Giant Panda (*Ailuropoda melanoleuca*) and Takin (*Budorcas taxicolor*).

Taiwan, Hainan Dao and the South China Sea islands

All these are in the tropical zone with the exception of the northern part of Taiwan, which is in the subtropical zone. The climate in this region is characterized by high temperatures and abundant rainfall. Tropical rainforest predominates. On the coastline, Common Bruguiera (*Bruguiera gymnorhiza*), Kandelia (*Kandelia candel*) and Sharpleaf Mangrove (*Rhizophora apiculata*) grow in the mud of the intertidal areas and are partially covered at high tide. These mangroves are especially interesting as the fruit germinates while it is still on the parent tree. After it has grown, a seedling drops off and either grows in the mud where it lands, or is carried by the water, sometimes for several years, before it is stranded on another mudbank. In this way the mangroves can effect a form of land reclamation.

Most of the South China Sea Islands are coral islands which were formed in the Quaternary period less than 2 million years ago, and as a result they have been colonized by relatively few species of plants. There are only 150 species of angiosperms on the Xisha Islands. Evergreen trees include *Pisonia grandis* and Velvetseed (*Guettarda speciosa*); evergreen bushes include *Scaevola sericea* and *Argusia argentea*.

Many species of animals that live on the mainland do not appear on the islands, but Hainan Dao Island has several animals that are found there and nowhere else in China; these include the Red-shanked Douc Monkey (*Pygathrix nemaeus*), Eld's Deer (*Cervus eldi*), the Hainan Hare (*Lepus hainanus*), the Hainan Flying Squirrel (*Petinomys electilis*), the Hainan Hill-Partridge (*Arborophila ardens*) and the Hainan Tree Frog (*Rhacophorus oxycephalus*). Endemic species in Taiwan include the Taiwan Macaque (*Macaca cyclopis*) and Swinhoe's Pheasant (*Lophura swinhoei*).

The fauna of the South China Sea Islands consists mainly of seabirds and migratory birds. There are 103 species of birds on the Xisha Islands, but only ten species breed there. These include the Red-footed Booby (*Sula sula*), the Brown Booby (*Sula leucogaster*), the Sooty Tern or Wide Awake (*Sterna fuscata*) and the White Tern (*Gygis alba*). During the breeding period vast numbers of these birds gather in colonies to nest and lay their eggs, and many islands have deep deposits of guano. The beaches are used as breeding grounds by Leatherback Sea Turtles (*Dermochelys coriacea*), Hawksbill Turtles (*Eretmochelys imbricata*) and Green Turtles (*Chelonia mydas*).

These sparsely inhabited coral islands, with their large populations of nesting seabirds, stretch 1500 kilometres (930 miles) from the coast of Hainan Dao Island, and bring the territory of China down almost as far as the Equator.

49

FORESTS 森林

The actual area of forest in China is not especially large. Seven countries have more forested land, and the fraction of the total country covered by forests is 13 per cent. Despite this, China has a great number of tree species, and more rare ones than in any other country. The forests are also the homes of many of the most interesting birds and animals, such as tragopans (*Tragopan*), the Golden Monkey (*Pygathrix roxellanae*) and the Giant Panda (*Ailuropoda melanoleuca*).

China's forests are not evenly distributed across the country, but are mainly situated in the eastern monsoon region. The types of forest fall into distinct bands from north to south according to climate, with cool-temperate coniferous forest in the north, then temperate coniferous and deciduous broad-leaved mixed forest, warm-temperate deciduous broad-leaved forest, subtropical evergreen broad-leaved forest and tropical monsoon rainforest and rainforest in the extreme south of the country.

There are more than 20,000 species of angiosperms in China, among which more than 8000 species are trees or shrubs. Among the 30 genera of coniferous trees in the world, about 200 species belonging to 20 genera grow in China. There are eight genera – Dawn Redwood (*Metasequoia*), Cathay Silver Fir (*Cathaya*), Golden Larch (*Pseudolarix*), Taiwania (*Taiwania hayata*), Chinese Deciduous Cypress (*Glyptostrobus*), Keteleeria (*Keteleeria*), Fukien Cypress (*Fokienia*), and Chinese Fir (*Cunninghamia*) – which only grow in China. There are even more broad-leaved species – some 200 genera in all. Many are endemic to China, such as Dove Tree (*Davidia involucrata*), Eucommia (*Eucommia*), Emmenopterys (*Emmenopterys*), False Pistachio (*Tapiscia*) and others. If the destruction of forests worldwide continues China's forest nature reserves will become increasingly important.

Cool-temperate coniferous forest

This type of forest is found at the southern end of the coniferous forest belt that lies across northern Eurasia, including Siberia. The Chinese section is mainly located in the country's northern mountains, and extends as far south as 46° 26′N on the gentle slopes of the Da Hinggan Mountains. However, most of the forest is on the mountains of Heilonjiang Province, where the altitude is generally about 1000 metres (3300 ft) above sea level. The rivers, such as the tributaries of the Heilong River, are deep and flow through wide, gently sloping valleys. Here, as in Siberia, it is very cold; the winter lasts for nine months, and the average annual temperature is below 0°C (32°F). There are only about 80 to 100 frost-free days each year, and in some parts of the northern forest there is permafrost – a layer of permanently frozen ground below the soil surface.

The coniferous species in the cool-temperate forest include the Dahurian Larch (*Larix gmelinii*), Mongolian Scots Pine (*Pinus sylvestris* var. *mongolica*) and Korean Spruce (*Picea koraiensis*). The dominant broad-leaved species include the Manchurian or Asian White Birch (*Betula platyphylla*), Dahurian Birch (*Betula dahurica*), Mongolian Oak (*Quercus mongolica*), and David's Poplar (*Populus davidiana*). Of all of them, the Dahurian Larch is best adapted to the cold and hence grows further north than the others. All these trees can produce leaves, flowers and seeds over a very short period, so completing their annual cycles in just a few months.

Dahurian Larches are common throughout the region, occupying about 50 per cent of the total forest area. They grow to a height of about 20 to 30 metres (65 to 100 ft), casting deep shade which restricts other vegetation. However, where they are destroyed by man-made or natural causes, broad-leaved trees such as Asian White Birch, David's Poplar, Dahurian Birch and Mongolian Oak often grow in their place, forming secondary

ABOVE: the dense, slender stems are typical of the closed canopy forest of David's Poplar (*Populus davidiana*), a common broad-leaved tree of the cool-temperate forest.
OPPOSITE: Dawn Redwood (*Metasequoia glyptostroboides*) is the only deciduous redwood; redwoods are native to China.

PREVIOUS PAGE: there are more than 8000 wide-ranging species of trees and shrubs in China, a significant number of which are quite rare. Many of these are protected in forest nature reserves.

forests. These currently occupy about 24 per cent of the forest area. Eventually, the Dahurian Larch will again replace them as they provide the necessary shade for its development. Among the former trees, Asian White Birch often predominates, sometimes forming its own forest.

Of the other coniferous trees, Mongolian Scots Pine is found mainly in the northern part of the Da Hinggan Mountains, generally on southern slopes at an altitude of 300 to 500 metres (1000 to 1600 ft). Korean Spruce is most commonly found growing on wet soils on the valley floors. On the edge of the forests, underneath the tree canopy, a variety of bushes and low shrubs grow, including Cowberry (*Vaccinium vitis-idaea*), Labrador Tea (*Ledum palustre*) and Dahurian Rhododendrons (*Rhododendron dauricum*), and many grasses (Gramineae), sedges (*Carex* spp.) and Red-flowered Pyrola (*Pyrola incarnata*). Some of the plants have commercial value; for example, jam and wine can be made from Cowberry.

Apart from the Scots Pine, Korean Spruce and a few others, most of these trees, even the coniferous species, shed their leaves in the cold winters, making the forests grey and desolate. The dark canopy favours mainly the growth of mosses and lichens, but various small shrubs, which flower in late spring and summer, also grow. It is often damp and boggy underfoot, but this presents no problem to the deer that frequent the forests.

Mixed coniferous and broad-leaved forests of the Changbai Mountains, with the typical contrasting colours of mixed vegetation.

Temperate coniferous and deciduous broad-leaved mixed forest

This type of forest is most widespread in the mountains of the north-eastern part of China, including the Xiao Hinggan and Changbai mountains. In places the forest covers over 40 per cent of the land area. This is one of the main forest areas in China, with forests covering the smooth and low Xiao Hinggan Mountains and all of the mountains in the Changbai range. The trees that grow here have to be able to withstand cold as the mean temperature in January is between −14°C (7°F) and −28°C (−18°F), and the temperature can fall to −40°C (−40°F). However, as this area is close to the Pacific Ocean the climate is significantly affected by the sea, and the summers are warm, with July and August highs in the range 20 to 24°C (68 to 75°F). Annual precipitation can reach 500 to 1000 mm (20 to 40 in.), being highest in the south-east and lowest in the north-west. Between 100 and 150 days of the year are usually frost-free. The warm summer temperatures and reasonable level of rainfall provide good growing conditions, and if it were not for human intervention the forests would be dense.

The main species of coniferous tree is the Korean Pine (*Pinus koraiensis*). The bark and wood are red, which made it popular for building temples, and have a distinctive but delicate odour. Further south the number of the broad-leaved trees increases, the main species being the Mongolian Oak (*Quercus mongolica*). Manchurian Ash (*Fraxinus mandshurica*), another common tree in these forests, has hard wood much favoured by furniture makers. The southern part also boasts several rare species of trees and shrubs including the Largeleaf Ash (*Fraxinus rhynchophylla*), several maples (*Acer*), *Kalopanax pictum*, and the Japanese Yew (*Taxus cuspidata* var. *latifolia*). There are many species of undershrubs; the commonest include Manchurian Filbert (*Corylus mandshurica*) and Many-prickled Acanthopanax (*Acanthopanax senticosus*). Manchurian Ash, Amur Cork Tree (*Phellodendron amurense*) and Japanese Yew are relict species of the Tertiary period. The Amur Cork Tree is a wide-branched tree which grows up to 15 metres (50 ft) high, its green leaves turning gold in autumn, when it carries an abundance of shiny black fruits. Various vines grow in the area, including Amur Grape (*Vitis amurensis*), Chinese Magnolia Vine (*Schisandra chinensis*), and species of actinidia

Chestnut-flanked White-eyes (*Zosterops erythropleura*) live in mountain forests of north-eastern China; all the white-eyes, which are found in Africa and Australia as well as Asia, have white rings of feathers around the eyes and are superficially similar to warblers in appearance.

(*Actinidia*), some of which produce fine fruits suitable for both wine- and jam-making.

The Changbai Mountains are home to various medicinal plants, including the well-known Ginseng (*Panax ginseng*). The root, stem, leaf and fruit are all said to give health and vigour to the body and to settle the stomach. Ginseng grows on the forest floor and is about 20 cm (8 in.) in height, with small, light yellowish-green flowers.

If these forests are destroyed and the area where they stood is left undisturbed, various types of secondary forest may grow. The most common is Mongolian Oak (*Quercus mongolica*) forest dominated by pioneer species such as David's Poplar (*Populus davidiana*) and Asian White Birch (*Betula platyphylla*), which germinate in sunny clearings once the mature forest is felled.

In the valleys there are meadows and patches of woodland, the main species of trees being the larch *Larix olgensis* and Asian White Birch.

According to pollen analysis, Korean Pine (*Pinus koraiensis*) began to grow in the north-eastern part of China about 10 million years ago and it is now so widespread in the Xiao Hinggan and Changbai mountains that the latter are known in China as the native home of Korean Pine. The trees are evergreen and grow to a height of 30 to 40 metres (100 to 130 ft); they make excellent timber for building purposes.

Warm-temperate deciduous broad-leaved forest

Although the warm-temperate broad-leaved forests cover a vast area of northern China, including the southern part of Liaoning Province, Shandong Province, the North China Plain and the Loess Plateau, the forests are sparsely distributed. The average annual temperature is 8 to 16°C (46 to 61°F) in these areas; it is hot and wet in summer, dry in winter, and spring is characterized by persistent dusty winds. Along the coast, the annual rainfall generally exceeds 800 mm (32 in.), although on the western coast it is only 400 mm (16 in.). About 70 per cent of the annual precipitation falls in summer.

In the past, this part of China was covered by dense forests and forest-steppe. However, the land here has long been used for agricultural purposes and the human population has consequently been very dense. Under these conditions the forests have been greatly reduced, so that now forest cover constitutes only 8 per cent of the landscape.

As a result of this destruction the main surviving species are typical of secondary forest: oaks (*Quercus*) and Chinese Pine (*Pinus tabulaeformis*). The Chinese Pine is the most common; it can live 400 or 500 years and grows to over 20 metres (65 ft). Examples of these long-lived trees can often be found near ancient buildings such as temples. Chinese Pines are also popular trees for the fascinating art of growing bonsai. The leaves of east Liaoning oaks are eaten by silkworms.

North and west of Beijing the forests make a magnificent sight when the leaves of the maple (*Acer*) trees turn red and gold in the autumn, in contrast to their green neighbours. On the low coastal mountains and hills where the climatic conditions are favourable, the forests were once destroyed, but are now growing back, due to both replanting and natural regeneration. Japanese Red Pine (*Pinus densiflora*) is the dominant species; the trunk is often crooked, but it may grow in a dense cover to over 35 metres (115 ft) tall. Above 1600 metres (5250 ft) in all the mountains the forest turns to cool-temperate, with species typical of that zone.

Commercial forestry prospers in the warm-temperate belt. Chinese Chestnut (*Castanea sativa*) and Chinese Walnut (*Juglans regia*) grow within the forests, and are also cultivated separately. Peaches (*Prunus persica*), apples (*Malus domestica*), persimmon (*Diospyros kaki*), Chinese Walnut and Chinese Chestnut all have commercial uses.

Subtropical evergreen broad-leaved forest

About a quarter of the country falls into the subtropical region, from the Qin Ling Mountains (34°N) and Huai River (32°N) in the north to almost as far south as the Tropic of Cancer. As well as stretching 12° of latitude, the region extends 28° of longitude, from the coast to the eastern edge of the Qinghai-Tibet Plateau.

The predominantly subtropical monsoon climate of this area is characterized by high temperatures and abundant rainfall. This region has not been much altered by climatic changes and glaciation for millions of years, and under these stable conditions the flora has become abundant and very diverse. According to current statistics, there are some 1700 genera of seed plants in this area, which is 56.9 per cent of the total number found in China. Of these, 77 are endemic, single-species genera of great antiquity and many relict species survive in this area as well. There are in all about 14,500 species of angiosperms in the subtropical area.

The oak family (Fagaceae), is the most important in the region, and its evergreen species account for a large proportion of the forest area. Evergreen chinquapins (*Castanopsis*), and Tanoak (*Lithocarpus*) of the family Fagaceae are among the 15 genera with over 100 species of the laurel family (Lauraceae) found in this area. The most important genus is *Machilus* followed by the spice-producing *Cryptocarya*, slugwoods (*Beilschmiedia*) and cinnamon (*Cinnamomum*).

Eleven or so genera and over 100 species of the tea family (Theaceae) are subdominant or common species in these forests, the main genera being *Schima*, *Adinandra* and *Anneslea*. Tea-producing plants (from the *Camellia* genus) are now grown commercially, and there are still a few wild tea plants. The tea plant *C. sinensis* has long been cultivated in China for use as a medical stimulant and as a popular beverage.

Bamboo proliferates in this type of forest, with some 26 genera and 300 species (including tropical species), of which the most valuable is Meso Bamboo (*Phyllostachys pubescens*).

Many varieties of pteridophytes (ferns) grow profusely in tropical and subtropical zones. There are about 45 families in the area, with 140 genera and over 1000 species, mainly flourishing on the ground layer of the forests. On the land cleared of forest and turned over to grass, *Dicranopteris dichetoma*, a relict species of the Mesozoic era, has become very common.

However, the main vegetation in this forest belt is subtropical broad-leaved evergreen trees, which thrive in the region, benefiting from the warm and humid climate; the mean January temperature is 5 to 12°C (41 to 54°F) and the July average 25 to 30°C (77 to 86°F). With the heavy monsoon rains, the annual precipitation is 1000 to 2000 mm (40 to 79 in.), which rises to 2600 mm (102 in.) in some places. But there is also a little rainfall in winter, enough to support broad-leaved evergreen plants. The forest is usually up to 20 metres (65 ft) high, sometimes 30 metres (100 ft), with several layers of canopy and shrubs and climbers beneath. It is one of the most vigorous forests in the world, with its impressive and luxuriant growth and rich fauna.

Endemic species of the subtropical zone in China are Bitter Evergreen Chinquapin (*Castanopsis sclerophylla*), Carles's Evergreen Chinquapin (*C. carlesii*), Farges' Evergreen Chinquapin (*C. fargesii*), Ford's Evergreen Chinquapin (*C. fordii*), Faber's Evergreen Chinquapin (*C. fabri*), Blue Japanese Oak (*Cyclobalanopsis glauca*) and members of the large beech and oak families: Schima (*Schima superba*), Red Nanmu (*Machilus thunbergii*), Golden-haired Tanoak (*Lithocarpus chrysocomas*) and michelias (*Michelia*). The Dove Tree (*Davidia involucrata*) is especially beautiful, and so-called because of its large, white flowers that look like doves perching on its branches. It is also remarkable for being a single-species genus in a single-genus family. Rare and relict species are also numerous, such as White Aril Yew (*Pseudotaxus chienii*), Chinese Golden Larch (*Pseudolarix amabilis*), Plum Yews (*Cephalotaxus fortunei*), hemlocks (*Tsuga*), Maire's Yew (*Taxus chinensis* var. *mairei*) and many others.

In 1943 examples of the Water Larch, or Dawn Redwood (*Metasequoia glyptostroboides*) were found in Lichuan County, Hubei Province. Water Larch originated 100 million years ago in arctic regions, and subsequently spread southwards to Europe, Asia and North America. Until this discovery, it was thought to be extinct, and the find so surprised the botanical world that the plant was honoured as a 'living fossil'. Now there are Water Larch forests covering 600 square kilometres (230 square miles) of the county with an average height of about 30 metres (100 ft), and some 300-year-old Water Larches have also been found in the nearby Longshan County. These rare and precious trees attract thousands of visitors every year.

Because of man's intervention very little of the natural evergreen broad-leaved forest can be found in its virgin state. Masson Pine (*Pinus massoniana*) forests, which can be found almost everywhere on hilly areas below 800 metres (2620 ft) above sea level, and Chinese Fir (*Cunninghamia lanceolata*) forests, which thrive in a humid climate where there is acidic yellow earth, are, although very widespread, mainly secondary or planted.

The northern part of the subtropical evergreen forest zone forms the transition between subtropical evergreen and warm-temperate deciduous forests. Here the zonal vegetation type is mixed evergreen and deciduous broad-leaved forest, and main species that grow are those of the beech and oak families, such as the deciduous Sawtooth Oak (*Quercus acutissima*) and Oriental Cork Oak (*Q. variabilis*), and the evergreen Bitter Evergreen Chinquapin (*Castanopsis sclerophylla*) and Blue Japanese Oak (*Cyclobalanopsis glauca*).

The virgin forest can only be found in small areas at high altitude, where it has remained inaccessible and undisturbed by human activities. Secondary forests like those of Masson's Pine and Chinese Fir provide the main coverage.

TOP: the Dove Tree (*Davidia involucrata*) has large, papery white bracts.
ABOVE CENTRE: the hard, round fruit of the Dove Tree.
ABOVE: early growth of the Dawn Redwood (*Metasequioa glyptostroboides*) with delicate yellow-green foliage edged with red-brown.

On some extensive and high mountain ranges of over 3000 metres (10,000 ft), such as the Qin Ling and Shennongjia mountains, the vegetation has obvious altitudinal zones, and contains a wide diversity of species. Many endemic plants, like Qin Ling Mountain Fir (*Abies chensiensis*), the shrubs Tangut Daphne (*Daphne tangutica*), Girald Lilac (*Syringa giraldiana*) and Diel's Abelia (*Abelia dielsii*), can be seen here. One mountain alone, the 3767 metre (12,359 ft) Taibai Mountain in the Qin Ling, has 29 single-species genera, one endemic genus and over 150 endemic species. Shennongjia Mountain, known as a 'Treasure House of Plants', is so called because it is so rich in species; of the trees found here, *Tetracentron*, *Dipteronia*, Wilsontree (*Sinowilsonia*), the flowering Dove Tree (*Davidia*) and *Heptacodium* are endemic and ancient genera. It is also a haven for many wild animals.

The southern part of the subtropical evergreen forest, near the Tropic of Cancer, is also a transition zone with some tropical vegetation. The western part of the subtropical zone, including Yunnan-Guizhou Plateau and the south-west of Sichuan Province, which is mostly above 2000 metres (6500 ft) above sea level, has a moderate climate with insignificant temperature variation during the year. The area does not have four distinct seasons, but only two: rainy and dry. Though the average annual temperature is 2°C (3.6°F) lower than that of the areas at similar latitudes in eastern parts of the subtropical zone, the Mongolian cold air current is blocked by the high mountains in the north, enabling plants to grow in winter. The flora is mixed temperate, tropical and Alpine plants. Due to the complexity of the landforms and variety of available habitats, many endemic species, genera and families can be found. Some endemic species, such as the Yunnan Pine (*Pinus yunnanensis*), Evelyn's Keteleeria (*Keteleeria evelyniana*), Schottky's Oak (*Cyclobalanopsis glaucoides*), Delavay's Oak (*Castanopsis delavayi*) and Smith's Fir (*Abies georgei*), are the main forest species.

Since the region has for a very long time been subject to the effects of widespread human activity, little primitive evergreen forest remains. Yunnan Pine, which will grow in the open exposed to bright sunlight and can thus thrive in a variety of habitats, is now the main and most widely distributed type, although it does not form whole forests. The branches do not open out but cling to the trunk, making the trees look like tall pillars. Armand's Pine (*Pinus armandii*) and Evelyn's Keteleeria are also widely distributed, mostly growing with Yunnan Pine in mixed forests. In the mountains and hills of eastern Yunnan, western Guangxi and most of Guizhou, the rock is of limestone, which does not hold water. Accordingly, the tree cover in the forests is sparse – mainly Ducloux's Cypress (*Cupressus duclouxiana*) and Taiwan Juniper or Prickly Cypress (*Juniperus formosana*).

Tropical monsoon rainforest and tropical rainforest

Tropical rainforests and tropical monsoon rainforests are found south of the Tropic of Cancer. The main difference between them is that tropical monsoon rainforests experience a dry season and the trees lose their leaves, whereas in the tropical rainforests the trees keep their leaves all year round.

Only 3 per cent of China falls into the tropical region – the southern part of Yunnan, Guangdong and Fujian provinces, the Zhuang Autonomous Region of Guangxi, Hainan Dao Island, Taiwan Island and the South Sea Islands, and only small parts are forested. The climate is typical monsoon tropical with high temperatures; the average annual temperature is 20 to 26.5°C (68 to 80°F) on the plains and abundant rainfall produces luxuriant plant growth.

Although this is the smallest zone, it has more plant species than any of the other zones of China; the higher plants (angiosperms) number well over 7000 species. Many of these are found nowhere else in the world. For example, there are more than 500 species on Hainan Dao Island, and more than 300 in Xishuangbanna in southern Yunnan. Of these species, many are rare and precious, and are given national protection. The forests are also rich in wildlife, with monkeys, snakes, elephants and large numbers of noisy, colourful birds.

Monsoon rainforest is distributed in the tropical zone where dry and wet seasons alternate, the dry season occurring from November to March. As well as differing in that the trees shed their leaves partly or even entirely in the dry season, this type of forest is distinctive from the rainforest to a small extent in the species that grow, and in the fact that rainforest species are purely tropical. Over 80 per cent are pan-tropical species (species found throughout the tropics of the world). There is no dominant species of tree, but a mix of predominantly the mulberry family (Moraceae), chinaberry family (Meliaceae), the soapberry family (Sapindaceae) which includes many lianas and the Lychee (*Litchi chinensis*), the lime or linden family (Tiliaceae), the trumpet creeper or bignonia family (Bignoniaceae), which are mainly lianas,

Tropical monsoon forest on Hainan Dao Island: few habitats could provide such a feast for naturalists' eyes.

spurge family (Euphorbiaceae), custardapple family (Annonaceae), including the Durians (Bombacaceae), and the sterculia family (Sterculiaceae), which are related to the African colas. The species in the gurjun family (Dipterocarpaceae) are rather few in number in the area, but some of them, such as Stellate-hair Vatica (*Vatica astrotricha*) and Kwangsi Parashorea (*Parashorea chinensis* var. *kwangsiensis*), are very important for they may grow in almost pure dipterocarp forests and are typical of the rainforest of the monsoon regions.

The tropical monsoon rainforest is rich in endemic species, such as Hainan Belltree (*Radermachera hainanensis*), Hainan Chaulmoogra Tree (*Hydnocarpus hainanensis*), Hainan Meyna (*Meyna hainanensis*) and Hainan Rosewood (*Dalbergia hainanensis*) on Hainan Dao Island, and the Hsienmu (*Burretiodendron hsienmu*), Garcinia (*Garcinia chevalieri*) of the widespread mangosteen family (Guttiferae), which produce drugs, dyes and fruits, and Naked-flowered Tetrameles (*Tetrameles nudiflora*) in Guangxi and Yunnan. There are also many deciduous species such as the kapok or silk cotton tree, the Common Bombax (*Bombax malabaricum*), Lebbek Albizzia (*Albizia lebbek*), a valuable timber tree of the pea family, and Chittagong Chickrassy (*Chukrasia tabularis*), one of the mahoganies.

The appearance and structure of the monsoon rainforest alter with the seasons as the climate changes from dry to wet. In the dry season, the highest trees drop most of their leaves due to shortage of water, and the canopy becomes sparse, allowing sunshine to reach the forest floor beneath. In the wet season, the canopy is so dense as to make the interior of the rainforest very dark. However, the undergrowth has adapted to survive and does not die away for lack of light. There are two to three sublayers of trees with an average height of less than 25 metres (80 ft), the tallest being about 35 metres (115 ft) high. Plank or buttress roots are generally not well developed except for those of the various fig trees (*Ficus*). There are fewer large woody climbers

Tropical rainforest trees will adapt to their habitat: these are buttress roots in Lianfeng Mountain Nature Reserve in Hainan Dao Island.

and epiphytes and they are less well developed than those in the true rainforest.

True rainforest has developed in the warmest and wettest tropical area of China, including the southern parts of Taiwan, Guangdong and Yunnan provinces, Guangxi Autonomous Region and south-eastern Tibet. The forest consists of evergreen tropical species, growing luxuriantly in a dense 'jungle'. Because of the tropical climate, ground litter decomposes quickly, so the recycling of nutrients is rapid. Sadly, only a small area of this extraordinarily rich, primitive forest remains, and many of the plant species, and a number of insects, reptiles and amphibians, are severely endangered.

The tropical monsoon rainforest has developed only in certain humid areas in river valleys and on the windward slopes of the lower mountains and hills. In the eastern part of the country, there is rainforest only below 500 metres (1650 ft); to the west this increases to 800 metres (2650 ft) in south-western Yunnan and to about 1000 metres (3300 ft) in south-eastern Tibet.

The Chinese rainforest is similar to the rainforest of South-east Asia. Trees of the gurjun family are commonly found in both areas. There are many rainforest species of a tropical nature; most can also be found in the monsoon rainforest, and there is no obvious dominant one in any part of the forest. Though the individual plants of Stellate-hair Vatica (*Vatica astrotricha*) and Small-leaved Heritiera (*Heritiera parvefolia*) are relatively common on Hainan Dao Island, for example, they are intermixed with other species.

The rainforest is also very similar to that of South-east Asia with respect to the form and structure of the forest. The trees are generally very tall, with an average height of 30 to 40 metres (100 to 130 ft). Some grow to 60 metres (200 ft) in height, true giants of the forest. The trees have straight trunks and greyish white, smooth bark. The forest can be divided into three layers; the shrubs form one layer, sometimes overlapping with the herb layer. The tree canopy forms the final layer and looks almost level from above, despite the great variety of tree species.

The rainforest is characterized by the abundance of large, woody climbers, the lianas (vines), which have adapted to germinate in deep shade but require bright light as they mature. Their slender stems are supported by the trees which they climb, eventually penetrating the dense canopy in order to reach open sunlight. In doing so they bind the forest trees so effectively that dead, broken trees are sometimes held upright by them for years.

Epiphytes survive in the gloom of the rainforest in a quite different way.

They germinate on the boughs of tall trees and reach high into the canopy. They have a network of long, trailing, aerial roots which catch debris and fallen leaves to provide the epiphytes with nutrients. There may be hundreds of epiphytes, of scores of species, on a single large tree.

These forests include species of fig trees (*Ficus*), breadfruits and jackfruits (*Artocarpus*), the custardapple family (Annonaceae) and the sapote family, which grow large and showy flowers and beautiful fruits from their trunks, rather than their branches. Woody climbers are always species of the pea family (Leguminosae), custardapple family and dogbane or periwinkle family (Apocynaceae), most of which climb up to the highest part of trees.

Saprophytes are able to live in deep shade, having no chlorophyll and therefore no need for sunlight to assimilate food. They live on decaying vegetable matter. Other forest plants are semi-parasitical, taking nutrients from the trees on which they grow. The stranglers, including the Lofty Fig (*Ficus altissima*), are initially attached to the host plant in which they have germinated, but take their nutrients and water from the air. Then they grow roots into the ground, circling the trunks of the trees within like cloaks. When they become strong enough, they may strangle the trees to death with their cloaks, and then grow independently. Some types of fern grow on the tops of trees, winding themselves round in nest-like shapes like young stranglers, taking water and nutrients from the ambient atmosphere. Many epiphytes flower very beautifully, giving rise to the name 'gardens in the air'.

All these species have developed their own unique means of survival in the rainforest, each having found a niche in one of the various habitats that are provided.

The bamboo groves are made up of woody, perennial bamboo plants belonging to the bamboo subfamily of the grass family (Gramineae). Most of the plants are small or medium-sized shrubs which grow in clusters. However, the highest bamboos may reach 20 to 30 metres (65 to 100 ft).

Usually the reproduction of bamboo is asexual. The stems spread underground over several metres, and have little nodules on them which turn into buds; the buds then become young bamboo shoots. The young bamboo grove is thus formed in the way that reeds (*Phragmites*) form reed beds. One bamboo plant may spread its subterranean stems over a large area; a bamboo grove is always a pure and dense stand of a single species of plant. Many species of bamboo are characterized by high, thick stalks and slender branches. The stalks are much like slender tree trunks so that the bamboo grove gives the appearance of a young forest, and is consequently called 'bamboo forest'. The young shoots are familiar to all those who enjoy Chinese food and have eaten bamboo shoots.

There are altogether 62 genera and over 1000 species of bamboo in the world, of which 37 genera and about 700 species grow in Asia. Twenty-seven genera are endemic. China has the greatest number of bamboo species, having 30 genera and no fewer than 300 species. Some species are very beautiful, with multi-coloured patterns on the stalks, and others have square stalks. China is also the home of many species such as Meso Bamboo (*Phyllostachys pubescens*, also known as *Phyllostachys edulis*), which is the highest and fastest growing species, Giant Timber Bamboo (*P. bambusoides*), Henon Bamboo (*P. nigra* var. *henomis*), Chinese Bamboo (*Sinobambusa tootsik*) and Tonkin Cane (*Pseudosasa amabilis*). Giant Timber Bamboo originated in China but is now also found both in Britain and in Japan. The area of bamboo groves in China is 3.2 million hectares (12,355 square miles), which is one fifth of the total bamboo grove coverage in the world.

Bamboo groves are widely distributed in China, the natural limits being between 18 and 35° N from the Yellow River catchment area to Hainan Dao Island, and between 85 and 122° E from the Nyalam region of Tibet to Taiwan Island. Cultivated bamboos are even more widely distributed

LEFT: this bamboo stand grows in the hot springs area of Huangshan like a dense young forest.
ABOVE: quite a different appearance is given by the fronds of Spiny Bamboo (*Bambusa arundinacea*) near Guilin.

throughout the country. For instance, *Bambusa remotiflora* and *Bambusa suavis* are planted in the Xisha Islands in the South China Sea. In Beijing (40°N), the bamboo *Phyllostachys viridis* is planted for ornamental purposes.

It should be emphasized here that, although the distribution of bamboo covers quite a large area of the country, the bamboo groves are concentrated mainly in tropical and subtropical zones; in other words, they flourish in the hills, low mountains and valleys south of the Yangtze (Chang) River where the climate is warm and humid. The only significant exception to this rule is the area north of the Yangtze River, up the Yellow (Huang) River, but here the distribution is patchy, the bamboos do not grow so thick or so high as further south, and they are found only in places that enjoy warm micro-climates. However, fountain bamboo (*Sinarundinaria*) does grow at the height of 1000 to 3000 metres (3300 to 10,000 ft) on the slopes of the Qin Ling Mountains.

The two main bamboo-growing regions are between the Yangtze River and the Nan Ling Mountains and south of the Nan Ling Mountains. In the former the bamboo growth is relatively sparse. The main species that grow in small groves are Omei Mountain Bamboo (*Dendrocalamus affins*), Rigid Bamboo (*Bambusa rigida*) and other species of the genus *Bambusa*. Those that are more widely dispersed include species of the genera *Pseudosasa* and *Indosasa*. South of the Nan Ling Mountains bamboo grows in groves mainly of *Bambusa* species such as Punting Pole Bamboo (*B. pervariabilis*) and Chinese Textile Bamboo (*B. textilis*).

Of all the species of bamboo, Meso Bamboo (*Phyllostachys pubescens*) is by far the most common in China. Meso Bamboo groves (including cultivated plants) make up 78 per cent of the total bamboo grove coverage in the country, and reach a higher percentage of the total growth in the provinces to the south of the Yangtze River. Meso Bamboo grows quickly up to a height of 10 metres (33 ft) and makes fine timber. Remarkably, it takes only two months to grow from the emergence of shoots into mature bamboo, and well-cultivated Meso Bamboo groves can produce 30 tonnes of timber per hectare (12 tons per acre) annually. The timber is valuable for building purposes and for making into furniture, and it is also of use to fishermen, who lash mesos together to make rafts.

Species of fountain bamboo (*Sinarundinaria*), such as China Cane (*Sinarundinaria nitida*), have gradually become the staple diet of the famous but critically endangered Giant Panda (*Ailuropoda melanoleuca*) over a long

Misty belts of fir (*Abies*) forests such as these are widespread in the mountains of north-western China.

evolutionary period. However, when they can find it, they prefer the rarer Fang Cane (*Sinarundinaria fangiana*).

Bamboo flowers after a period of several years, the exact time varying from species to species. Some fountain bamboos flower only once about every 100 years. As they belong to the grass family (Gramineae), bamboo flowers are not spectacularly coloured, but shortly after flowering the bamboo plant dies. If large areas flower at one time, there can follow a sudden shortage of mature bamboo, and this has created serious food shortages for the Giant Pandas.

The use of bamboo in China goes back far into prehistory. Bamboo-woven wares have been unearthed among the remains of a primitive society of 6000 to 7000 years ago, at Hemuda, Yuyao, in Zhejiang Province. It has become ever more widely exploited with the progress of civilization, and the range of bamboo-made wares available has become increasingly diverse. Nowadays the woven-bamboo art of China is justly celebrated both at home and abroad for its delicacy and charm.

North-western mountain forest

Apart from the five forest zones so far discussed, there are forests on some of the great mountains in the north-western arid zone of China, for, despite desert and near-desert conditions in the plains, there can be reasonable rainfall on the middle and upper parts of mountains (see The Geography of China). Coniferous forests of spruce (*Picea*) and fir (*Abies*) are widespread on the Altai, Tien, Qilian, Helan and Daqing mountains. The most interesting are the trees on the Tien Mountains. On the northern slopes, a band of mountainous cold-temperate coniferous forest grows between 1500 and 2700 metres (4900 and 8900 ft). The southern slopes are very dry, so the forest has only developed in patches in shady valleys or valley bottoms between 2300 and 3000 metres (7500 and 9800 ft) above sea level. The predominant tree in this area is Schrenk's Spruce (*Picea schrenkiana*), which is distributed most widely in the western Yili region, where it grows to a height of 60 to 70 metres (200 to 230 ft) and develops a trunk diameter of over 1 metre (3 ft). Sievers's Apple (*Malus sieversii*), Persian (English) Walnut (*Juglans regia*), Cherry Plum (*Prunus sogdiana*) and Taishan Mountain Maple (*Acer semenovii*), which are all found in the Yili region, are relicts from the temperate broad-leaved forest of the Tertiary period 50 million years ago. Nature reserves have been set up in the area to ensure the continuing survival of the Sievers's Apple.

The climate in the north-west is generally too dry to support a varied flora but a few forest shrubs and the thick layers of lichen and moss on the trees are able to survive the arid conditions.

Wildlife of the forests

Forests are complicated and comprehensive ecosystems where differing climatic conditions, soils and aspects have encouraged the growth of different types of plants and the evolution of a wide variety of animals; in a virgin forest, many and various flora and fauna have evolved, taking advantage of the numerous ecological environments which are available. China also has the advantage of encompassing two great animal regions – the Oriental region and the Palaearctic region – and includes animal groups of the cool-temperate, warm-temperate and tropical zones. The great diversity of forest types, together with the fact that most of the surviving mountain forests are virtually inaccessible to the depredations of man, has made the forests havens for wildlife, and it is therefore in the forested regions that the majority of China's wildlife can be found.

Mammals

It is unlikely that you would catch sight of many of the forest mammals during the day, as they are mainly nocturnal. The chief exceptions are squirrels and rats, which are widespread.

Tree Shrews

The Tree Shrew (*Tupaia glis*) is a species of small mammal living in tropical forests in Yunnan, Guangxi and on Hainan Dao Island. The shape and behaviour of Tree Shrews are similar to those of squirrels and, like squirrels, they are active by day. They differ in their long, sharp snouts and short, round ears. Most of them look for insects on low trees, around stems of vines and on the ground, but they eat fruit, seeds and some small animals as well. For a long time it was considered that these unusual small mammals should be classified in the order Insectivora; however, some scientists consider that they belong to the lowest class of primates – the order that includes human beings. Other evidence suggests, however, that they may be closer to the common ancestors of all placental mammals.

Monkeys and gibbons

China's subtropical and tropical forests provide among the world's best environments for monkeys.

The Slow Loris (*Nycticebus coucang*), one of the prosimians (lower primates), can be found in Yunnan and the southern part of Guangxi. It lives in trees, sleeps in the morning and is active at night. It moves rather slowly as it searches for the eggs of birds and insects, hence its name.

The brown and red Rhesus Macaque (*Macaca mulatta*) is the most widely distributed monkey in China, the northern boundary of its range being as far as the northern mountains of Hebei Province. It lives in groups of ten or so. Stump-tailed Monkeys (*M. speciosae*) live on the high mountains of the south-western and southern part of China and are characterized by an unusually short tail, a well-developed, long beard at the lower jaw and a human appearance. A widespread modern belief has it that a primitive wild man lives in the mountains and since 1980 various supposed examples have been captured and exhibited, but in each case it has been found that the specimen was merely one of these Stump-tailed Monkeys.

The Black Leaf Monkey (*Presbytis francoisi*) and Grey Leaf Monkey (*P. pileatus*) have long forelegs and long tails. They live on tender leaves, flowers and fruits. These animals are exceedingly good at negotiating steep rocks, and swing from tree to tree with great agility.

The Golden Monkey (*Pygathrix roxellanae*) is an endemic and endangered species, with a head and body length of about 60 to 85 cm (24 to 33 in.). It is perhaps the most beautiful monkey in the world, with long, thick, golden brown fur, which is as long as 10 cm (4 in.) or more on the shoulder and at the back. The tail almost equals the length of the body. The skin on the face is a blue colour and the nostrils tilt upward, giving a distinctive and appealing facial expression. Golden Monkeys inhabit high mountains about 3000 metres (9800 ft) above sea level, in Sichuan, the southern part of Gansu and the southern part of Shaanxi. They live in small groups in broad-leaved forests dominated by oaks (*Quercus*) and chestnuts (*Castanea*) and eat wild fruits and tender leaves.

Two other monkeys, Biet's Snub-nosed Monkey (*Pygathrix bieti*) in the north-western part of Yunnan and Brelich's Snub-nosed Monkey (*P. brelichi*) in Guizhou, have blackish fur. They are also endemic and endangered species, and are very similar to the Golden Monkey. Indeed, both are so similar in all but colour that they are sometimes considered races of the Golden Monkey.

OPPOSITE LEFT: the Rhesus Macaque (*Macaca mulatta*) is the commonest monkey of southern mountain forests.
OPPOSITE RIGHT: the beautiful Golden Monkey (*Pygathrix roxellanae*) is now very rare and, sadly, endangered in the wild.
OPPOSITE BELOW: the 'King of the Monkeys' is Père David's Macaque (*Macaca thibetana*), photographed here in the Huang Mountains.

ABOVE: Slow Lorises (*Nycticebus coucang*) are sleepy creatures that become more active after dark, their large eyes being adapted for night vision.

THE DECLINE OF THE GIANT PANDA

One of the reasons for the decline of the Giant Panda (*Ailuropoda melanoleuca*) is its highly specialized diet, which depends largely on fountain bamboo. The bamboo periodically flowers and dies, depriving the Giant Panda of its main food. This has a significant effect on the population as the pandas are not widely distributed. Unfortunately, roads and human settlements have restricted them to small areas and they do not have enough choice of breeding partners to maintain a healthy population.

ABOVE: the Giant Panda (*Ailuropoda melanoleuca*).
LEFT: flowering bamboo in Wolong Nature Reserve, already nutritionally useless.

Gibbons (*Hylobates*) are interesting and remarkable animals, found in tropical forests. There are three species in China, namely the White-browed or Hoolock Gibbon (*H. hoolock*), the Lar or Common Gibbon (*H. lar*) and the Concolor, Crested or White-cheeked Gibbon (*H. concolor*), all living in the southern part of Yunnan Province and on Hainan Dao Island. Their short tails are usually invisible, their front limbs are noticeably longer than the back ones and their body weight is about 5 to 13 kg (11 to 28 lb). They can move about rapidly, and swing from branch to branch, hanging on with their long, powerful front limbs and leaping several metres (10 to 15 ft) from tree to tree. Gibbons are noisy, sociable, and fascinating to watch. They live mainly on leaves, flowers, fruits and insects.

Pandas

One of the most famous animals in China, and one of the most popular in the world, the Giant Panda (*Ailuropoda melanoleuca*) is also highly endangered. It is only found in China, and then only in three places, although in prehistoric times it was widespread. At present, Giant Pandas only exist in the bamboo groves of mountainous areas near the boundary of Sichuan, Shaanxi and Gansu provinces between 3000 and 4000 metres (9800 and 13,000 ft) above sea level. They eat mainly the stems and leaves of various bamboos, including China Cane (*Sinarundinaria nitida*), Swollen-jointed Cane (*Qiongzhuea tumidinoda*) and bamboos in the genus *Phyllostachys*. They will also eat fruits, bamboo rats and the remains of dead animals. From the structure of their teeth, pandas would appear to be carnivores, and it seems that when they were much more widespread some species adapted to specialized diets. It is one of these adapted species that has survived, eating primarily bamboo. A method of attracting and capturing them with meat bait has succeeded in Wolong Nature Reserve, and this appetite for meat may reflect their carnivorous ancestry.

Giant Pandas often move about alone, travelling slowly like bears. Using radio-tracking, it has been discovered that the panda's forage range is about 10 to 30 hectares (24 to 74 acres). The current densities of Giant Pandas are one animal per 3.3 to 3.8 square kilometres (1.3 to 1.5 square miles) at Wolong, Sichuan Province, one panda per 2.3 square kilometres (0.9 square miles) at Mabian, one per 4.8 to 9.7 square kilometres (1.9 to 3.7 square miles) at Wanglang and one per 2.9 square kilometres (1.1 square miles) in the Qin Ling Mountains, Shaanxi Province.

Pandas do not reproduce rapidly; pregnancies last five months, and usually a single cub is born in September. When two babies are born, it is common for only one of them to survive. Studies at Beijing Zoo showed that the mother would drop one cub while picking up the other, and inadvertently sit on the first. The newborn pandas are physically poorly developed, and they weigh only about 100 grammes (3.5 oz), while an adult weighs about 100 kg (220 lb). They reach sexual maturity at the age of six or seven and live another 20 years or so.

In 1980, in some parts of Sichuan Province, the Giant Panda's main food, fountain bamboos (*Sinarundinaria*), died over a very large area after flowering, which resulted in the death of a large number of Giant Pandas. However, according to research carried out by zoologists in recent years, this dependency on one type of food may not be the determining factor for the animal's disastrous decline. A more likely cause is that their habitats are becoming restricted and separated from each other by human activities, such as road building. One solution to these problems would be to develop ways for the panda communities to interconnect with each other, which must include the provision of 'corridors' of bamboo to allow movement from one core area to another.

The Red Panda (*Ailurus fulgens*) is not in fact in the same family as the

The large Hoolock Gibbon (*Hylobates hoolock*), now very rare in the forests of Yunnan, exudes an air of power and importance.

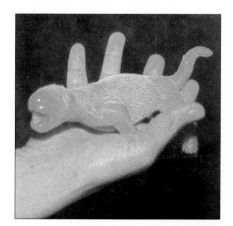

The new-born Giant Panda is small enough to be held in the palm of the hand.

There is very little resemblance, and no relationship, between the Red Panda (*Ailurus fulgens*) and its more famous namesake the Giant Panda (*Ailuropodus melanoleuca*).

Giant Panda. There is little resemblance except for a striking facial mask, and it is a much smaller animal at 60 cm (2 ft) long. It is a representative of the family Procyonidae and inhabits the mountainous forests and bamboo groves of the south-western region. The Red Panda also likes to eat the stems and leaves of fountain bamboo as well as fruits and birds' eggs. It is characterized by mostly dark red-brown fur, short legs and a long tail, and it is skilled at climbing. The breeding period begins in April or May; gestation lasts for 60 days and the female gives birth to two or three cubs at a time.

Bears, Red Dogs and civets

The Asiatic Black Bear (*Selenarctos thibetanus*) is commonly seen in coniferous and broad-leaved mixed forests. It is quite small in size and some male bears weigh as little as 100 kg (220 lb). Both sexes are black in colour, with a white 'V' on the chest. Asiatic Black Bears are also found in the southern evergreen broad-leaved forests and tropical rainforests and in the Himalayas at an elevation of 4000 metres (13,000 ft). In the northern part of China, after October, they choose large tree holes to hibernate in until spring of the following year. They are mild mannered unless attacked. They are omnivorous, with plants as their staple food, and have a special liking for honey. They are active in the daytime and are skilled at climbing trees. Generally speaking, these animals are solitary except for family groups. Their mating season is in summer and gestation lasts seven months, with two cubs being the norm. Asiatic Black Bears reach sexual maturity at the age of three and their lifespan is about 30 years.

Brown Bears (*Ursus arctos*) live only in the mountain forests of north-eastern, north-western and south-western China, living as high as 5000 metres (16,400 ft) above sea level. They are relatively large bears – males often weigh over 200 kg (440 lb). They hibernate in winter from November to March in caves. They are solitary, the mother looking after cubs on her own, and they live for about 40 years. Their characteristics and habits are quite similar to those of the Asiatic Black Bears, but Brown Bears are more formidable animals.

The Red Dog or Asian Wild Dog (*Cuon alpinus*) is a wolf-like animal that is widely distributed in forests, especially in southern China. In appearance it is quite similar to a large dog, with a head and body length of about 1 metre (3 ft). It is red-brown all over apart from the tip of the tail, which is black. It lives and hunts in groups of about ten, and can capture and kill animals much larger than itself, such as Tufted Deer (*Elaphodus cephalophus*), Wild Boar (*Sus scrofa*) and even young Water Buffalo (*Bubalus bubalis*).

Expert climbers, civets are common in China. They are grey with black marks and about the size of a fox, but with shorter legs. They are solitary and live mainly on small animals and wild fruits. Common Chinese species include the Large Indian Civet (*Viverra zibetha*), Small Indian Civet (*Viverricula indica*) and Masked Palm Civet (*Paguma larvata*).

Although quite small for a bear, the Asiatic Black Bear (*Selenarctos thibetanus*) has all the typical attributes of its family, including a liking for honey.

Cats

The Leopard Cat (*Felis bengalensis*) is the most widely distributed of China's nine forest species, inhabiting mountain forests in many areas. It weighs 3 to 7 kg (6.5 to 15 lb), has a brown body with black spots and stripes, and looks a little like a leopard. The Asiatic Golden Cat (*F. temmincki*) is similar but is larger, with a weight of 10 to 15 kg (22 to 33 lb). It is found chiefly in areas to the south of the Yangtze (Chang) River. The Lynx (*F. lynx*) is seen mainly in the mountainous forests of northern and south-western China. It weighs about 20 kg (44 lb) and is an agile animal, good at climbing trees and swimming. Unfortunately, it is heavily hunted for its fur.

Clouded Leopards (*Neofelis nebulosa*) inhabit the mountainous forest to the south of the Qin Ling Mountains. They are smaller than the familiar Leopard (*Panthera pardus*), with a body weight of about 20 to 30 kg (44 to 66 lb). Clouded Leopards have a less defined pattern with much larger spots than the Leopard, and are remarkably attractive animals. Leopards are widely distributed in mountainous forests, but they are now drastically reduced in numbers and very rare.

At one time Tigers (*Panthera tigris*) were widespread in China, but now their numbers are very small. Three subspecies are found today; the Siberian Tiger (*P. t. altaica*) and the South Chinese Tiger (*P. t. amoyensis*) are the best known. The Siberian Tiger is the largest – the body weight of the male can be as much as 200 kg (440 lb). It is limited to several northern mountainous areas in the eastern part of Heilongjiang Province and the south-eastern part of Jilin Province, and is a seriously endangered species – only a hundred or so Siberian Tigers remain.

The South Chinese Tigers are even more endangered as there are fewer than 40 of them. They are smaller than Siberian Tigers, and their fur is orange-ochre in colour. They are mainly distributed in the mountains of southern China, where they live on goats, wild pigs, badgers, bears and pheasants. Females reach sexual maturity at three and a half years. Clearly, urgent measures are needed to save them from extinction.

ABOVE LEFT: the Clouded Leopard (*Neofelis nebulosa*) of the tropical forests.
ABOVE: the Lynx (*Felis lynx*) is very much more widespread in Eurasia.
FAR LEFT: much smaller, but quite splendidly patterned, is the Leopard Cat (*Felis bengalensis*).
LEFT: the Siberian race of the Tiger (*Panthera tigris altaica*) now numbers only 100 or so individuals in China.

Deer, Takin and Gaur

The deer in China range in size from the tiny to the enormous, and include the rare as well as the common. The Lesser Mouse Deer (*Tragulus javanicus*) can be taken for a rabbit rather than a deer, and it weighs less than 2 kg (4¼ lb). This, the smallest deer in China, lives in the forests of the southern part of Yunnan Province. Musk Deer (*Moschus moschiferus*) are much more widely distributed, being found in many broad-leaved forests. They have given their name to the substance used in perfume and Chinese medicine, which is secreted by glands of the male deer. Tufted Deer (*Elaphodus cephalophus*) belong to the subtropical region in hills and high mountains south of the Qin Ling Mountains, while Red Deer or Wapiti (*Cerrus elaphus*) are found only in the north. The Red Deer is the larger, weighing about 250 kg (550 lb). While the Red Deer is common, the Thorold's or White-lipped Deer (*C. albirostris*), which is endemic to China, is endangered. It lives only in high-altitude forests on the Qinghai-Tibet Plateau at an elevation of 4000 metres (13,000 ft). Its body-weight is about 200 kg (440 lb). The winter coat of Thorold's Deer is much lighter in colour than its summer coat. Elk (*Alces alces*) can be seen only in the forests of the Da Hinggan Mountains, where they live on leaves from broad-leaved trees, and they like to be near water. They are huge animals: a mature male can easily weigh 700 kg (1540 lb). Their other distinguishing features are the flat horns and the large upper lip that is used to seize leaves.

TOP: mountain forests in northern China hold Red Deer (Wapiti) (*Cervus elephas*).
ABOVE LEFT: the Lesser Mouse Deer (*Tragulus javanicus*) is found in the south of Yunnan.
ABOVE RIGHT: Musk Deer (*Moschus moschiferus*) are widely distributed.
OPPOSITE ABOVE: the Takin (*Budorcas taxicolor*) is a mountain creature of Sichuan, Shaanxi and Tibet.
OPPOSITE BELOW: the huge Gaur (*Bos gaurus*) inhabits the tropical forests of southern Yunnan Province.

A large, heavy ruminant, the Takin (*Budorcas taxicolor*) is an endemic species in China distributed in Sichuan, the southern part of Shaanxi, and even in parts of Tibet. The weight of a Takin is as much as 300 kg (660 lb) and the colour of the body is brownish white. The shape of the horn is unusual, twisting upwards and outwards. These animals frequently gather in small groups and feed at an elevation of around 3000 metres (9800 ft).

Gaur (*Bos gaurus*) inhabit the tropical forests of the southern part of Yunnan Province. Looking like a huge wild bull, the Gaur is an impressive sight. A typical animal weighs 700 to 1000 kg (1540 to 2200 lb); the colour of the body is blackish brown. The lower part of the limbs is white. They are ferocious, but this has not prevented their numbers from becoming very small. They will charge aggressors and attack them with their horns.

Elephants

The world's second largest land mammal, the Indian Elephant (*Elephas maximus*) can be found in small numbers (about 200) in the tropical forest of Xishuangbanna. Unlike the African Elephant, it has only one prehensile lip, or pupilla, at the end of its trunk, and it also has smaller ears. A mature adult weighs about 3 to 4 tonnes and has a lifespan of about 120 years. They live in herds of 20 or 30, and are active in the early mornings and evenings, when

Living on ants in the forests of southern China, the Chinese Pangolin (*Manis pentadactyla*) is a real curiosity.

they go looking for tree bark, tender branches and the Bajoa Banana. Gestation lasts for about 20 months, but they give birth to only a single calf and give birth only once every five or six years. There is considerable evidence to suggest that Indian Elephants used to be spread over a much larger area of eastern China.

Pangolins

The Chinese Pangolin (*Manis pentadactyla*) is an extraordinary creature belonging to the order pholidota of mammals that look like reptiles. Its appearance is similar to that of a large lizard with cuticle scales (scales formed from a layer of skin) all over the body. Pangolins have a very long tongue and long, curved, toeless paws with which they dig holes to make their burrows and to get their food. They have no teeth, but can stretch their long tongues into the nests of termites (white ants). Chinese Pangolins are found in the mountains south of the Yangtze (Chang) River; another species, the Indian Pangolin (*M. crassicaudata*), is restricted to Guangxi and the southern part of Yunnan. One cause of their decline is that their flesh is considered to be a delicacy, and many are trapped.

The Red and White Giant Flying Squirrel (*Petaurista alborufus*) is a nocturnal animal.

Squirrels, rodents and bamboo rats

Squirrels are mammals mainly living in trees. The Red Squirrel (*Sciurus vulgaris*) is the most numerous in northern China while Pallas's Squirrel (*Callosciurus erythraeus*) is common in southern China. The Red Giant Flying Squirrel (*Petaurista petaurista*) can glide among the trees, borne on large membranes that stretch from the front to the back legs. They are distributed in the subtropical to tropical forests.

Rodents are the most plentiful of forest animals. The Grey Red-backed Vole (*Clethrionomys rufocanus*) and Northern Red-backed Vole (*C. rutilus*) are widely distributed in the forests of the northern part of China. They nibble bark and pine cones and are harmful to forestry, especially saplings. Other common rodents of the northern forests include the Common Field Mouse (*Apodemus speciosus*), and in southern forests the Chestnut Rat (*Niviventer fulvescens*), White-bellied Rat (*N. confucianus*) and Edward's Rat (*Leopoldamys edwardsi*) are widespread.

There are three species of bamboo rat (*Rhizomys*) in China, namely the large Bamboo Rat (*R. sumatrensis*), the Chinese Bamboo Rat (*R. sinensis*) and the Hoary Bamboo Rat (*R. pruinosus*). All of them are distributed in the bamboo groves to the south of the Yangtze (Chang) River. They burrow tunnels underground and eat the underground stems and the tender twigs of bamboo.

The Chinese Porcupine (*Hystrix hodgsoni*) is a large species of rodent with a body-weight of 17 to 27 kg (37 to 59 lb). A part of the fur at the back of the body has adapted to become hard, thorn-like quills, which are 20 cm (8 in.) long and hollow in the middle. They serve as powerful protection when the animal rolls into a ball. It is widely distributed in the southern provinces.

Birds

China has nearly 1200 species of breeding and non-breeding birds, which is about twice the number found in either Europe, the USSR or the USA. The majority of these species can be found on mountain slopes.

Game birds

China has one of the largest varieties of pheasants and other game birds found in any country in the world. There are altogether 49 species of the family Phasianidae and 16 pheasants listed as endangered species in the *Red Data Book* (published by the International Council for Bird Preservation, King, 1981) are to be found in China. Most of them are Chinese endemics which live in the forests all the year round.

The Black-billed Capercaillie (*Tetrao parvirostris*) and Black Grouse (*Lyrurus tetrix*) are representative species of the grouse family (Tetraonidae), found in China only in the cool-temperate mixed forest of Xinjiang and the north-eastern region. The male Black-billed Capercaillie is in fact mostly black, with bands of white spots on the wings and above the tail. It weighs 2 to 2.5 kg (4.4 to 5.5 lb). It inhabits larch (*Larix*), and sometimes Korean Pine (*Pinus koraiensis*) or fir (*Abies*) forests, where it lives on tree seeds and the buds and tips of the twigs of the birch (*Betula*) which grows nearby. In summer, it also eats various kinds of berries and insects. In winter, it is often found near riverbanks, which are kept clear of snowdrifts for the birds' protection in very cold weather.

ABOVE: Black-billed Capercaillie (*Tetrao parvirostris*) eggs and chicks. The eggs take about 24 days to hatch.
BELOW: the rare Chinese Hazel Grouse (*Tetrastes sewerzowi*). A few remain in Gansu, Qinghai and Sichuan provinces.

The Black-billed Capercaillie's breeding period is from late March to early June. Males display at special 'leks' (groups of birds involved in communal courtship display) around dawn, with fanned tails and drooped wings, calling to attract and impress the females, which the dominant male will mate. Males fight fiercely for the right to mate. One male will mate several females, which then choose a secluded place to make nests of leaves, moss and feathers. Six to ten eggs are laid and they hatch after about 24 days. Females tend the eggs and the chicks, which are able to run within two or three hours of hatching, without assistance from the males.

The feathers of male Black Grouse are mainly black, with the outer tail feathers curved into a distinctive lyre shape. They live on open ground near pine, birch and poplar forests and their behaviour is similar to the Black-billed Capercaillie's. The breeding period begins in late March, and lasts for six to seven weeks. During this period, a dozen or so males gather together on the open ground in leks where the cock birds spar and call, uttering a distinctive, bubbling, pigeon-like sound, but they rarely come to physical combat. The dominant birds, usually near the centre of the lek, will attract the females which watch secretively nearby. The mated female makes a simple nest on the ground and lays eight to ten eggs in a clutch. The eggs hatch after 19 to 25 days. The boundary of Black Grouse distribution is further south than that of the Black-billed Capercaillie, in the eastern part of China, and the bird can be found in Weichang, Hebei Province, in large numbers.

There are two kinds of Hazel Grouse in China, namely the Hazel Grouse

(*Tetrastes bonasia*) and the Chinese or Severtzov's Hazel Grouse (*T. sewerzowi*). The latter is found only in China, and was until recently widely believed to be extinct. However, a few still survive in the southern part of Gansu Province as well as some parts of Qinghai and Sichuan provinces. The characteristics of their nests and eggs, and their general behaviour, have been known only since the mid-1980s. They live in coniferous forests in northeastern China. The tips of twigs and the buds of birches and David's Poplar (*Populus davidiana*) are staple food and pine seeds, hazel nuts and acorns the preferred foods. They often gather in small groups and build nests on the ground, laying seven to 14 eggs which hatch after about 25 days. Hazel Grouse were once abundant, but centuries of hunting have taken their toll. In the past, they were offered to the Imperial palace as tribute, and were well known as 'flying dragons'. In recent years, due to the reduced size of their preferred habitat and to overhunting, their numbers have been dramatically reduced, and they are now protected birds. Conservation work in the forest region of the Da Hinggan Mountains has ensured that populations of several hundreds have been successfully maintained.

China has ten species of hill partridges (*Arborophila*). They are insectivores, and are sparsely distributed in the mountain forests of tropical and subtropical zones. Hill partridges are chicken-like birds, with short legs, short tails and an upright stance. They occupy wooded areas, from wet jungle to dry hillside scrub. The Hainan Hill Partridge (*A. ardens*), Taiwan (Formosan) Hill Partridge (*A. crudigularis*) and Sichuan (Boulton's) Hill Partridge (*A. rufipectus*) are endemic. The Common Hill Partridge (*A. torqueola*) can be found up to a height of about 3600 metres (11,800 ft) in the Himalayas.

The Blood Pheasant (*Ithaginis cruentus*) inhabits high mountain forests in the south-west. During the non-breeding period Blood Pheasants gather in groups, subsisting mainly on leaves, flowers, seeds, berries, moss and mushrooms. In winter, they live in subalpine coniferous forests at a height of 2500 to 3000 metres (8200 to 9800 ft) above sea level; in summer they move up to 4500 metres (14,800 ft) among rhododendrons, junipers, alpine forest and scrub. There are several races, each found in a small area, but merging with others where their ranges meet.

All five of the world's tragopans are found in China; all are rare and require special efforts to protect them and their habitats. Tragopans are spectacular Himalayan birds, with vivid and beautiful red, black and white markings on their plumage. Males have striking, fleshy horns which become erect in display and at the same time a fleshy lappet spreads smoothly down from the throat, covering the whole chest. This lappet has a red and sapphire blue pattern. Although rare and precious birds, tragopans are eagerly hunted. Due to loss of habitat and overhunting, most of them are listed as endangered species.

Among the five species of tragopans, the Chinese Tragopan (*Tragopan caboti*) is a Chinese endemic species found in the subtropical forest of the south-east from 1000 to 1400 metres (3300 to 4600 ft) above sea level. Of the five species, it lives at the lowest altitude. Temminck's Tragopan (*T. temminckii*) is mainly confined to China as well, but it extends to Burma and Vietnam. It is found in south-western China, especially in mountainous forests from 2200 to 3500 metres (7200 to 11,500 ft).

Little was known about tragopans' habits and characteristics in the wild until the early 1980s, when long-term investigation on them began. Radio-tracking has been useful in tracing them: it is now known that they live in regions where the dominant vegetation is mainly composed of the beech family (Fagaceae), laurel family (Lauraceae), tea family (Theaceae), and holly family (Aquifoliaceae). In their typical habitats, the population density is about 0.15 per hectare (0.06 per acre), and their normal forage area covers about 0.24 square kilometres (0.09 square miles). However, the forage area

This Hazel Grouse (*Tetrastes bonasia*) is calling in courtship.

OPPOSITE: the male Temminck's Tragopan (*Tragopan temminckii*) is one of the world's most glorious birds, never more so than in his courtship display. Loss of habitat and excessive hunting threaten the survival of all the tragopans worldwide.

TOP: the large, pale eggs of the Chinese Tragopan (*Tragopan caboti*) in a tree-fork nest.

TOP RIGHT: a female Chinese Tragopan (*Tragopan caboti*) incubating eggs.

ABOVE: subalpine coniferous forests and alpine shrub are the home of the Blue Eared-Pheasant (*Crossoptilon auritum*).

increases in winter because of the shortage of food. *Daphniphyllum macropodum* trees seem to determine the distribution of Chinese Tragopans, because the berries are their main food in autumn and in winter. When the ground is frozen, the birds snap the ice off the leaves with their beaks before eating them. One of the authors of this book has seen a Chinese Tragopan eat those leaves for three complete hours and then fall asleep, only to feast again on waking. The breeding period begins in late March. The birds make nests in trees; the clutch size varies from two to six eggs with an average clutch size between three and four; incubation lasts 28 days. During the hatching period, predators often take eggs, especially the Jay (*Garrulus glandarius*) and Grey Treepie (*Dendrocitta formosae*); other predators will also take chicks and adult females.

Monal pheasants (*Lophophorus*) are also mainly found in China, and the Chinese Monal Pheasant (*L. lhuysii*), a beautiful iridescent blue, green, copper and white bird, is endemic to the country. They live in the bushy grassland of the south-western mountains, their range extending up to 4000 metres (13,000 ft) in summer. In winter, they move down to 2000 to 3500 metres (6500 to 11,500 ft), into the mixed forest. These birds eat the corms and tubers of plants, especially the bulb of Fritillary (*Fritillaria thunbergii*). The Fritillary is very familiar to the Chinese because of its medicinal properties; Chinese Monal Pheasants are also known as 'Fritillary Birds'. They make their nests on the ground, where the female lays three to eight eggs at a time and incubates them for 25 to 26 days. Monal pheasants are endangered species, and populations are at a critically low level.

There are three species of eared-pheasants (*Crossoptilon*) in the world and all of these are mainly distributed in China. The Tibetan or White Eared-Pheasant (*C. crossoptilon*) and Blue Eared-Pheasant (*C. auritum*) are mainly found in the subalpine coniferous forests and alpine shrubs in Qinghai, Tibet, Sichuan and Yunnan at the altitude of 3500 metres (11,500 ft) above sea level. The Brown Eared-Pheasant (*C. mantchuricum*) is found only in the mountains in Shanxi and Hebei provinces.

Between autumn and winter, eared-pheasants gather in groups. Their breeding season begins in April and fierce fighting occurs among the males at that time. The birds make their nests on the ground, laying eight to ten eggs in a clutch, and the hatching period is 26 days.

The Silver Pheasant (*Lophura nycthemera*) is widely distributed and separated into eight subspecies. It is commonly seen in China, living in the

KILLED FOR THEIR LOOKS

One of the causes of the decline of various species in China has been overhunting, and some birds have been killed solely for their plumage. In pre-Revolutionary times the Imperial house gave the horse-tail-like plumes of the tails of Brown Eared-Pheasants (*Crossoptilon mantchuricum*) to their generals as awards for valour. These feathers were much prized and would be prominently displayed in the generals' hats. The plumes of other colourful birds, such as Lady Amherst's Pheasant (*Chrysolophus amherstiae*), have also been widely sought for decorative purposes.

ABOVE: the Brown Eared-Pheasant (*Crossoptilon mantchuricum*).
RIGHT: Lady Amherst's Pheasant (*Chrysolophus amherstiae*).

southern mountains in mixed coniferous and broad-leaved forests and bamboo groves, from the foot of the mountains to 1500 metres (5000 ft) or more. They frequently gather in family groups, running rapidly through the forests. The male of this much celebrated species has long and beautiful white tail feathers and has been nicknamed the 'White Phoenix'. The birds nest on the ground, laying large clutches of nine to 14 eggs, and the hatching time is about 23 days.

The Taiwan Blue Pheasant or Swinhoe's Pheasant (*L. swinhoei*) is an extremely rare Chinese endemic species from the mixed coniferous and broad-leaved forests at an elevation of 300 to 2200 metres (980 to 7200 ft) in Taiwan. Their habits and characteristics are similar to those of the Silver Pheasant. In 1958 only 120 remained in the wild; introductions from captive-bred stock have since supplemented the population.

The Koklass Pheasant (*Pucrasia macrolopha*) is widely distributed from central China to the south-western mountains in various types of forests, from 700 to 4000 metres (2300 to 13,000 ft) above sea level. During the courtship period, the male birds occupy the top of a hill, beginning to crow loudly at dawn and raising their short crest erect. They make their nests on the ground, laying four to seven eggs in each clutch.

One of the most familiar game birds in the west, Common (Ring-necked) Pheasants (*Phasianus colchicus*) originated in China and were widely introduced into Europe and America both as wild and as domestic birds. However, although there are 19 subspecies distributed in different regions, their numbers declined considerably in China until the Special Product Research Institute in Jilin Province succeeded in breeding the bird in captivity and establishing a stable breeding population.

ABOVE CENTRE: the Silver Pheasant (*Lophura nycthemera*) of southern China.
ABOVE: the Koklass Pheasant (*Pucrasia macrolopha*) is distributed from central to south-western China.

Of all the pheasants the Common Pheasant (*Phasianus colchicus*) is the best known, favoured worldwide as a bird for artificial rearing and shooting.

The Red Junglefowl (*Gallus gallus*) is distributed in the subtropical zone of Yunnan, Guangxi and Hainan Dao Island and has two subspecies. They are the ancestors of the farmyard hen, which was first domesticated, according to the latest evidence, 7000 years ago. Charles Darwin believed Red Junglefowl came from India and were taken to China, but archaeological evidence has since suggested that the opposite is the case. They are thinner than their farmyard cousins, mainly a brown-red colour, with longer spurs and shorter combs. The number of surviving birds is very small.

There are four species of Long-tailed Pheasants (*Syrmaticus*), among which Reeves's (*S. reevesii*), Elliot's (*S. ellioti*) and Mikado Pheasants (*S. mikado*) are endemic to China. Mrs Hume's Pheasant (*S. humiae*) is resident in south-western China, living in dry forest, scrub oak and grassy clearings. The male bird is most attractively patterned with brown, metallic blue, copper, black and white. The tail-plumes of the males are quite beautiful, and as long as 1.4 metres (55 in.); they are used as head decorations for generals in the Beijing opera. Because of overhunting, only a very small number of these birds still exist. They live in the mountain forests of central and south-western China at an altitude of 400 to 2000 metres (1300 to 6500 ft). The fruits and seeds of various plants are their staple food, and they build their nests on the ground.

Elliot's Pheasants have shorter tail-plumes. They are found in the hilly and low mountainous area of south-eastern China. These birds live near agricultural areas, and the exploitation and reduction of forests means that their number is decreasing markedly. On the basis of recent research, Chinese scientists have suggested that this is an endangered species which must be strictly protected, but the problem of habitat loss remains serious.

The Mikado Pheasant is mainly black, with metallic purple-blue feather edgings above, and white bars on the tail. This species lives in dense mixed forest at an altitude of 1600 to 3300 metres (5200 to 10,800 ft). The breeding period is from February to June and the clutch size is two to eight eggs, which are incubated for 28 days. It is estimated that only a few thousand survive.

Two very beautiful pheasants which used to be found in large numbers are Lady Amherst's Pheasant (*Chrysolophus amherstiae*) and the Golden Pheasant (*C. pictus*). Both are splendid birds of mixed forests from 1500 to 4000 metres (4900 to 13,000 ft) high in the southern part of the country. Male Golden Pheasants have mainly red and vivid yellow body-feathers with golden feathers on the tops of their heads. They inhabit mountains in the south-western part of China, farther north than Lady Amherst's.

Lady Amherst's Pheasant is a very elegant bird; the adult male has an exceptionally long, arched tail and the head and body are boldly marked with

OPPOSITE ABOVE: Elliot's Pheasant (*Syrmaticus ellioti*) is rarely shown to advantage in identification paintings, but is in reality a very beautiful bird.
OPPOSITE BELOW: the Golden Pheasant (*Chrysolophus pictus*) is a colourful bird, yet can be difficult to see in its dense and dark natural habitat.

83

ABOVE: rare and beautiful, the Green Peafowl (*Pavo muticus*) is restricted to Yunnan.

RIGHT: streaks on the underside of this Northern Goshawk (*Accipiter gentilis*) indicate immaturity.

green, blue, red, yellow and white. Broad bars of white feathers, edged neatly with black, form a lacy pattern on the back of the neck. Its habits and characteristics are similar to those of the Golden Pheasant. Natural hybrids have been found where the distribution of these two species overlaps. Because the plumes of both species are so beautiful, they have been used widely for decorative purposes, and overhunting has reduced their numbers; they are now listed for protection.

The typical pheasants of the Chinese tropical forests are the Grey Peacock-Pheasant (*Polyplectron bicalcaratum*) and Green Peafowl (*Pavo muticus*). Both are distributed in the southern part of Yunnan Province and the Grey Peacock-Pheasant is also found on Hainan Dao Island. They are very rare and little is known about their habits and characteristics. The Green Peafowl is recognizably similar to the familiar Peafowl (*Pavo cristatus*), but males have metallic bronze instead of blue on the neck, iridescent green on the back (each feather brilliantly blue in the centre) and a sensational train; they look, if anything, even more beautiful.

Birds of prey

There are 56 species of birds of prey found in China, and most of them live in mountain forests. Hawks and falcons are the most common, nesting in large trees and preying on small birds, rodents and lizards.

Crested Honey Buzzards (*Pernis ptilorhynchus*) live on bees, wasps and their larvae, honey and wax, as well as on other small animals. There are usually distinct crests on their heads, but otherwise they resemble the Honey Buzzard (*P. apivorus*) of Europe. They make their nests in tall trees, using small sticks as building material. In late May, they lay one to three eggs which hatch after 30 to 35 days.

Sparrowhawks (*Accipiter nisus*) are commonly seen in China. They breed in the forests of the north-east and spread over the eastern coast of China during their migration to wintering grounds south of Shanghai. The Besra Sparrowhawk (*A. virgatus*) is a similar species, but smaller, with a black chin stripe. It flies above the forests, sometimes making a high-pitched trilling sound, and over more open ground, especially above bushes and grassland, on the lookout for small birds such as sparrows for food. The Besra

Sparrowhawk nests on large trees and usually lays two to five eggs in a clutch, incubating them for 32 to 34 days.

About the same size as the Sparrowhawk, the Hobby (*Falco subbuteo*) is the most widespread species of falcon in the country's forests. It flies gracefully above forest clearings, taking large insects in its feet in mid-air; it is also capable of flying fast enough to catch agile birds like swallows and swifts. Hobbies often make use of the old nests of other birds, such as other kinds of birds of prey, crows and magpies.

The Red-footed Falcon (*F. vespertinus*) is commonly seen in forests of the north-eastern region. The males are mostly grey with red legs. Research has shown that insects account for 90 per cent of their food, the rest being lizards and small animals. They like to take over magpies' and crows' nests and they will fight the owners for several days until they drive them away; the number of eggs they then lay is three to five, and the incubation period is 28 days.

The Kestrel (*F. tinnunculus*) is another species of falcon commonly found in mountain forests in various parts of China. The Kestrels' shape and habits are similar to Red-footed Falcons. Their body feathers are rust-coloured with black-brown spots or bars and the male has a grey head and tail. They are very widely distributed in mountains, from low mountain areas to the Qinghai-Tibet Plateau up to an altitude of 4270 metres (14,000 ft). Lesser Kestrels (*F. naumanni*) breed in the north and appear elsewhere on migration to and from Africa.

Tree ducks

There are only three species of ducks that nest in tree holes in the forests of China: the Lesser Whistling or Lesser Tree Duck (*Dendrocygna javanica*), Chinese Merganser (*Mergus squamatus*) and the Mandarin Duck (*Aix galericulata*). They select holes in tall trees at the edge of the forests near lakes or rivers and line them with leaves, fur and matted feathers. When the nestlings hatch they jump from the tree holes straight into the water, and are instantly able to look for food with their parents. Lesser Whistling Ducks are southern species distributed only in tropical and subtropical forests. The Chinese (or Scaly-sided) Merganser is an endemic and endangered species, which breeds only in the Changbai Mountains. It prefers turbulent mountain streams. It was once thought that the Mandarin Duck only bred in the north-eastern region and wintered in areas south of the Yangtze (Chang) River. However, in recent years, these birds have also been found to breed and winter in the mountainous area of Guizhou Province. Mandarin Ducks have been introduced into Britain and it has been suggested that there are now as many in England as there are remaining in China, where they have suffered severely through loss of forest.

The Grass Owl (*Tyto capensis*) has the typical monkey-shaped face of the three owls in the family Tytonidae found in China. It is widespread from South Africa to India, Burma, China and Australasia.

Owls, nightjars and cuckoos

Most of the 25 species of owls in China are found in forests. The Grass Owl (*Tyto capensis*) is a typical tropical owl and is closely related to the Barn Owl (*T. alba*). Their heads look like those of monkeys, with heart-shaped faces and slanting black eyes. Grass Owls nest in the thick growth of grass at the edge of forests, preying mainly on rodents. Barn Owls prefer buildings for nest sites and they are found in many cities. Scops Owls (*Otus scops*) are widely distributed in mountainous forests in the eastern part of China. They are small for an owl, only 19 cm (7.5 in.) long, and live mainly on insects. They nest in tree holes.

Collared Scops Owls (*O. bakkamoena*) are also widely distributed in mountainous forests in eastern China. They are similar in their habits to Scops Owls, but are rather larger. Cuckoo or Asian Barred Owlets (*Glaucidium castanopterum*) are commonly seen in mountainous forests to the south of the Yangtze (Chang) River and look rather like Scops Owls, but they lack the

feathery 'ear tufts' of the latter. They are a black-brown colour with close barring on head, back and breast, and white around each eye. They prey on small birds in the daytime and also eat rodents, snakes, lizards, frogs and insects. They lay their eggs in the holes of trees.

The Eagle Owl (*Bubo bubo*) is widespread but nowhere common. It is very big, standing almost 70 cm (28 in.) high and having an enormous wingspan of 1.8 metres (6 ft). Finally, the Brown Fish Owl (*Ketupa zeylonensis*) is a very rare bird which lives around the coasts and streams of the north-east catching fish and crabs for food.

There are eight species of nightjars in China, all of them live on the edge of forests and are active at night. The most commonly seen species is the Grey Nightjar (*Caprimulgus indicus*). Widely distributed in the forests of the eastern regions, it can be recognized by the band of white on its tail. Nightjars are extraordinary birds, with elongated bodies, rather broad, flattened heads, tiny bills and very small legs. Their long wings and broad,

ABOVE LEFT: Scops Owls (*Otus scops*) do not begin hunting until dark but call loudly at dusk.
TOP: the Collared Scops Owl (*O. bakkamoena*) is common in mountain forests in eastern China.
ABOVE: the Long-eared Owl (*Asio otus*), which is very widespread in Eurasia, breeds in the north and moves south in winter, when flocks of up to 100 roost together in thickets on the plains.

movable tails make them highly acrobatic in flight and their wide bills, surrounded by stiff bristles arranged like a kind of net, make them very efficient at catching moths and other insects in flight. During the day they remain silent and motionless, relying on their barred and spotted plumage to give them perfect camouflage. They lie along a bare branch or crouch on the ground among dead leaves, and are extremely hard to see. Each evening, after sunset, they make their presence known by characteristic songs, which are far-carrying, repetitive trilling or whistling calls.

China has 17 species of cuckoos, most of them in the forests of the south. Among them, the most commonly seen are the Common Cuckoo (*Cuculus canorus*), Indian Cuckoo (*C. micropterus*) and Large Hawk Cuckoo (*C. sparverioides*). These birds lay an egg in the nest of another bird. The cuckoo nestling instinctively lifts the eggs or nestlings of the host birds on to its back and throws them out. It then enjoys the full attention of the duped parent birds, which continue to feed it. Other cuckoos mainly use Brown Shrike (*Lanius cristatus*), Willow Warbler (*Phylloscopus trochillus*) and Azure-winged Magpie (*Cyanopica cyanus*) nests, but which birds were inflicted with hosting China's Large Hawk Cuckoos was not clear until quite recently, when one of the authors found that they are the Magpie (*Pica pica*) and Red-billed Blue Magpie (*Urocissa erythrorhyncha*).

The Violet Cuckoo (*Chrysococcyx xanthorhynchus*), Koel (*Eudynamys scolopacea*), Greater Coucal (*Centropus sinensis*) and Lesser Coucal (*C. bengalensis*) are relatives of the true cuckoos which are distributed in the southern tropical forests. Although these birds have the same breeding strategy, the nestlings do not throw out the eggs and nestlings of the hosts, but are simply accepted by their hosts together with their own offspring as if they properly belong in the same nest. But these invaders develop very fast and eventually monopolize the food with the result that the other chicks starve.

Woodpeckers and rollers

Woodpeckers are typical forest birds. They are able to climb vertical tree trunks, pecking for insects beneath the bark. To increase their grip on rounded surfaces, their feet have two claws pointing forwards and two back claws (the outer one of those usually long and splayed out sideways). Thirty-six species are found in China, all of them listed as protected birds, but many have declined with the clearance of woodland. The largest is the Black Woodpecker (*Dryocopus martius*), which is typically found in the cool-temperate coniferous forests. It is about as big as a Rook, with a black body, except for a vivid red forehead and crown in the male, and a small red patch on the female's nape. The Grey-headed Woodpecker (*Picus canus*), the Great Spotted Woodpecker (*Dendrocopos major*) and Grey-capped Woodpecker (*Picoides canicapillus*) are widely distributed in forests in eastern China, and the Bay Woodpecker (*Blythipicus pyrrhotis*) in southern tropical areas in tall evergreen forest. It is largely a brown-cinnamon colour with many black horizontal bars, and has a long yellow bill. As with other woodpeckers, the familiar sound of the drumming on tree trunks is a feature of its courtship display and it has various contact calls. In the southern areas, the breeding period begins between February and March.

The Common Golden-backed Woodpecker (*Dinopium javanense*) is a large, striking species found in the humid forests in the south-west, while the Speckled Piculet (*Picumnus innominatus*) and White-browed Piculet (*Sasia ochracea*) are tiny, Goldcrest-sized (90 mm (3½ in.)) birds of bamboo thickets in the south.

There are three species of rollers in China, among them the Eastern Broad-billed Roller or Dollarbird (*Eurystomus orientalis*), which is widely distributed in forests of the eastern parts in China. Dollarbirds are about 25 cm (10 in.) long, with beautiful blue-green and black feathers, rather short red

BELOW: the Rufous-bellied Woodpecker (*Picoides hyperythrus*) inhabits coniferous or mixed mountain forests in central China.
BOTTOM: the Eastern Broad-billed Roller or Dollarbird (*Eurystomus orientalis*) is a bird of the higher forests in the eastern mountains, where it hunts above the trees for insects.

bills and red legs. They wheel around rapidly over forests, catching insects. Their wings show round, transparent patches in flight – the 'dollars'. They nest in tree holes or use the old nests of magpies for laying their four eggs.

The Indian Roller (*Coracias benghalensis*) looks like several other species of roller in Europe and Africa, being particularly beautiful in flight, when the wings show a dazzling pattern of purple, blue and turquoise.

ABOVE LEFT: an Indian Roller (*Coracias benghalensis*) shows its typical roller blues and turquoise.
ABOVE RIGHT: Lord Derby's Parakeet (*Psittacula derbiana*) is a fairly common, large parakeet of tropical forests.

Hornbills and parrots

The hornbills and parrots are typical birds of tropical forest all around the world. The four species of hornbills in China are all restricted to the southern part of Yunnan Province. Among them, the Indian Pied Hornbill (*Anthracoceros malabaricus*) and Great Pied Hornbill (*Buceros bicornis*) are the more common. They have huge bills, tapered to a curved point and topped by a massive casque, or helmet, which looks cumbersome but is actually spongy and very light. Fruits and seeds are their staple food and they make their nests in tree holes. The clutch size is two or three eggs. While incubating on the nest, the female blocks the entrance hole with mud and droppings, leaving a narrow crack through which the male feeds her. This prevents predators, such as monkeys and snakes, from reaching the nest inside. The female breaks an exit hole when the young birds are ready to leave the nest.

Parrots are found in the tropical forests of the southern part of Yunnan and Guangxi, and on Hainan Dao Island. The Red-breasted or Moustached Parakeet (*Psittacula alexandri*) and Lord Derby's Parakeet (*P. derbiana*) are the most common of the seven species found. They gather in areas from low mountains to 4000 metres (13,000 ft), the former in dry woodland, the latter in pines, mixed forest and rhododendrons. As many as one hundred or more

ABOVE: unfortunately extremely rare, the Oriental Pied Hornbill (*Anthracoceros coronatus*) is found only in the tropical forests of southern Yunnan Province. RIGHT: the Great Pied Hornbill (*Buceros bicornis*) is also found in southern Yunnan Province. Hornbills are among the biggest and most spectacular of forest birds.

in a group may still be seen in favoured areas, often moving noisily over the forest with loud, squealing calls. At night, they often roost with Crested Mynahs (*Acridotheres cristatellus*) and crows in mixed flocks. These parrots eat fruits and seeds of plants and make their nests in tree holes. The Vernal Hanging Parrot (*Loriculus vernalis*), only 12.5 cm (5 in.) long, is a tiny green and red parrot of flowering forest trees in the south. It sleeps at night hanging from a branch like a bat.

Doves and pigeons

Doves and pigeons are familiar birds, though many species are quite elusive. Rufous Turtle Doves (*Streptopelia orientalis*), Spotted Doves (*S. chinensis*) and Red Turtle Doves (*S. tranquebarica*) are widely distributed in the forests of eastern and southern regions of China.

Eight species of green pigeons, including the Pompadour Green Pigeon (*Treron pompadora*), the Wedge-tailed Green Pigeon (*T. sphenurus*), the Green Imperial Pigeon (*Ducula aenea*) and the Mountain Imperial Pigeon (*D. budia*), are all species of tropical forests, distributed only in the southern part of Yunnan, the southern part of Guangxi and Hainan Dao Island. Outside the breeding period, they often gather in large groups, living mainly on fruits and seeds of plants. They make simple and crude nests in trees with dead twigs. Male and female pigeons feed nestlings on a sweet white liquid known as 'pigeon milk' which is secreted from the parents' crop and stored there until it is disgorged for the young.

Pittas

Pittas are rarely seen, small, ground-living birds of tropical forests, where they run through the undergrowth searching for insects, and weave large, untidy, ball-shaped nests among the branches. They are brilliantly coloured jade-blue, brown, yellow, black, white and green, and are hence colloquially known as 'eight-coloured thrushes'. In China, there are seven species. The only one with a relatively wide distribution is the Fairy Pitta (*Pitta nympha*) in eastern China. The Lesser Blue-winged Pitta (*P. brachyura*), has been seen in mangroves in southern Yunnan; the Blue Pitta (*P. cyanea*) in evergreen forests and bamboo groves in Xishuangbanna in the same region.

Songbirds

By far the largest number of birds living in forests are songbirds, in the great order of passerines or perching birds. They include most of the small, familiar groups such as warblers, finches and thrushes and larger species up to the size of the crows. They are common and found in great variety in differing types of forest, in areas of grassland between forests and by streams. Nevertheless, over very large areas of China, where the land is intensively farmed and the human population large, the range of species is very restricted and numbers of birds often small.

Bulbuls are frequently found in forests or bamboo groves of low southern mountains. There are 20 species in China. Among them, the Chinese or Light-vented Bulbul (*Pycnonotus sinensis*) is the most widely distributed, commonly found on plains or mountains to the south of the Yangtze (Chang) River in gardens and scrub. Bulbuls are omnivorous birds but their staple food is seeds and fruits. They make their bowl-like nests in trees, laying four to six purple-spotted eggs in a clutch. Bulbuls are often detected by their loud, cheerful, fluting calls.

Shrikes are small birds, about the size of a thrush, but they are able to catch other small birds, rodents, lizards, frogs and insects. After they have killed them, they often impale their prey on sharp thorns so that they can more easily tear them up to eat; prey remains are frequently found on the branches in areas where these birds are active. The main species found in

BELOW LEFT: the Green Imperial Pigeon (*Ducula aenea*) is a typical large pigeon of Chinese tropical forest.
BELOW: the Lesser Blue-winged Pitta (*Pitta brachyura*) lives on the forest floor in the jungles of south-eastern China.

northern China are Brown Shrikes (*Lanius cristatus*) and Bull-headed Shrikes (*L. bucephalus*). The former breeds in summer on the plains and foothills and is widespread in eastern China in winter; the latter is found in the alpine areas of the north-east. The large Rufous-backed or Long-tailed Shrike (*L. schach*) lives on the plains or in the low mountains to the south of the Yangtze River, and does not migrate.

There are five species of orioles in China, all in low mountain forests. Among them, Mell's Maroon Oriole (*Oriolus mellianus*) is an endemic species. Black-naped Orioles (*O. chinensis*) are widely distributed in forests on plains or low mountains of the eastern part of China. The males are almost wholly vivid yellow apart from a black band across the head and black on the wings and tail, but, like other yellow orioles, they are surprisingly inconspicuous. Orioles' nests are slung between two branches inside a horizontal fork,

Many of the Old World orioles of Eurasia and Africa share a basic yellow and black pattern but are still hard to detect in thick foliage; the Black-naped Oriole (*Oriolus chinensis*) is no exception.

ABOVE LEFT: these captive Rusty-cheeked
Scimitar Babblers (*Pomatorhinus
erythrogenys*) come from the bamboo groves
and bushes south of the Yangtze River.
ABOVE TOP: the Hill Mynah (*Gracula
religiosa*) is more familiar as a caged bird.
ABOVE: Elliot's Laughing Thrush
(*Garrulax elliotii*) is equally likely to find its
way into captivity.

looking like hanging baskets. Their eggs are white with beautiful pink spots.

Drongos are also birds of tropical forests. The distribution of the Black Drongo (*Dicrurus macrocercus*), Ashy Drongo (*D. leucophaeus*) and Hair-crested Drongo (*D. hottentottus*) is generally northern. The Lesser Racquet-tailed Drongo (*D. remifer*) and Greater Racquet-tailed Drongo (*D. paradiseus*) can be found only in the tropical forests of the southern part of Yunnan Province. Their outer tail feathers are extremely long, mostly thin, bare shafts with broad, spoon-like tips. The latter species moves through bamboo and teak forest with mixed parties of birds, eating insects and nectar.

There are 16 species of starlings in China, the most commonly seen ones being Silky or Red-billed Starlings (*Sturnus sericeus*) in the south and Grey or White-cheeked Starlings (*S. cineraceus*) in the north. Other important southern species are the Crested Mynah (*Acridotheres cristatellus*) and Hill Mynah (*Gracula religiosa*). Mynahs are famous for their extraordinary ability to mimic other bird species, and even human voices, which has made them popular the world over as pets. All these starlings nest in tree holes.

Of China's 80 species of robins, chats and thrushes, half are forest birds. Common representatives include the Daurian Redstart (*Phoenicurus auroreus*), a bird of forests and dense scrub in northern and central China, the White-crowned Forktail (*Enicurus leschenaulti*) and Little Forktail (*E. scouleri*), rather wagtail-like birds of upland torrents with long, forked, black and white tails, the Blue Rock Thrush (*Monticola solitarius*), Blue Whistling Thrush (*Myiophoneus caeruleus*) and Blackbird (*Turdus merula*). The Daurian Redstart is insectivorous and can easily be attracted to artificial nest boxes, which have been placed in various forests to encourage it to become established there.

China has a large number of species of babblers of the family Timaliidae – 129 species in all – and most of them are resident birds, including many endemic species. These birds live mainly in southern China, inhabiting woodland and scrub. They are fine songbirds and very large numbers are trapped to sell as caged birds. Thousands pass daily through the bird markets of Chinese cities, often held in lamentable conditions.

The Ashy Laughing Thrush (*Garrulax cineraceus*), Hwamei (*G. canorus*), Rusty-cheeked Scimitar Babbler (*Pomatorhinus erythrogenys*), Rufous-necked or Streak-breasted Scimitar Babbler (*P. ruficollis*) and Red-billed Leiothrix or Pekin Robin (*Leiothrix lutea*) are all widely distributed in bushes or bamboo groves to the south of the Yangtze River, and are typical members of this very large and varied group of distinctively Chinese birds.

Parrotbills (also known as crow-tits) are small, long-tailed birds related to

the Eurasian Bearded Tit. Unlike that species they have short, curved bills like parrots. They frequently gather in groups and are active in thickets, bamboos and tall grasses in the foothills. There are 13 species in China; among them, the Chinese or Yangtze Parrotbill (*Paradoxornis heudei*) is one of the world's endangered species, and is also an endemic species of China. Recent research into its habitats and breeding and wintering habits have established that now it only exists in reed beds beside streams in the Lianyungang region, from Nanjing to 95 kilometres (56 miles) below Zhenjiang and around Hangzhou. The most widely distributed of these birds is the Vinous-throated Parrotbill (*P. webbianus*), which lives in the tea gardens, bamboo groves and shrubs of the eastern and southern parts of China.

Warblers (Sylviidae) are almost as abundant in China as babblers, with 84 species, most of them migratory. They are small, usually olive-green, grey or cinnamon in colour with various combinations of eye stripes and wing bars. They are insect eaters, mainly living in shrubs and trees, and weaving ball- or cup-shaped nests in shrubs or on the ground. Common ones in China are the Yellow-browed Warbler (*Phylloscopus inornatus*), Goldcrest (*Regulus regulus*), Chestnut-crowned Warbler (*Seicercus castaniceps*), Fan-tailed Warbler (*Cisticola juncidis*) and Tawny-flanked Prinia (*Prinia subflava*). With the exception of the Yellow-browed Warbler and Goldcrest, which sometimes breed in the north, most of the warblers live in the south of the country.

Three species of tailor birds (*Orthotomus*) inhabit southern mountainous forests. They are small warblers with pointed bills and long, cocked tails. They build their nests in a remarkable way, folding a leaf into a 'pocket' and sewing the sides together with plant fibre, then making a nest inside the hanging pouch.

The Yellow-rumped Flycatcher (*Ficedula zanthopygia*) and Asian Paradise-Flycatcher (*Terpsiphone paradisi*) are the representatives of the Old World flycatcher family (Muscicapidae) that breed in the eastern area of China. The tail of the male Paradise-Flycatcher is four times longer than the body. Other flycatchers include the Narcissus Flycatcher (*Ficedula narcissina*) of waterside woodland and mangroves, the Large Niltava (*Niltava grandis*) which occupies dense evergreen forest in Yunnan, the Pale Blue Flycatcher (*N. unicolor*), a lovely bird of humid and bamboo forests, and the splendid azure-blue Black-naped Monarch Flycatcher (*Monarcha azurea*).

Titmice are distributed worldwide and 21 species are found in China. The Great Tit (*Parus major*) and Marsh Tit (*P. palustris*) are the most widespread. The Rufous-vented Tit (*P. rubidiventris*) and Grey-crested Tit (*P. dichrous*) are mountain birds, and live only on the Himalayas and Hengduan Mountains in thick evergreen forest and rhododendron scrub. Sultan Tits (*Melanochlora sultanea*) are found only in tropical forest tree-tops; they are large, rather bulbul-like birds with yellow crests.

The flowerpeckers (Dicaeidae) are tiny, mostly brightly coloured birds which flit about in flowering trees and vines in forests and secondary scrub, gardens and parks. They feed on insects, nectar, pollen and berries and build beautiful nests which are domed or hanging, and are made of silky plant fibres. The male Yellow-bellied Flowerpecker (*Dicaeum melanozanthum*) of the forests of central China is mostly slate black and yellow in colour with a white throat; the male Fire-breasted Flowerpecker (*D. ignipectus*) is glossy steel blue above and yellow buff below with a vivid red patch on the breast and a black stripe on the belly. It occupies tea plantations and forest up to 4000 metres (13,000 ft) in summer.

Sunbirds (Nectariniidae) resemble the hummingbirds of the Americas and feed on nectar and insects, but they do not hover, simply clinging to flower stems to feed. Typical sunbirds are tiny, with thin, curved bills, like the Ruby-cheeked Sunbird (*Anthreptes singalensis*), 10 cm (4 in.) long, of moist

OPPOSITE: Asian Paradise-Flycatchers (*Terpsiphone paradisi*) may be dark with long, trailing tail feathers. They are very similar to close relatives in Africa. In China they breed in the forests of the eastern mountains.

forests in south-west China, but another group, the spiderhunters, is represented in China by two species which are larger, heavier-billed birds. The Streaked Spiderhunter (*Arachnothera magna*) is 19 cm (7½ in.) long and is found in forests with wild plantains and vines in the south-west.

Most of the 85 species of finches (Fringillidae) and buntings (Emberizidae) in China are northern types, but they also breed in south-western mountain forests. The common ones are the Oriental Greenfinch (*Carduelis sinica*), Red Crossbill (*Loxia curvirostra*) and Black-tailed or Yellow-billed Hawfinch (*Coccothraustes migratorius*) among the finches, and the Rock Bunting (*Emberiza cia*) and Meadow Bunting (*E. cioides*). The Rock Bunting and Meadow Bunting are widely distributed on rock and grass slopes in the hills, and are very similar to one another in shape and behaviour. On the basis of investigations carried out in the Qin Ling Mountains and the most mountainous areas of northern China, it is clear that each of them dominates in a certain altitudinal belt. The Rock Bunting is generally found at higher altitudes, above 1100 to 1200 metres (3600 to 3900 ft).

ABOVE: the Red Crossbill (*Loxia curvirostra*) is found all over Europe and Asia in a variety of subtly different forms. It feeds on seeds from conifers.
ABOVE RIGHT: the Rock Bunting (*Emberiza cia*) is almost equally widely distributed, but more southerly, in mountainous regions.

Reptiles, amphibians and insects

Colourful and fascinating tree frogs (*Rhacophorus*) are commonly seen in subtropical and tropical forests, including *R. dennysi*, *R. omeimontis*, *R. chenfui* and many others. They have flat suction disks at the ends of their toes which enable them to climb along trunks or among stems and leaves. They are found mainly in forests close to streams or other watery environments. During the breeding period, the females hang balls of frog spawn from among the leaves, and when the tadpoles hatch, they drop into the water below. Wood frogs – the Common Eurasian Frog (*Rana temporaria*) and *R. japonica* – are common species in forests from north-eastern to central China. Frogs contribute significantly to the dusk chorus in many Chinese forests.

The Chinese Xenosaur (*Shinisaurus crocodilurus*) is an endemic and rare lizard in China, mainly distributed in Yaoshan Mountain in Guangxi. It is about 50 cm (20 in.) in length, with a flat tail which is longer than the body. The scales are of various sizes, the larger ones bead-like in shape; these stand proud from the body and form rows. They live on trees near streams, eating small fish, insects and tadpoles.

Finally, there is a great variety and abundance of insects in the forests of China, and among them are many endemic species. Of the many interesting species, the Palaearctic Snout Butterfly (*Libythea celtis*), an endemic species of China, merits special attention. It is a very ancient species, widely found today in northern China. Up to now, only one species similar to the Palaearctic Snout Butterfly has been found, in South America.

ABOVE: a mating pair of Great Tree Frogs (*Rhacophorus dennysi*) in the tropical forest. LEFT: the eggs hang over a suitable pond in frothy clusters, and the hatching tadpoles fall into the water below where they grow into baby frogs.

RIVERS, LAKES AND SEA COASTS

河湖与海岸

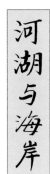

Water has played a varied part in China's history, providing the site and means of one of the earliest flowerings of civilization along the Yellow (Huang) River several thousand years ago. China's waters also need constant management to control flooding, or require careful eking out in irrigation. Lakes, rivers and coasts have constantly provided homes for large numbers of birds – most characteristically storks and cranes – and today feature prominently in the impressive list of Chinese nature reserves. They also harbour some of the strangest and rarest animals such as Chinese Alligators, Chinese River Dolphins and the Chinese Giant Salamander. China's mighty rivers, the Yellow and the Yangtze (Chang), extend over a considerable area of the country, reaching from their icy mountain sources down to sluggish, flat estuaries. Variety is equally the keynote of the many lakes, which offer both fertile, tropical pools and the shrunken remains of prehistoric seas, the high salinity of which is inimical to most forms of life.

PREVIOUS PAGE: a stunning view of Geladandong Snow Mountain where the Yangtze (Chang) River begins.
ABOVE: a magnificent waterfall at the northern end of Tianchi (Heaven) Lake in the Changbai Mountains.

Rivers

China's rich surface water resources include more than 50,000 rivers, each of which drain a catchment area of some 100 square kilometres (40 square miles) and, of these, 1600 carry off superfluous water from an area of more than 1000 square kilometres (400 square miles) each. Approximately 64 per cent of the country's total area is drained by rivers flowing to the sea. The remaining 36 per cent is drained by rivers that run into lakes from which the water evaporates. All the large rivers rise in important mountain areas: the famous Yangtze and Yellow Rivers in the Qinghai-Tibet Plateau; the Heilong and Liao, Huai and Xi have their sources in the Da Hinggan Mountains, the Taihang Mountains and the Yunnan-Guizhou Plateau respectively; and the Yalu, Tumen, Qiantang, Ou, Min, Han, Dong and Bei Rivers originate in the Changbai Mountains and in the south-eastern coastal mountains. These rivers are of great value for their hydroelectric potential: each drops in altitude dramatically over a short distance. The three largest rivers, described in detail below and following, are major features in the geography of the country and provide a variety of habitat for plant and animal life.

The Yangtze (Chang) River

The largest river in China and the third largest river in the world, the Yangtze River flows 6300 kilometres (4000 miles) west–east across the southern part of China. Its dimensions give an idea of its importance. It has a catchment area of 1.8 million square kilometres (450,000 square miles), and its annual flow to the sea averages 979,350 million cubic metres (3.4585 US billion cubic ft). With a total fall of more than 6600 metres (21,600 ft) from source to estuary and a high level of rainfall in its catchment area, it has enormous hydroelectric power potential, and is used to generate 170 million kilowatts, or 40 per cent of the country's total hydroelectric power output. It starts in the Tanggula Mountains which straddle the Qinghai-Tibet border, flows through Qinghai, Tibet, Yunnan, Sichuan, Hubei, Hunan, Jiangxi, Anhui, Jiangsu and Shanghai, and finally enters the East China Sea at Chongming Island near Shanghai. The upper reaches of the Yangtze are normally defined from its headwaters in the Tanggula Mountains to Yichang in Hubei Province, the middle reaches cover from there to Hukou in Jiangxi Province, and the lower reaches run from Hukou to its estuary.

The 2308 kilometre (1440 mile) section of the river from Yushu in southern Qinghai to Yibin City in Sichuan is called the Jinsha River. The river flows south from Yushu and courses through the Hengduan Mountains between Sichuan and Tibet, where the turbulent flow has cut a deep and spectacular valley. The water is too rough for any fish or their predators to

remain in this stretch. The Yangtze abruptly turns north-east from Shigu in Yunnan, and enters the precipitous Hutiao, or 'Tiger Leaping', Canyon. This section is lined on both banks by numerous snow-covered mountains with peaks 3000 metres (9800 ft) high above the river, while the river is only tens of metres wide – a narrow breadth for the tremendous amount of water thundering through it. Within a mere 16 kilometres (10 miles) the river falls 200 metres (660 ft), creating roaring torrents. White fronted Geese (*Anser albifrons*) survive the winter in the lower reaches of the Yangtze.

The so-called Yangtze River proper starts at the confluence of the Min and Jinsha rivers at Yibin, where they enter the Sichuan Basin. From Yibin to Yichang the Yangtze flows through hills of red sandy shale, while from Wanxian County the mountains become steeper, culminating in the Yangtze Gorges area in the east of Fengjie. This stretch covers the 200 kilometre (125 mile) section from Baidicheng in Fengjie, Sichuan, to Nanjinguan in Yichang, Hubei. Here the Yangtze River cuts deeply into the limestone and forms many gorges, but the area (Qutang Xia Wu Xia) is named after the three most famous and spectacular ones, Qutang Gorge, Wuxia Gorge and Xiling Gorge. There has been a proposal to build a high dam so as to develop hydroelectricity and irrigation as well as to prevent flooding. However, the project has caused much controversy since it would entail

The upper reaches of the Yangtze (Chang) River fall 200 metres (650 ft) over a course of just 16 kilometres (10 miles) through the Hutiao Canyon, after turning to a north-easterly course from Shigu. The 3000 metre (11,250 ft) peaks create a wilderness where wildlife can still survive largely undisturbed.

flooding the three gorges and further research concerning various aspects of this large project is being carried out.

Deep, steep-sided gorges alternate with shallow open sections through this area, and the river is full of twists and turns. In the gorge sections both banks are precipitous, overshadowed by high, steep peaks, generally more than 500 metres (1600 ft) above the river. The river itself narrows down to 100 metres or so at the narrowest points. The current is swift, and the maximum flow rate is 7 to 8 metres (23 to 27 ft) per second during the flood period.

From Yichang the Yangtze enters its alluvial plain. Here it becomes much wider, the slope of the river bed decreases considerably, and the flow is much more even and less turbulent. The river bed meanders in wide, sinuous bends, especially in the section from Zhijiang in Hubei to Chenglingji in Hunan, which is generally known as 'Nine Intestine-like Bends'. In this section the slower flow on the inside of each bend deposits a large amount of sediment, while the fast flow on the outside of the bends undercuts the soft banks. The channel gradually changes course through this process of erosion and infilling, and leaves a low, flat bed of rich sediment in a typical alluvial plain, which regularly floods during summer. This is one of the Yangtze's problematical flood control areas. Wild ducks live on the lakes near the river, and in winter they are joined by thousands of egrets and geese migrating from the north. The Chinese River (or Whitefin) Dolphin (*Lipotes vexillifer*), which weighs 100 kg (220 lb) or more, is the only aquatic animal powerful enough to live in these waters.

The lower reaches, from Hukou downstream, run through a gentle landscape, particularly after Zhenjiang city where the Yangtze's river delta starts. The delta is characterized by drainage networks dotted with lakes, and is famous for its profusion of rivers and lakes. From Jiangjin the river widens into a broad fan, 80 kilometres (50 miles) across at its widest point. It finally empties into the East China Sea, with many mud flats and sandbanks created by its sediment over a large area. Chongming Island lies in the estuary, also created by the river's sediment. Of all the islands off China's coast, this island is exceeded in size only by Taiwan and Hainan Dao.

The Yellow (Huang) River

The second largest river in China, the Yellow River is famous throughout the world. It has its source in the Bayan Har Mountains in Qinghai, and flows for 5464 kilometres (3415 miles) through Qinghai, Sichuan, Gansu, Ningxia, Inner Mongolia, Shanxi, Shaanxi, Henan and Shandong, until it empties into the Bo Hai Sea. The gigantic river drains an area of 750,000 square kilometres (300,000 square miles).

The upper reaches of the Yellow River flow from its source to Togtoh County in Inner Mongolia, a length of 3472 kilometres (2170 miles). In two places in this section the river opens out to form lakes where a species of inland gull, the Brown-headed Gull (*Larus brunnicephalus*), can be found. Wild asses roam in the surrounding grassy plains. The middle reaches of the river cover the 1122 kilometre (1011 mile) stretch from Togtoh to Mengjin in Henan. It veers south from Togtoh, cuts through a group of gorges in Shanxi and Shaanxi, and reaches Longmen. In one 718 kilometre (446 mile) section, the drop is a substantial 611 metres (2000 ft). A famous waterfall, Hukou Falls, is located on this section of the river with a drop of 17 metres (55 ft). Hukou means 'mouth of the pot' in Chinese, so-called because the river above the falls is 250 metres (810 ft) wide, but tapers at the Hukou Falls into a 50 metre (160 ft) wide torrent, roaring down into magnificent swirling waters below.

Up to this point the Yellow River is a clear, sparkling stream, but this soon changes in the 130 kilometre (80 mile) section from Longmen to Tongguan, where it is joined by tributaries such as the Fen, Lue, Jing and Wei rivers.

A stretch of the Yangtze (Chang) River, its discoloured water muddied by sediment and its banks heavily eroded.

ABOVE: the huge, sweeping meanders of the Yellow (Huang) River swing between banks of fertile sediment and the edge of the formidable Tengger Desert.
LEFT: one of the most famous rivers of the world, the Yellow River is the second longest of China's great watercourses. Here, near Lanzhou, it is a very broad, deceptively placid river with a spectacular mountain backdrop.

The flow is greatly increased but it carries with it large amounts of sediment. This is most evident in the middle reaches of the Yellow River which pass through the Loess Plateau, picking up vast amounts of the yellow, silty and easily eroded soil; 89 per cent of the river's sediment load is collected in this section. It is at this point that the river becomes yellow in appearance, giving it its English name. According to records made in Shanxian County, the river's average sediment yield has been as high as 37 kilograms per cubic metre (2 lb 14 oz per cubic foot) which is the highest of the major rivers of the world.

In a stretch measuring 870 kilometres (530 miles), the lower section runs from Mengjin downstream to the sea. In this section the Yellow River flows slowly and smoothly through the North China Plain, where its river bed widens and large quantities of silt are deposited. As a result, the river bed has risen 4 to 5 metres (13 to 16 ft) above the original banks, so the river has had to be embanked, leading to its Chinese name here, the 'Above-Ground River'. The embankment is undermined by badgers that make their sets in it. The Government now encourages people to fill in these sets and thousands have now been so treated.

Due to the enormous quantity of sediment deposited at the river mouth it is too shallow to be navigated by cargo ships. The course of the river also changes frequently as the channel meanders to and fro across the mud flats; the last major change in the river's direction was in 1976.

THE GREAT SILTED RIVERS

Both the Yellow (Huang) and the Yangtze (Chang) rivers gather large amounts of silt in the middle reaches of their long courses. The fine silt is deposited on the river beds and banks when the force of the current is no longer powerful enough to carry it along. Both rivers have extensive and sluggish lower reaches where the fall is low. These shallow, broad stretches produce large mud flats. Silt in the Yellow River is so thick that it appreciably lowers the oxygen level, and a popular story has it that carp leap from the water in order to breathe.

BELOW: at Hukou Falls the Yellow River cascades in a bubbling mass of silt-laden water.
RIGHT: on the coastal plain at Chenchow the Yellow River is wider and its flow more sedate.
BELOW RIGHT: Xiling Gorge on the Yangtze River.

The Amur (Heilong) River

China's third largest river is also its most northerly point, as its middle section serves as the boundary between north-eastern China and the Soviet Union.

The river gives its name to the north-eastern province of China, Heilongjiang – 'jiang' meaning 'river'. The upper stream of the Amur River is from Luoguhe on the Sino-Soviet border to Aihui 900 kilometres (540 miles) further along the border. The middle section runs from here to the convergence with the Wusuli, from where the river continues its course to the sea through the Soviet Union and becomes the Ussuri River.

The Amur River system drains mostly densely forested areas which absorb rainfall and release water to the river slowly, with little erosion. Consequently, the river contains little sediment. The river system has the fast and deep flows ideal for hydroelectric generators – a resource that has been much exploited. The hydroelectric power generated is as much as 6 million kilowatts. The wide and deep trunk stream and tributaries of the Amur are also good for navigation, and the river is rich in aquatic resources such as the famed Kaluga Sturgeon (*Huso dauricus*) and Chum or Dog Salmon (*Oncorhyncus keta*). However, at present flood danger is still a threat in the Amur catchment area, so reservoirs are needed in the river system to tame the natural cycle. The river is frozen for the duration of the five-month winter, with ice so thick that it can bear the weight of cars driven across it.

Lakes

Although China has no huge lakes, there are over 2800 of one square kilometre (about ⅜ square mile) or more in the country, covering a total area of 80,000 square kilometres (30,890 square miles). They are mainly in the eastern plain and the Qinghai-Tibet Plateau, but there are also a number in the Yunnan-Guizhou Plateau, the Inner Mongolian Plateau and Xinjiang. Rich in aquatic resources, freshwater lakes, such as Poyang, Dongting, Taihu, Hongze and Chaohu, normally drain (eventually) into the sea. Most of the lakes which drain by evaporation are salt lakes which are also rich in soda, mirabilite, gypsum, lithium and boron deposits from the evaporation of stagnant water in an inland basin. These lakes include Qinghai, Hulun Nur, Nam and Siling Co.

Lakes of the Yangtze (Chang) and other river plains

Lakes of the plain formed by the lower half of the middle reaches of the Yangtze River are all freshwater lakes, and cover a total area of 22,161 square kilometres (11,606 square miles). This is approximately one quarter of the total surface area of the country that is covered by lakes.

Situated in Jiangxi, Poyang Lake is the largest freshwater lake in China, with an area of 3583 square kilometres (1878 square miles). It moderates the flow of the Yangtze River to some extent. There is a magnificent nature reserve, especially famous for its geese and cranes, at Poyang Lake, and it is rich in fish. Located in northern Hunan and covering an area of 2820 square kilometres (1478 square miles), Dongting Lake is the second largest freshwater lake in China. It is known as 'Dongting of Eight Hundred Li' (a 'Li' is half a kilometre – approximately quarter of a mile). It is formed by the Yangtze, and the sediments from that great river make it very shallow, so much so that islands appear in winter when the river flow is reduced.

As the third largest freshwater lake in China, Hongze Lake, situated in the middle-lower Huai River plain, has an area of 2069 square kilometres (1084 square miles). Due to heavy silting, the lake bed is several metres above the level of the Lixia River on the eastern side, where it has had to be dammed, making it a raised lake.

Qinghai Lake, high on the Qinghai-Tibet Plateau, is China's largest salt lake; the Common Cormorant (*Phalacrocorax carbo*) breeds on the rocky shores or in trees, the large population sustained by the plentiful supply of fish.

In addition, Nansi Lake in the Yellow (Huang) River, in western Shangdong, and Beiyangdian, in the Hai River catchment area, are gradually being silted up, and choked with reed.

Lakes of north-eastern China

North-eastern China has both mountain and lowland lakes, with a total area of 3722 square kilometres (1949 square miles), 4.6 per cent of the country's total. This region is characterized by volcanic barrier lakes such as Jingpo Lake. A crater lake on top of Mount Baitou, Tianchi (Heaven) Lake, has an elevation of 2155 metres (7074 ft) and is up to 373 metres (1224 ft) deep. It also serves as the boundary between China and Korea, and its scenery is beautiful, with the edges of the volcano dropping sharply into the lake. It is too cold for fish, but this does not stop some people believing that, like Loch Ness, it has a prehistoric monster living in it! A large waterfall on one side of the lake is the source of the Songhua River. By the side of the lake are hot springs, which are a popular tourist attraction.

On the Sino-Soviet border, Xingkai Lake has an area of 4380 square kilometres (2293 square miles), and its huge Chum Salmon (*Oncorhynchus keta*) are a special delicacy.

Lakes of the Yunnan-Guizhou Plateau

Among the freshwater lakes on this plateau Dianchi is the largest, while Erhai and Fuxian lakes are stunningly beautiful, with steep banks, straight shorelines and deep water. Fuxian Lake is 151 metres (490 ft) deep. The area owes much of its beauty to the climate; high temperatures are moderated by the high altitude, leading to spring weather conditions all year round.

Lakes of Inner Mongolia and Xinjiang

The Inner Mongolian Plateau and Xinjiang have 22,450 square kilometres (11,700 square miles) of lakes, 27.8 per cent of the country's total. Since many of the rivers that flow into the lakes in Xinjiang tend to change course either for natural or man-made reasons, lakes in this region frequently dry up, as has happened to Manas Lake. Historically, it changed its position many times before disappearing finally over the last 20 years. Most of these lakes are shallow and very salty.

Lakes of the Qinghai-Tibet Plateau

The Qinghai-Tibet Plateau is the region with the most lakes in China, and also has more lakes than any comparable plateau in the world. The lakes have a total surface area of 30,974 square kilometres (16,228 square miles), which is approximately 38.4 per cent of the total lake surface area of China. There are more than 1500 lakes in the Tibet Autonomous Region alone.

This is a very cold region, and melt-water from the lofty snow-covered mountains supplies most of the lakes. A high concentration of salt results in salt lakes, the salinity of the rivers being generally 1.5 to 2.5 grammes per litre (¼ to ⅓ oz per gallon). The largest saltwater lake in China, Qinghai Lake, has a salinity of 12.49 grammes per litre (nearly 2 oz per gallon). This compares with about 3 grammes per litre (½ oz per gallon) for the sea. On the western bank of Qinghai Lake is Bird Island, a nature reserve famous for geese, and the lake itself is rich in carp.

Aquatic plants

Fresh water lakes are the best places to look for aquatic plants, of which all or part grow under water. According to their physical and ecological characteristics, the plants can be classified into three types.

The three types of aquatic plants are submerged plants, floating plants and emergent plants. The stems and leaves of the submerged plants are

In south-eastern Xinjiang, on the lower reaches of the Miran River, lie numerous small, shallow lakes, many of which are of an ephemeral nature.

immersed in water and most have roots anchored in the mud. The leaves are leathery or silky, thin and soft. These characteristics reduce resistance to flowing water, and hence the damage caused by it. The most common of these plants include Bamboo-leaved Pondweed (*Potamogeton malaianus*), Ottelia (*Ottelia* spp.), *Vallisneria gigantea* and Litter Naiad (*Najas minor*), a valuable fish food, but a nuisance in irrigation ditches.

Plants that float on the water surface, or plants attached to the bottom but with their leaves on the surface of the water, form the second group. Free-floating forms drift with the wind, such as Common Duckweed (*Lemna minor*), Common Ducksmeat (*Spirodela polyrhiza*), and *Azolla imbricata*. Plants anchored firmly in the mud include *Nymphoides indicum*, Cristate Floating-heart (*Nymphoides cristatum*) and the large Golden Waterlily (*Euryale ferox*), whose seeds yield arrowroot. They have slender and soft leafstalks, some as long as one or two metres (3 to 6 ft), which lengthen or curl automatically with the rise or fall of the water level so that their leaves are always floating on the water surface.

The emergent aquatic plants have their roots in the mud and the upper part of the plants or the leaves stand out above the surface. Common examples are Woolly Philydrum (*Philydrum lanuginosum*), Wild Calla or Water Arum (*Calla palustris*) and the famed Hindu or Sacred Lotus (*Nelumbo nucifera*). Celebrated for their pink and white flowers, all are found mainly in shallow waters.

Most of the aquatic plants can be used as animal foodstuff or fertilizer, or for human consumption. Singharanut (*Trapa bispinosa*), a water chestnut, is a good foodstuff, as is the Hindu or Sacred Lotus, which is abundant in the shallow water lakes of the Yangtze (Chang) River system. Lotus seeds are edible and can also be used for medicinal purposes. The rhizomes of the Lotus are rich in starch and can be served as vegetables or ground up to produce lotus powder; the Lotus is therefore in heavy demand by the food industries on account of its versatility.

Great Black-headed Gulls (*Larus icthyaetus*) are among the largest and most spectacular of the world's gulls. Large numbers breed at Qinghai Lake high in the Qinghai-Tibet Plateau, resplendent in their jet black hoods and vividly coloured bills of spring. Their hoods and bills lose colour in the winter, when the gulls migrate to the south-west.

Bogs and marshlands

Marshes in China are found mainly in the flat north-east; bogs, in lesser numbers, are mainly confined to the Qinghai-Tibet Plateau and the north-eastern high mountains, although some are also found in the eastern plains and on sea coasts. In the north-east, the Sanjiang Plain has the most marshes, and is the chief wetland area in China, covering 8640 square kilometres (4525 square miles). Another major wetland region extends over an area of 3000 square kilometres (1570 square miles) in the Aba Tibetan Autonomous Prefecture of north-western Sichuan. Here the bogs are herbaceous with a layer of peat 2 to 3 metres (6 to 10 ft) thick, and up to 8 to 9 metres (26 to 30 ft) in the thickest parts.

The Sanjiang Plain is naturally rich in wild flowers. The marshes form grassy ponds speckled with flowers – particularly the purple, multiflower-headed *Sanguisorba parviflora*, the white flowers of *Polygonum nodosum*, also with a multiflowered head, and the light blue flowers of *Iris*. Many birds migrate here in summer, including geese, cranes, Mallard and Mandarin ducks.

Wetland vegetation

Vegetation grows well in all the temperate or cool wetland regions. There are about 100 families of plants represented altogether, mainly grasses (Gramineae) and sedges (Cyperaceae), but also buttercups (Ranunculaceae), arum lilies (Araceae), knotweeds (Polygonaceae), bladderworts (Lentibulariaceae) and arrowgrasses (Juncaginaceae).

Commonly found trees are Chinese Deciduous Cypress (*Glyptostrobus pensilis*), which is a relict plant of the Tertiary period, and Trabeculate Alder (*Alnus trabeculosa*). Bushes and shrubs or herbs include Altai Birch (*Betula fruticosa*) and Cranberry (*Vaccinium microcarpum*). Of the herbaceous plants, most are perennials such as the sedge *Carex limosa*, the marsh plant *Ischaemum rugosum* var. *segetum*, the reed grass *Glyceria triflora* and the Chinese water chestnut *Eleocharis tuberosa*. Annual and biennial plants make up only about one sixth of the total numbers. They include Red Shanks (*Polygonum persicaria*) and Water Pepper (*Polygonum hydropiper*). Vines are also common – especially the pitcher plant Common Nepenthes (*Nepenthes mirabilis*) and the gourd Common Schizopepon (*Schizopepon bryoniifolium*).

The most commonly found plant is the cosmopolitan common reed *Phragmites australis*. It grows on every available site around lakes, ponds and river banks, from the temperate Sanjiang Plain in the north-east to the subtropical plains in the middle and lower reaches of the Yangtze (Chang) River, and from the humid south-eastern coast to the arid drainage of the Tarim Basin in Xinjiang. The reeds are firmly rooted in mud and spread with well-developed underground roots and stems, and they mostly form dense reed beds with few other plants intermixed. Most grow to a height of 1.5 to 4 metres (5 to 13 ft), and they cover 70 to 90 per cent of the land where they grow. The common reed is a good fibre plant which can be harvested to use in paper production as well as for weaving and thatching.

Sea coasts

The coast of China forms the very eastern edge of the Asian continent and faces the Pacific Ocean. Four seas – the Bo Hai, the Yellow, the East China and the South China seas – constitute the coastal waters. Cranes settle beside them, and turtles swim in the southern waters.

The Bo Hai is an inland sea with an area of about 97,000 square kilometres (about 50,000 square miles) and an average depth of 26 metres (85 ft).

This colourful display of flowers and blue water is in a shallow, swampy depression in the sand dunes of Horqin Youyi Qianqi in Inner Mongolia.

Enclosed on three sides by land, the salinity and depth of the Bo Hai is influenced by the continent: the salt content of the sea is low because of the rivers draining into it, and they deposit sediment that makes it shallower. In winter the coastal waters are regularly frozen. It is rich in fish, including lobsters.

The Yellow (Huang) Sea is a half-enclosed, shallow sea, with an average depth of 44 metres (145 ft) over an area of about 400,000 square kilometres (209,000 square miles). There is a south-east to north-west trench in the middle of the sea, with a depth of up to 80 metres (260 ft). The maximum depth of the sea is only 140 metres (455 ft). The coastline is very flat because of deposits from the Yellow River.

The East China (Dong) Sea has a rocky coastline with many coves and bays and several ports. The sea covers an area of about 800,000 square kilometres (419,000 square miles) and has an average depth of 370 metres (1200 ft). It is an open sea, and its seabed has a complicated topography, with the continental shelf lying under two thirds of the total sea area. Commercial fishing is widespread, exploiting the extensive fish reserves.

The South China (Nan) Sea is a typical deep-sea basin partially surrounded by the continent and has a rough coastline with peninsulas and islands. Its area is about 3,500,000 square kilometres (1,837,000 square miles), and its average depth 1212 metres (4000 ft). Situated in the tropical zone, the South

China Sea has a relatively high temperature and a high degree of salinity, and is full of tropical fish and sharks. The Green Turtle (*Chelonia mydas*) can sometimes be seen from the cliffs and dolphins from coastal boats. Boobies, close relatives of the gannet (family Sulidae) of the North Atlantic, are fish-eating seabirds found in this area.

China has a very long coastline, totalling about 18,900 kilometres (11,250 miles) with rich and diverse marine resources. The coastline falls into one of three types – flat sedimentary coast, rocky coast or a mixture of mangrove and coral reefs.

North of Hangzhou Bay, which is just south of Shanghai, most of the coasts are flat except for the Liaodong Peninsula and the Shandong Peninsula, which have rocky headlands. South of Hangzhou Bay, the coastline is predominantly rocky, with some low-lying shores in the bays. The mangrove swamps and coral reefs are found on some of the shorelines of the South China Sea. South of the Penghu Islands are 64 islands with coral reefs, and there are more coral reefs off the south-east coast of Taiwan and the islands nearby. The reefs are inhabited by a vast array of brightly coloured fish, sea anemones, sea urchins and so on.

Mangroves play an important role in the formation of the coasts where they grow, as their roots hold the sand and silt brought up by the tide, thereby eventually extending the shoreline out into the shallow seas. Dune plants abound on all the beaches. On the sandy beaches and platforms of the Bo Hai

ABOVE LEFT: small waders, like these Dunlin (*Calidris alpina*), are common migrants along the coasts of China.
ABOVE: the South China Sea has coral reefs, feared by sailors but rich in colourful marine life.

and the Yellow seas in northern China, there are many grasses and grass-like plants which can tolerate moist, salty conditions, such as the sedge *Carex kobomugi*, the bindweed *Calystegia soldanella*, the daisy *Ixeris repens*, the grass *Elymus mollis* and the pea *Lathyrus maritimus*. In the north the sand is quite stable, being sedimentary, but on the coasts of the South China Sea, where the sand is loose, the dominant plants are the rapidly growing, branched, creeping shrubs *Ipomoeacaprae*, related to the Sweet Potato *I. batatas*, and *Vitex trifolia*, related to the verbenas. On low-lying beaches the grasses *Fimbristylis complanata*, *Spinifex littoreux* and *Cymbopogon caesius* grow. On the inner side of the dunes plants which have adapted to the environment include *Imperata cylindrica*, *Wedelia prostrata*, *Alysicarpus vaginalis*, *Desmodium heterophyllum*, *Launaea sarmentosa* and *Saccaharum arundinaceum*, which is closely related to Sugar Cane (*S. officinarum*).

Mammals of the wetlands

Of the few mammals that live in aquatic environments, the Himalayan Water Shrew and the Common Otter are the most widespread. A number of unusual or very rare species of mammals can be found in China, especially in the middle to lower reaches of the Yangtze (Chang) River.

The Himalayan Water Shrew and Common Otter

A tiny mammal, the Himalayan Water Shrew (*Chimarrogale platycephala*) is widely distributed in the mountainous waters in the south. In appearance and size it is rather like a rat, but it has a pointed snout and webbed toes, and feeds on aquatic insects, little fish and shrimps. It is agile and thoroughly at home in rapid streams.

Found in northern fresh waters, the Common Otter (*Lutra lutra*) feeds mainly on fish, and is the same creature that we know in Europe. In China it is hunted for its fur.

Beavers and muskrats

Inhabiting only the upper reaches of forested rivers in north-eastern Xinjiang, the Eurasian Beaver (*Castor fiber*) builds banks with tree stems and gravel to dam streams and adjust the depth of water in lakes and ponds. It eats primarily bark and aquatic plants, and stores food in autumn to help it survive the icy winter.

After entering Xinjiang from the Soviet Union in the 1950s by means of the rivers, Muskrats (*Ondatra zibethicus*) became established in north and north-east China, spreading rapidly. Muskrats nest in holes in marshes and swamps, and feed on aquatic insects, small animals and plants. They have a high-quality fur, and 'muskrat spice' which is taken from the glands near the anus, is also very precious, though is not to be confused with musk, which comes from musk deer (*Mochus* spp.). It is, however, a serious pest in areas with riverside embankments and dams, which can be damaged by its burrowing activities.

Wild Boar and Red Deer

These two mammals were once widely distributed in forested areas close to waters in plains, hills and mountains. However, the forests in China's plains and nearby mountains have been converted into farmland, and the dense human population and the popularity of hunting have contributed to a significant reduction in their distribution and numbers. According to research, Wild Boar (*Sus scrofa*) and Red Deer (*Cervus elaphus*) still live in considerable numbers on the wide reed beds of the Tarim River catchment area in Xinjiang. They spend most of their time hidden among the reeds,

Very local in its distribution, the Eurasian Beaver (*Castor fiber*) still survives in the remote rivers of Xinjiang, where it exerts an influence on the landscape unexpected for an animal of its size, creating lakes and ponds.

leaving cover to feed on crops. One of the authors of this book was lucky enough to see the largest Wild Boar recorded on a field trip. The male boar was not much smaller than an ass, and was sighted in the Tarim River in August 1975. If disturbed, Wild Boars will silently move away rather than offer aggression, but if cornered and attacked they can put up a fierce resistance, fighting with their strong tusks.

Seals and dolphins

There are 20 or more species of sea mammals in China, but each species is few in number and inadequately researched. Species include the Lesser Rorqual (*Balaenoptera acutorostrata*), which is much like a dolphin in appearance, is under 1 metre (3 ft) long and lives in inshore waters. About 2 metres (6 ft) long, the Black Finless Porpoise (*Neophocaena phocaenoides*) lives in estuaries, and swims upstream to freshwater regions along the Yangtze (Chang) River. The widespread Common Seal (*Phoca vitulina*) dwells primarily in the coastal waters in Liaoning. It breeds between January and February, when male and female may often be seen together resting on an ice floe.

The placid Dugong (*Dugong dugon*) is a large, superficially seal-like herbivore 2 metres (6 ft) long, with the horizontal tail typical of an aquatic mammal. It is the only truly sea-dwelling vegetarian mammal, and eats underwater sea grasses. Small numbers live in the sea coasts off Guangxi, Guangdong, Hainan Dao Island and Taiwan.

The Chinese River Dolphin (*Lipotes vexillifer*) is a great rarity. It is endemic in China, and is also an endangered species. The present population is a mere 300, which survive in limited sections of the middle to lower Yangtze River, eating mainly fish. Water pollution, fishing and ships' propellers are chief causes of injury, and considerable efforts are being made to preserve the species. No other river in the world harbours more than one species of cetacean but, interestingly, the Black Finless Porpoise does not seem to compete with the Chinese River Dolphin for food and thus is not a contributory factor in its decline.

The Yangtze River is home to one of the great rarities of China, the endemic Chinese River Dolphin (*Lipotes vexillifer*) which lives in the middle reaches of the great river. The long, slender 'beak' and domed head are very distinctive features.

Spot-billed Pelicans (*Pelecanus philippensis*) and Black-crowned Night Herons (*Nycticorax nycticorax*) make a dramatic sight against the setting sun at Zhalong Nature Reserve in Heilongjiang Province. The Black-crowned Night Herons, true to their name, become active as dusk falls, emerging from dense trees where they spend the day in small flocks.

Birds of the wetlands

An abundant supply of water plants provides not only food for birds, but also somewhere for them to rest and hide from predators. Most swamp birds are migratory.

Grebes

Five species of grebes breed in small numbers in the freshwater and lake areas of China. Breeding in Xinjiang, the Slavonian or Horned Grebe (*Podiceps auritus*) migrates to north-east China, north China, and the Yangtze (Chang) River catchment area for the winter. The rather similar Black-necked or Eared Grebe (*P. nigricollis*) breeds from Heilongjiang south to Liaoning and in parts of western China, and winters in the valley of the Yangtze. The much larger Great Crested Grebe (*P. cristatus*) breeds in the north and in Tibet and moves south in winter. Red-necked Grebes (*P. grisegena*) breed in Manchuria. Little Grebes (*P. ruficollis*) live in most parts of China the whole year round. Little Grebes look like small, round ducks, but have pointed bills, particularly short tails and lobed feet. They dive beneath the surface of the water to catch fish. They make their nests from water weeds and attach them to growing reeds and emergent bushes so that the completed nests float on the water. They produce four to seven cream-coloured eggs, which hatch after 18 to 24 days. When the mother leaves the nest she covers the eggs o hide them from predators. The nestlings can swim and dive almost immediately, but depend on their parents for food for several weeks.

Pelicans, boobies and cormorants

Two species of pelicans (*Pelecanus*) are recorded in China but the status of the Great White Pelican (*P. onocrotalus*) is uncertain. The Spot-billed Pelican (*P. philippensis*) is the more common; it breeds around Lop Nur Lake of Xinjiang and the lower reaches of the Yangtze (Chang) River. Both species feed mainly on fish, make their nests in trees near water, and lay one to four eggs which they incubate for four or five weeks. The nestlings must be fed by their parents for about 30 days before leaving the nest to fish for themselves.

The species of boobies found in China include the Red-footed Booby (*Sula sula*) and Brown Booby (*S. leucogaster*). They nest in treetop colonies, with 20 or 30 pairs per tree, and their droppings make it hazardous to walk under the trees. The rich feeding around the tropical Xisha Islands of the South China Sea allows the boobies to breed more than once a year. Similarly streamlined, boobies are closely related to gannets and, like their larger relatives, plunge headlong in pursuit of fish.

The Common Cormorant (*Phalacrocorax carbo*) is a freshwater bird which can be found in the plateau lakes in the north-western and south-western parts of China. The largest colony is in the 'Bird Island' of Qinghai Lake in Qinghai Province, where it congregates in thousands. These birds feed mainly on fish and make nests on the rocks, cliffs and in trees. Two to four eggs are laid in a clutch, and the incubation period is 25 days. The nestlings leave the nest after 21 days. Common Cormorants used to be domesticated to catch fish, a practice dating back hundreds of years, but they were so good at hunting that they were depleting fish resources. Consequently domestication was outlawed after the founding of the People's Republic, although many traditional fishing flocks can still be seen.

Bird Island in Qinghai has a thriving colony of Common Cormorants (*Phalacrocorax carbo*), which also nest in north-western and south-western China. These large birds have long been domesticated for fishing.

EGRETS, STORKS AND CRANES

Although separate genera, egrets (*Egretta*), storks (*Ciconia*) and cranes (*Grus*) are quite similar in appearance. The easiest to differentiate is the egret, which has an 'S'-shaped neck when standing, which it draws back into its shoulders when flying.

Storks and cranes look remarkably similar in flight. Both stretch their necks out before them, but storks normally rise into the air by gracefully gliding up on thermals, while cranes ascend like most other birds by the power of their wingbeats. At rest the crane is an elegant bird, with head, neck and body tapering into each other with no clear division between them. By contrast, in the stork the three elements are altogether much more distinct.

RIGHT: the White-naped Crane (*Grus vipio*) breeds in Inner Mongolia.
BELOW LEFT: the Great White Egret (*Egretta alba*).
BELOW RIGHT: the White Stork (*Ciconia ciconia*).

Herons, storks, ibises and the Spoonbill

The most common heron in China is the very large Grey Heron (*Ardea cinerea*). The Purple Heron (*Ardea purpurea*), Green Heron (*Butorides striatus*), Black-crowned Night Heron (*Nycticorax nycticorax*) and the Chinese Pond Heron (*Ardeola bacchus*) also breed in China, building large, untidy nests of branches and leaves in trees or in reeds near water. Four to six eggs are laid at a time, and the incubation period is about three weeks. It takes another 50 days or so before the noisy and unruly nestlings are able to fly.

Egrets (*Egretta*) are elegant white herons with slender, curved necks and pointed bills. They feed on fish and large insects. In flight, like herons, they trail their long legs and large feet behind them, but draw back their heads onto the shoulders.

The rare White Stork (*Ciconia ciconia*) and Black Stork (*C. nigra*) are both endangered species. The White Stork lives in the fresh waters from northeast China to Xinjiang, and in recent years has been found to breed in the Zhalong Nature Reserve of Heilongjiang Province. Storks migrate from many areas to spend the winter around Poyang Lake and along the middle to lower reaches of the Yangtze River. Black Storks breed near lakes and rivers in the mountains of the northern part of China. They make their bulky nests of sticks on steep cliffs. In recent years detailed research has been carried out into the distribution, numbers and breeding habits of the Black Stork in the Pangchuan Creek Nature Reserve in Shanxi.

Although they have shorter legs and curved beaks, ibises otherwise look

ABOVE: the Black Stork (*Ciconia nigra*) is more elegant than the White Stork (*Ciconia ciconia*) and has a black head and neck.
TOP RIGHT: the Black-crowned Night Heron (*Nycticorax nycticorax*) is widely distributed around the world.
RIGHT: the Purple Heron (*Ardea purpurea*) breeds in China and is also quite common in warmer parts of Europe and Asia.

similar to storks. They nest either in trees or on the ground. The Sacred Ibis (*Threskiornis aethiopicus melanocephalus*) breeds only in the Zhalong Nature Reserve, nesting in groups in the reed beds. It winters in Guangdong and Fujian provinces in the far south of China. With only 40 or so birds left, the Japanese Crested Ibis (*Nipponia nippon*) is an extremely endangered species, and one of the rarest birds in the world. It breeds at an altitude of 1200 to 1400 metres (3900 to 4500 ft) in the Qin Ling Mountains in central China. Its plumage is almost wholly white, and its bill, bare face and feet are red, making it a striking and very beautiful bird. Its nest of dead branches is built in high waterside trees. A clutch has two to four eggs, which hatch after about 30 days. This ibis preys mainly on small fish and on other small aquatic animals, but it has proved vulnerable to pesticides that find their way into the water, mainly from nearby ricefields, and these are the chief threat to the survival of this species.

Lastly, the White Spoonbill (*Platalea leucorodia*) used to breed widely in north-east China and Xinjiang, but in recent years a large breeding colony has been found only in the Zhalong Nature Reserve. Spoonbills move about in groups, and feed on invertebrates and small fish in shallow water. They have long, flattened bills which broaden out into a 'spoon' shape at the tip. By sweeping them, partly opened, from side to side in shallow water, they find prey by touch.

ABOVE: this captive Japanese Crested Ibis (*Nipponia nippon*) is one of very few left in the world; there is a population of about 20 in the Qin Ling Mountains.

ABOVE RIGHT: the Zhalong Nature Reserve in Heilongjiang, north-eastern China, is the only breeding place of the Sacred Ibis (*Threskiornis aethiopicus melanocephalus*).

Geese, swans and ducks

Forty-six species of wildfowl (Anatidae) are found in China, 27 of them breeding in freshwater areas. The others breed in the Soviet Union and elsewhere but migrate through most of eastern China in large flocks, and live through the winter on the Yangtze (Chang) River and in the lakes and marshes to the south. They have been popular in the past with hunters, making protection necessary. The preservation of the wetland habitats and the establishment of winter reserves in China play an important part in the worldwide conservation of many species.

The Swan Goose (*Anser cygnoides*), Bean Goose (*A. fabalis*) and Greylag Goose (*A. anser*) breed commonly in north-east and north-west China. Bar-headed Geese (*A. indicus*) reproduce around the freshwater lakes in the Qinghai-Tibet Plateau. The 'Bird Island' of Qinghai Lake has the largest colony of about 5000 Barheaded Geese, approximately three times the number recorded in 1960. Promising as this seems, one reason for the increase is that the geese have left some of their other habitats. They make their nests in large groups and lay eight to ten eggs in a clutch. Artificial incubation and captive breeding have been successfully implemented with the birds from Qinghai Lake.

China has three species of swans. Whooper Swans (*Cygnus cygnus*),

Bewick's Swans (*C. columbianus Bewickii*) and Mute Swans (*C. olor*) breed in the wetlands of northern China. The Bayanbulak Nature Reserve in Xinjiang has the largest breeding population of Whooper Swans. Mute Swans, which are a little larger and have orange and black (rather than yellow and black) bills, breed in Inner Mongolia. The Falcated Teal (*Anas falcata*), Mallard (*A. platyrhynchos*), Spotbilled Duck (*A. poecilorhyncha*), Garganey (*A. querquedula*) and Shoveler (*A. clypeata*) breed in eastern and north-eastern China. These are all surface-feeding, or dabbling, ducks. The Red-crested Pochard (*Netta rufina*) breeds in Wuliangsuhai in Inner Mongolia. Of the diving ducks, which feed by diving underwater, Goldeneye (*Bucephala clangula*) winter along the sea coasts in southern China, and breed in Inner Mongolia. Nestlings were collected in Hulun Buir in 1963, but eggs have not yet been found. There are five species of pochard ducks (*Aythya*) in China, including the Shoveler (*Anas clypeata*). The Common Pochard (*Aythya ferina*), Ferruginous Duck (*A. nyroca*), Baer's Pochard (*A. baeri*) and Tufted Duck (*A. fuligula*) nest near rivers of north-western and north-eastern China.

The Chinese Merganser (*Mergus squamatus*), endemic in China, has a serrated, hooked beak, green head and black back. This duck, and also the Mandarin Duck (*Aix galericulata*) and the Lesser Whistling Duck (*Dendrocygna javanica*), breed in tree holes in riverside forests, and are all endangered because of loss of habitat. (See the chapter on Forests.)

ABOVE LEFT: Swan Geese (*Anser cygnoides*) breed in Heilongjiang.
ABOVE: Whooper Swans (*Cygnus cygnus*) nest in north-western China.

BELOW: these are the eggs of the Spot-billed Duck (*Anas poecilorhyncha*).
BOTTOM: Mandarin Ducks (*Aix galericulata*) are now very rare because their habitat has been reduced.

LEFT: Qinghai Lake has a fine range of breeding birds including Brown-headed Gulls (*Larus brunnicephalus*).
ABOVE: Avocets (*Recurvirostra avosetta*) are also to be found on Qinghai Lake.
RIGHT: nests of Saunders's Gulls (*Larus saundersi*) have recently been discovered for the first time at Yancheng; this bird is a juvenile calling to be fed.

Waders (shorebirds), gulls and terns

Except for a few species that breed in China, most of the 56 species of waders (shorebirds) found in the country migrate along the sea coasts, and live through the winter on the Yangtze River and in the region to its south, having migrated from the USSR and northern Japan.

The Pheasant-tailed Jacana (*Hydrophasianus chirurgus*) nests in marshes south of the Yangtze River. It has long, slender toes for walking on lotus leaves. Oystercatchers (*Haematopus ostralegus*) breed in north-east China. Ringed Plovers (*Charadrius hiaticula*) and Little Ringed Plovers (*C. dubius*) are widespread breeding birds found almost throughout the country. They lay four well-camouflaged eggs in simple, unlined, shallow scrapes in riverside sand and shingle. Common Redshanks (*Tringa totanus*) and Common Sandpipers (*Actitis hypoleucos*) breed in north-western China. Black-winged Stilts (*Himantopus himantopus*) nest mainly on the plateaux of north-western China, but recently nests and eggs have been collected in Jilin. Breeding in eastern China, the Oriental (or Eastern) Pratincole (*Glareola maldivarum*) is commonly found and feeds on locusts. It is a slender, tern-like bird with a short, forked tail and long, pointed wings which give it an elegant flight when hawking for insects on the wing. The Black-tailed Gull (*Larus crassirostris*) and Saunders's Gull (*L. saundersi*) breed in the coastal islands off eastern China. The latter is an endangered species, and its nest was first found as recently as 1984 by Chinese ornithologists who found groups breeding in the saltmarshes near Yancheng in Jiangsu. Living around the Qinghai-Tibet Plateau salt-water lakes, the spectacular Great Black-headed Gull (*L. ichthyaetus*) and the much smaller Brown-headed Gull (*L. brunnicephalus*) breed mainly on Qinghai Lake. The Ancient Murrelet (*Synthliboramphus antiquus*) is scarce but can sometimes be seen on rocky coasts. Chinese ornithologists have recently found nests on some coastal islands near Shandong and Shanghai.

Cranes, egrets and coots

China abounds with cranes. Among the 15 species worldwide, nine are found in China, which is not only one of the main breeding areas for them, but also an important area for overwintering flocks. For example, 2000 Great White or Siberian Cranes (*Grus leucogeranus*) have been found during the winter at the famous reserve at Poyang Lake. The very rare Japanese or Red-crowned Crane (*G. japonensis*) breeds in Inner Mongolia, Heilongjiang, Jilin and Liaoning, and winters in the Yangtze River catchment area. According to recent studies there are now 600 or so Japanese Cranes breeding in the wild in Heilongjiang. Larger numbers breed in Zhalong Nature Reserve, the main breeding site, but this is largely due to captive breeding and a successful policy of protection. Birds reared in this reserve have, however, lost the instinctive urge to migrate, and remain there all year. Another popular species, the White-naped Crane (*G. vipio*), has similar breeding and over-wintering sites. Common Cranes (*G. grus*) breed around the lakes of the north-western grassland and migrate over much of China for the winter, and are more partial to wet areas than other cranes. A small number of the smaller and even more elegant Demoiselle Cranes (*Anthropoides virgo*) breed in Inner Mongolia and north-east China, their habitat including plains, high plateaux and deserts up to 5000 metres (15,500 ft) above sea level. Hooded Cranes (*G. monacha*) breed in north-eastern China but little is known about them; in winter some visit the lower Yangtze.

The Black-necked Crane (*G. nigricollis*) is an endemic species in China and is also endangered. It is the only species which breeds and stays throughout the year in the plateau wetlands. According to surveys in the mid-1980s in Qinghai, Tibet and Gansu, about 800 birds survive there. Black-necked Cranes have also been bred in captivity, the first success being achieved in Beijing Zoo in 1988, where six nestlings were reared. Breeding areas are around highland lakes up to 4300 metres (13,300 ft) above sea level; in winter they descend to abandoned rice fields at 1375 metres (4000 ft) above sea level.

All cranes make their nests with dried grass on flat, open ground near water or in swamps. They lay one or two eggs, and incubate them for 31 to 33 days. Cranes migrate south for the winter in family parties and then come back to their original breeding sites in spring.

Egrets feed on fish, shrimps and aquatic insects. Three species are common in China – the Great Egret (*Egretta alba*), the Intermediate Egret (*E. intermedia*) and the Little Egret (*E. garzetta*). All have white plumage and the long feathers on their backs were once much prized as ornaments. They have downy feathers near their tails, which, when they rub their dirty heads, necks and bills on them, crumble into powder and soak up fish slime from their outer feathers. Then they scratch the dirty powder off with a special claw on the feet, using it like a comb, before applying preen oil. They nest in colonies in trees, often with a mixture of egret species in the same tree.

Apart from size, which is 90 cm (36 in.) from head to tail for the Great Egret, 55 cm (22 in.) for the Little Egret and 68 cm (27 in.) for the Intermediate Egret, there are few obvious differences in appearance between them. The Little Egret has a black bill and legs, but yellow feet; the Intermediate Egret has all-black legs and feet and, in winter, a yellow bill; the Great Egret has black legs which flush yellow or red in spring and a blackish bill which becomes wholly yellow outside the breeding season. The Great Egret is widely distributed from the north-east of China to Yunnan and Hainan Dao Island and the Intermediate and Little are found in central China south of the Yangtze; the Little is also found in eastern China.

The Coot (*Fulica atra*) is widely hunted in China. It migrates through eastern China, stopping frequently on different waters, and lives through the winter in the Yangtze River catchment area. It breeds in Inner Mongolia and

TOP: a family of Japanese Cranes (*Grus japonensis*) at the nest in the Zhalong Nature Reserve, Heilongjiang. Japanese Cranes are capable of flying over great distances.
ABOVE: a Demoiselle Crane (*Anthropoides virgo*) in typically elegant pose. Demoiselle Cranes breed in north-eastern China and Inner Mongolia.

RIGHT: the Black-necked Cranes (*Grus nigricollis*) take off into a blue sky from their year-round home in the Qinghai-Tibet Plateau.

the north-east. The large flocks can cause damage when they are migrating as they sometimes descend on sorghum fields. They live on fish, insects and aquatic plants, which they find by diving underwater.

Kingfishers

Pied Kingfishers (*Ceryle lugubris*), Lesser Pied Kingfishers (*C. rudis*), Ruddy Kingfishers (*Halcyon coromanda*), White-breasted Kingfishers (*H. smyrnensis*) and Black-capped Kingfishers (*H. pileata*) are generally found near low mountain creeks in southern China. The Common Kingfisher (*Alcedo atthis*) is scattered over plains and around low mountain waters all over the country and can often be seen darting into rivers.

Kingfishers nest alone or in pairs, and make their nests by digging holes deep into firm banks. They use fishbones to line a chamber where they lay as many as eight eggs. The Lesser Pied Kingfisher frequently hovers before diving; the White-breasted is more frequently seen away from water where it catches insects, lizards and crabs.

The Black-capped Kingfisher (*Halcyon pileata*) breeds near creeks in the lower reaches of the mountains in southern China. It is less dependent on water for its food than the smaller Common Kingfisher (*Alcedo atthis*), and in its diet resembles the White-breasted Kingfisher (*Halcyon smyrnensis*) which eats crabs, lizards and insects away from the water's edge.

Harriers and the Osprey (Fish Hawk)

The common species of harriers in China, the Hen Harrier, or Marsh Hawk (*Circus cyaneus*), the Pied Harrier (*C. melanoleucos*) and the Marsh Harrier (*C. aeruginosus*), breed in the northern part of north-east China, but the Marsh Harrier is also spread throughout most of northern China. Harriers catch small birds and mammals in long grass or reeds or from the surface of pools by deftly picking them up in flight in their needle-sharp claws. The Osprey or Fish Hawk (*Pandion haliaetus*) is a rare species in China, but is one of the most widespread birds in the world. It hovers over lakes and dives into the water to catch fish. The headlong dive ends with a great splash, and the fish is held in the feet and carried off to be eaten on a suitable perch. This bird is said to breed in northern China and the southernmost part of south China, but nests have not yet been located.

Reed warblers and the Penduline Tit

The Great Reed Warbler (*Acrocephalus arundinaceus*), the Black-browed Reed Warbler (*A. bistrigiceps*), the Paddy-field Warbler (*A. agricola*) and the Thick-billed Reed Warbler (*A. aedon*) are the common species of these small waterside birds in China. Great Reed Warblers can often be heard singing their strident notes beside reedy ponds. All species nest in the reed swamps of eastern China, but the Black-browed Reed Warbler is frequently found nesting in drier places. Nests in reeds are popular with Common Cuckoos (*Cuculus canorus*), which lay an egg for the warbler to hatch. The Penduline Tit (*Remiz pendulinus*), which breeds in the wetland regions of north-eastern China, weaves a soft, delicate, flask-shaped nest from the silky down of willow and poplar flowers which it enters from a narrow opening to the side.

Great Reed Warblers (*Acrocephalus arundinaceus*) build cupped nests slung between several reed stems; the nests are often found by Common Cuckoos (*Cuculus canorus*) which lay an egg in them.

Amphibians and reptiles of the wetlands

Of the many frogs and toads in China's rivers and lakes, the rain frog *Kaloula borealis*, the frogs *Rana nigromacula*, *R. planoyi*, *R. limnocharis* and *R. guentheri*, and the toads *Bufo bufo*, *B. melanostictus* and *B. raddei* are the most common species. *Cynops orientalis* and *Pachytriton brevipes* are common salamanders. The Chinese Giant Salamander (*Andrias davidianus*) is found in the mountains. (See Mountains.)

The Chinese Soft-shelled Turtle (*Trionyx sinensis*) is widely distributed in fresh waters. Instead of a shell it has a hard, leathery skin. It lays its white eggs in sandy parts of river edges. Distributed south of the Yangtze (Chang) River, the Three-lined Box Turtle (*Cuora trifasciata*) is a typical oriental species. The large sea turtles, the Leatherback Sea Turtle (*Dermochelys coriacea*), the Green Turtle (*Chelonia mydas*) and the Hawksbill Turtle (*Eretmochelys imbricata*), are primarily found in the warm waters of the South China Sea. Apart from the Soft-shelled Turtle, which eats fish, and the vegetarian Green Turtle, they eat mainly invertebrates.

FAR LEFT: the Big-headed Turtle (*Platysternon megacephalum*) lives in mountain waterfalls.
LEFT: common on the plains, the Chinese Soft-shelled Turtle (*Trionyx sinensis*) is often captured for food.

LEFT: a female Chinese Alligator (*Alligator sinensis*) is clearing the top of her nest away to expose the eggs just before they hatch. During the past several decades the population of this rare species has decreased annually.

ABOVE LEFT: China's rivers and lakes provide a habitat for many species of frogs. *Rana planoyi* is a rare species of the lowlands.
ABOVE: *Rana nigromaculata* is the most common frog species in the plains.

The mature adult Chinese Alligator (*Alligator sinensis*) is about 1.5 metres (60 in.) long. It is endemic to China and is also an endangered species. Concentrated in the Yangtze River catchment area in southern Anhui, it inhabits the rivers in hills and mountains, and burrows holes in the banks to live in, siting its home at water level so that the river water just comes in. The holes are complex, becoming deep burrows with air vents to the bank above. It feeds on fish, shrimps, river snails and aquatic insects, and also preys on ducks, frogs and small animals. It makes a nest 40 to 60 cm (16 to 24 in.) in diameter and 50 to 70 cm (20 to 28 in.) high, using dried weeds, and lays 20 to 50 eggs. These are incubated by the warmth of the sun and the heat generated by the decaying nest material. They hatch after 60 to 70 days. A Chinese Alligator Nature Reserve and Reproduction Research Centre has been set up in Xuancheng, Anhui, and has succeeded in artificial propagation on a scale sufficient to make a substantial difference to the (admittedly very small) Chinese Alligator population.

Fish

Many of the freshwater fish farmed or bred worldwide originated in the rivers of the plains of eastern China. These include the Common Carp (*Cyprinus carpio*), Goldfish (*Carassius auratus*), Silver Carp (*Hypophthalmichthys molitrix*), Bighead Carp (*Aristichthys nobilis*) and Grass Carp (*Ctenopharyngodon idella*). The Goldfish is now common worldwide, while Grass Carp are used to control aquatic weeds, which they eat. Altogether over 2000 seafish and about 700 freshwater fish are found in the rivers, lakes and coastal waters of China.

Cold freshwater fish in the north include large numbers of graylings (Thymallidae), salmon and trout (Salmonidae) and pike (Esocidae), as well as the less well-known Burbot (*Lota lota*). Species of barbel (*Noemacheilus*) and the widespread sub-family of snow trout (Schizothoracinae) are widespread in the north-west. Several species of carp are the most common fish in the rivers and lakes of eastern China. The typical fish of southern China belong to the families Gyrinocheilidae, Akysidae, Heteropneustidae, Olyridae and Clari-idae. The Hairtail (*Trichiurus haumela*), Japanese Mackerel (*Pneumatophorus japonicus*), Large Yellow Croaker (*Pseudosciaena crocea*), Little Yellow Croaker (*P. polyactis*) and porgies, or sea breams (Sparidae), are all common in the waters off China. The Marine Eel (*Muranesox cinereus*), the swordfish Green Gar (*Tylosaurus anastomella*), the Halfbeak Fish (*Hyporhamphus sajor*) and shoals of Flying Fish (*Cypselurus rondeletii*) also proliferate.

MOUNTAINS 山地

Mountains and hills account for a large proportion of the Chinese landscape, covering about 43 per cent of the total land area. Because most of the plains of China have been cultivated for many centuries it is to the mountains, and the forests on them, that one has to look for most of the country's wild animals and plants.

Mountain range orientation

The orientation of the Chinese mountain ranges is important because it has a significant effect on the climate, and hence on the distribution of both plants and animals. Most lie generally from north-east to south-west and from west to east with fewer ranges north-west to south-east. Only a few in the middle of China run predominantly north to south.

There are three groups of mountains that run west to east. The most northerly is composed of the Tien and Yin mountain ranges. The middle group includes the Kunlun, Qilian and Dabie ranges, while the southern group consists of only the Nan Ling range. All these west-to-east ranges are important geographical boundaries.

Most of the ranges that run north-east to south-west consist of medium and low mountains and lie in the east of China. They also include three major groups: the Da Hinggan and Taihang mountains and Xuefeng Mountain in the middle of China; the Changbai Mountains, Shandong Hills and Wuyi Mountains in the east; and the Taiwan mountain ranges offshore.

The north-west to south-east ranges include the highest mountains, being mainly distributed in the high-altitude west of the country. They are the Altai in the north-west and the Himalayas in the south-west. Most of the mountains that run through the middle of China run north to south; these include the Helan, Liupan and Hengduan mountains.

Climatic effects

Just as chains of islands deflect ocean currents, mountain ranges impede the flow of air currents; as a result they have a significant effect on the climate. Every winter, cold dry air from Siberia and the Mongolian Plateau spills southwards into China, but the effect of this air mass gets weaker as it moves south because it has to overcome the series of west-to-east oriented mountain ranges. These mountains therefore act as boundaries between temperature and vegetation zones, and their flora and fauna reflect this.

The Tien mountain range resists the cold winter currents from Siberia as well as what is left of the humid air from the Atlantic and Arctic oceans, and therefore acts as the divide between the temperate desert zone to the north and the warm-temperate desert zone to the south of the range. The Yin range also obstructs the cold current from moving southward, and forms a boundary between temperate prairie to the north and warm-temperate prairie to the south. The Qin Ling range separates the warm-temperate deciduous broad-leaved forest zone from the subtropical evergreen broad-leaved forest zone. Although not very high, the Nan Ling range also plays a role in obstructing the cold currents from the north, and divides the middle subtropical zone from the southern subtropical zone.

The Himalayas are the highest barrier of all, and almost completely cut off the interior of the Qinghai-Tibet Plateau from the moist air of the south-west monsoon which moves in from the Indian Ocean; as a result there is heavy rainfall and hence dense forests on the southern slopes of the range, but dry, prairie conditions on the northern slopes. The contrast is very marked.

The mountain ranges that run from north-east to south-west resist the south-east monsoon which moves in over eastern China from the Pacific. It successively meets the Changbai, Qian, Da Hinggan and Taihang mountains,

Colourful Rhododendrons (*Rhododendron*) grow at high altitudes and are widely distributed in the Hengduan Mountains, Yunnan.

PREVIOUS PAGE: Fanling Mountain Nature Reserve in Guizhou Province. The nature of the vegetation growing on mountains depends on altitude.

The blooms of this delicate rhododendron are just opening on the slopes of the Emei Mountains.

and is obstructed on the Loess Plateau by the Luliang, Helan and Liupan mountains. Since the south-west monsoon is resisted by the Himalayas and the Qinghai-Tibet Plateau, very little moist air reaches the north-west and the resulting arid climate has led to the development of the vast desert areas, including the Gobi in Mongolia.

The directions faced by mountain slopes have a considerable influence on plant distribution, but the influence of this factor is profoundly modified by the prevailing air currents. For example, both the Tien Mountains and the Himalayas extend in part from west to east, but the influence of the local prevailing winds means that they have very different characteristics. The northern slopes of the Tien are affected by moist air from the Arctic Ocean and support groves of Schrenk's Spruce (*Picea schrenkiana*), but the southern slopes are sheltered and quite dry, with arid mountain steppe vegetation. By contrast, the southern slopes of the Himalayas are on the windward side, and

TOP LEFT: Spruce (*Picea*) forests on the northern slopes of the Tien Mountains become blanketed in snow in winter.
TOP RIGHT: the Da Hinggan Mountains in north-eastern China are lower lying than the Tien with much smoother, gentler slopes where forests of Dahurian Larch (*Larix dauricum*) are dominant.
ABOVE: this extraordinary bug was photographed in the Chang Mountains near Dali, Yunnan.

exposed to the south-west monsoon; as a result they support several varieties of forest. The north slopes, on the other hand, are on the rain-sheltered side, so they are characterized by dry mountain steppe.

In several places high mountains act as protective screens, turning large areas into sheltered 'walled gardens'. An example of this is the Sichuan Basin. This is on the same latitude as the middle and lower reaches of the Yangtze (Chang) River, but because it is surrounded by mountains with an elevation of 1000 to 3000 metres (3280 to 9840 ft), which shelter it from the cold winds that blow off Siberia, it has a milder climate. The Sichuan Basin has a natural vegetation of evergreen broad-leaved forests composed of cinnamon (*Cinnamomum*), plants of the tea family (Theaceae) and evergreen oaks (*Quercus*), and Sugar Cane (*Saccaharum officinarum*) and citruses can be grown, together with lychees and bananas. None of these plants are found on the plains of the middle and lower reaches of the Yangtze which lie on much the same latitude – the reason being that the plains are not protected by high mountains and there is nothing to stop the cold winter air currents from blowing southwards.

The influence of the mountain ranges on the climate also affects the distribution of animals. The northern parts of the Da Hinggan and Altai ranges are the southern limit of most of the animals that survive in a cold-temperate climate – roughly consistent with the southern boundary of the distribution of Reindeer (*Rangifer tarandus*) in the Arctic. North of this boundary the variety of animals is reduced because of the cold conditions.

The Yin and Yan mountains, which are at 41 to 42°N, roughly delineate the northern limit of the warm-temperate zone. South of this the climate is heavily influenced by the south-east monsoon so the average temperature is quite high, and some species more typical of the subtropical zone occur in this region. For example, Rhesus Macaques (*Macaca mulatta*) can be seen on Xinglong Mountain in northern Hebei Province. At 41°N this is the most northerly distribution recorded for present-day primates. The boundary of the warm-temperate zone is also roughly consistent with the northern limit of distribution of civets (Viverridae) and tortoises (Testudinidae).

The Qin Ling mountain range is a major regional boundary since it separates the Palearctic region from the Oriental region in the east of China. Some subtropical species stay south of these mountains even though some, such as tree frogs (Rhacophoridae), porcupines (Hystricidae) and bamboo rats (Rhizomyinae), can be found further north. Conversely, some northern creatures, such as sandgrouse (Pteroclididae) and bustards (Otididae), are not found immediately south of the Qin Ling range.

The Himalayas are the biggest boundary between distribution zones. Like the Qin Ling they separate the Palearctic region of the north from the Oriental region of the south, but because the mountain range is longer it is effective as a barrier over a much broader front.

Vertical zonation in the mountains

The nature of the vegetation growing on mountains changes according to altitude, forming a series of vegetation zones that run, ribbon-like, around each mountain. These vertical zones are also affected by latitude and the climatic conditions over the whole area. As a result two types of vertical zonation can be recognized: humid and arid.

The humid type of vertical zonation is found among the mountains of the humid monsoon zone of east China. From the Da Hinggan Mountains to Wuzhi Mountain on Hainan Dao Island and Yü Mountain in Taiwan, the vegetation is dominated by forest, with scrub and meadows on peaks and high mountains.

China boasts some superb scenery, none more so than that in the valley of the Yangtze (Chang) River where it runs through the Hengduan Mountains. The main peak is Yalong, with an altitude of 5596 metres (18,187 ft); this is the southernmost permanent ice and snow in China, at 27° 10′ N. The vertical zonation in vegetation and associated wildlife species is very evident here.

The height above sea level of every vertical zone gets higher from north to south. For example, the upper distributional limit of coniferous forest is 1000 metres (3280 ft) in the cold-temperate zone, 1100 to 1800 metres (3610 to 5900 ft) in the temperate zone, 2000 to 2600 metres (6560 to 8530 ft) in the northern part of the warm-temperate zone, 2600 to 3500 metres (8530 to 11,480 ft) in the southern part of the warm-temperate zone and 3000 to 4200 metres (9840 to 13,780 ft) in the subtropical zone.

The sequence of vertical zonation becomes more complicated from north to south too. There are only two or three vertical zones in the northern part of the Da Hinggan range, but four to five in the temperate and subtropical zones and six to seven in the tropical zone. The structures of the plant communities and the number of different plant species in each zone also become more complicated southwards, especially in the evergreen broad-leaved forests of the subtropical and tropical mountains.

The arid type of vertical zonation is found in the dry areas of the north-west and in the interior of the Qinghai-Tibet Plateau. The vegetation here is dominated by mountain grassland and desert plants, and the few forests are comparatively sparse. Cold-resistant ground-hugging plants and kobresia meadows occur on the high peaks.

The actual height of each vertical zone depends on the humidity, rising as the moisture content of the air decreases. On the north slope of the Altun Mountains, for example, where it is very dry, the desert zone reaches to 3800 metres (12,470 ft) above sea level. Directly above this zone are the cold prairies and ground-hugging plants of the high peaks.

A wonderfully exotic-looking Pleione (*Pleione*) flower in the Chang Mountains near Dali, in Yunnan.

The Changbai Mountains

The Changbai Mountains are a series of parallel mountain ranges running north-east to south-west in the north-east of China. The westernmost series, the Dahei range, consists of low mountains and hills about 400 metres (1310 ft) high. Further east lie the Zhangguangcai Mountains, 800 to 1000 metres (2620 to 3280 ft) high, while the easternmost series is composed of Laoye Mountain, Taiping Mountain and Mount Baitou, which are some 600 to 1000 metres (1970 to 3280 ft) above sea level.

Mount Baitou is a volcano, with a large volcanic cone which is a classic example of a volcanic landform. It has erupted three times in the last 500 years: in August 1597, April 1668 and April 1702. The cone is composed of rock in which tiny pieces of quartz-trachyte are embedded. It has a crater lake called Tianchi (Heaven) Lake; this is 373 metres (1224 ft) deep, which makes it the deepest lake in China (see Chapter 4, Rivers, Lakes and Sea Coasts).

Ten or so high peaks are scattered around the lake, which is on the border between China and Korea. The highest peak inside Chinese territory in this area and in all north-east China is Baiyun Peak, with a summit 2691 metres (8830 ft) above sea level. The landscape here is quite beautiful, with a waterfall 68 metres (223 ft) high at the northern end of Tianchi Lake and many small volcanic cones and warm-water springs.

The Changbai range receives large amounts of rain, and it is the source of three rivers. The mountains support several dense forests, each rich in plant and animal species: there are more than 50 species of mammals and over 300 species of birds. In fact, the ecosystem of this range is worth studying in detail as an example of a mountain area in the temperate zone.

The natural richness of the region was recognized when the Changbai Mountain Nature Reserve was founded in 1961, making it one of the first nature reserves in China. It has an area of 190,000 hectares (469,500 acres) and a complex, diverse vegetation. It includes many ancient plants that were thriving in the Tertiary period, over 10 million years ago, as well as plants of

European and Siberian origin and elements of the adjacent Korean and Japanese flora. Polar plants which colonized the area during the Quaternary ice ages have survived on the cold mountain plateaux, while subtropical plants more typical of southern China occur in the valleys. It is this combination of components from these very different origins that makes the Changbai flora special. From the river valleys to the high peaks, there are examples of all the major types of plants from the temperate zone (with some subtropical elements) to the tundra zone. It is an ideal place to study the formation, climate, soil, vegetation and wildlife of mountains in the temperate zone.

The vertical zonation of vegetation in the Changbai range is very marked. In order, from low to high, there are mixed forests of conifer and broad-leaved trees, coniferous forest, birch forest and finally mountain tundra.

The mixed forests of conifers and broad-leaved trees are distributed from 600 metres (1970 ft), in the river valley areas, to 1100 metres (3610 ft). Throughout this band the climate is mild and humid. The conifers are mainly Korean Pines (*Pinus koraiensis*) which have straight trunks about 30 to 40 metres (98 to 130 ft) tall. These are interspersed with other coniferous and broad-leaved trees such as Mongolian Oaks (*Quercus mongolica*), Manchurian Ash (*Fraxinus mandshurica*) and a variety of spruces. There are no cold-temperate zone conifers. A variety of Japanese Yew (*Taxus cuspidata* var. *latifolia*) grows in some profusion beneath the leaf canopy; its trunk is short, finely textured and fragrant.

Alongside the yews grow Changbai Red Pines (*Pinus densiflora* var. *sylvestriformis*), which reach some 20 to 30 metres (66 to 98 ft) and are colloquially called 'Beauty Pines' for their beautiful straight trunks and perfect, canopy-shaped branches. Mixed with the temperate Korean Pines and the broad-leaved trees are subtropical plants, including lianas which grow beneath the tree cover, various yangtao trees, Manchurian Dutchman's Pipe (*Aristolochia mandshuriensis*) and others. One group of yangtao vine species –

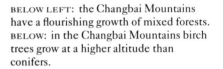

BELOW LEFT: the Changbai Mountains have a flourishing growth of mixed forests. BELOW: in the Changbai Mountains birch trees grow at a higher altitude than conifers.

Actinidia chinensis and *A. arguta* – has achieved fame under another guise. It has been widely planted in New Zealand, where its light brown, egg-shaped fruits are picked and exported as kiwi fruit. The vine's other name more accurately reflects its origin: Chinese Gooseberry.

There are numerous interesting species of herbs; many of these are of medicinal value, such as Ginseng (*Panax ginseng*), Manchurian Wild Ginger (*Asarum heterotropoides*) and Tall Gastrodia (*Gastrodia elata*), the dried roots of which are popularly used to cure headaches in China.

At 1100 to 1800 metres (3600 to 5900 ft) above sea level lies a zone of cold-temperate conifers. The temperature is lower, and in general the climate is cold in winter and cool in summer. Most of the tree species that prefer warm areas give way to forests of cold-resistant spruces (*Picea*) and firs (*Abies*).

Two subzones can be recognized in this zone. From 1100 to 1500 metres (3600 to 4920 ft) up lies the coniferous forest subzone, consisting mainly of Korean Pines (*Pinus koraiensis*), Yeddo (Yezo) Spruces (*Picea yezoensis*), Siberian Spruces (*P. obovata*), Khingan Firs (*Abies nephrolepis*) and larches (*Larix*). From 1500 to 1800 metres (4920 to 5900 ft) above sea level the climate becomes colder and more humid, and Yeddo Spruces and Khingan Firs become dominant. In this subzone conditions are dark and damp under the dense tree canopy, and only a few species of herbs and small shrubs can survive. A 10 cm (4 in.) layer of moss covers 40 to 80 per cent of the ground, and makes a thick, green carpet underfoot.

From 1800 to 2100 metres (5900 to 6890 ft) above sea level the terrain is steep and strong winds chill the air. Erman's (Russian Rock) Birch (*Betula ermanii*) is the dominant tree species in this zone. This can thrive on poor soils, and tends to branch at ground level to resist the effects of continuous wind and snow cover. The trees grow sparsely and their branches are windcut to form a very characteristic open canopy, below which grow a variety of herbaceous mountain plants including Grass of Parnassus (*Parnassia palustris*) and Japanese Globe Flower (*Trollius japonicus*).

Above 2100 metres (6900 ft) the ground is covered with snow for six months each year and it is very windy. The conditions are too cold for trees, and the slopes are clothed in mountain tundra vegetation with low-growing shrubs and herbs. Most of the plants are mountain species, of which the most striking are the abundant azalea species such as *Rhododendron redowskianum* and *R. conferrissimum*. Pink-flowering Bog Bilberry or Whortleberry (*Vaccinium uliginosum*), Cowberry (*V. vitis-idaea*) and Changbai Willow (*Salix tschanbaischanica*), a form of willow that grows as a shrub, can also be found at these altitudes.

The short mountain summer means that these plants tend to flower at much the same time to take advantage of the mild conditions. The peak period is July, when the whole mountain-top is a riot of glorious colour.

The Qin Ling Mountains

The Qin Ling range runs from west to east in central China, and is 2000 to 3000 metres (6560 to 9840 ft) high. Its highest peak, Taibai Mountain, is 3767 metres (12,360 ft) above sea level and rises majestically above the plain 3000 metres (9840 ft) below. These mountains are a very important climatic boundary: the northern slopes are in the warm-temperate zone, but the southern slopes are in the subtropical zone. The range borders the Qinghai-Tibet Plateau in the west and rises above the North China Plain in the east, so it has a mixture of plants and animals from several areas and climatic zones. As a result the range as a whole can boast a wide variety of species.

The dominant vegetation consists of mixed evergreen and deciduous forest, with deciduous trees in the majority. Sawtooth Oaks (*Quercus acutissima*) and Chinese Cork Oaks (*Q. variabilis*) are the principal species in these mixed forests. Other species include Bitter Evergreen Chinquapins (*Castanopsis sclerophylla*), Blue Japanese Oaks (*Cyclobalanopsis glauca*) and Masson Pines (*Pinus massoniana*).

Between 1200 and 2600 metres (3940 to 8530 ft) mixed forest of conifers and deciduous broad-leaved trees is distributed. In this belt, Armand Pine (*Pinus armandi*), East Liaoni Oak (*Quercus liaotungensis*) and Chinese Cork Oak (*Quercus variabilis*) are the most numerous trees between 1200 and 1800 metres (3940 to 5000 ft); between 1800 and 2600 metres (5000 to 8350 ft) Armand Pine, Chinapaper Birch (*Betula albo-sinensis*), Shingleaf Birch (*B. luminfera*) and Turczaninow Hornbeam (*Carpinus turczaninowii*) are the main species. From 2600 to 3000 metres (8530 to 9840 ft) the mountainside is clothed in fir forest composed of Farges's Fir (*Abies fargesii*) and Shensi Fir (*A. chensiensis*). Above 3000 metres (9840 ft) these give way to forests of Chinese Larch (*Larix chinensis*), and above 3400 metres (11,150 ft) the high-mountain shrubs take over, including colourful species such as the Autumn Purple Rhododendron (*Rhododendron fastigiatum*).

Owing to the particular nature of the conditions in the mountain range, there are several plant species found here and nowhere else; the Shensi Fir (*Abies chensiensis*) is one of these, as is Girald Lilac (*Syringa giraldiana*). In and adjacent to Taibai Mountain there are 29 single-species (monotypic) genera, one endemic genus and over 150 endemic species.

There are over 230 species of birds and 40 species of mammals, reptiles and amphibians in the mountains, including the Giant Panda (*Ailuropoda melanoleuca*) and the Japanese Ibis (*Nipponia nippon*). The presence of these rare species has encouraged the establishment of preservation areas on Taibai Mountain and in Foping (Shaanxi Province).

DISTRIBUTION OF VEGETATION IN THE QIN LING MOUNTAINS	
Height above sea level	*Predominant vegetation*
Below 1200 m (3940 ft)	Oaks
1200–1800 m (3940–5900 ft)	Oaks and pines
1800–2600 m (5900–8530 ft)	Pines and birches
2600–3000 m (8530–9840 ft)	Firs
3000–3400 m (9840–11,150 ft)	Larches
Above 3400 m (11,150 ft)	Mountain shrubs

The Taiwan mountain ranges

The Taiwan Mountains lie near the junction of the Eurasian and Philippine plates, and the area experiences frequent earthquakes. There are volcanoes around T'aipei, but they are dormant. The main mountain ranges are the Zhongyang, Yü and Ali Mountains. Of these, Yü Mountain is the highest at 3997 metres (13,114 ft) – the highest peak in eastern China.

Taiwan Island is surrounded by warm seas, and the Tropic of Cancer runs near the summit of Yü Mountain. Most of the mountains are in the sub-tropical zone, but the southern part of the range is in the tropical zone. Rainfall is plentiful: the mean annual rainfall of Huoshaoliao is 6378 mm (251 in.) and in 1912 the rainfall reached a maximum of 8507 mm (335 in.). Both figures are the highest in the country.

The dominant vegetation up to 1800 metres (5900 ft) consists of broad-leaved subtropical monsoon forest, mainly made up of Carles's Evergreen Chinquapin (*Castanopsis carlesii*) and *C. borneensis*, Chinese Cryptocarya (*Cryptocarya chinensis*), Banyan (*Ficus microcarpa*), the Camphor (*Cinnamomum camphora*), Taiwan Engelhardtia (*Engelhardtia formosana*) and Taiwan Helicia (*Helicia formosana*). The forest has some of the characteristics of rainforest, with luxuriant lianas such as Climbing Entada (*Entada phaseoloides*). Large herbaceous plants include the wild banana *Musa formosana* and the Taiwan Tree Fern (*Cyathea tauwabuaba*), which grows up to 30 metres (98 ft).

Higher up the mountains, from 1800 to 3000 metres (5900 to 9840 ft), the typical plants are Formosan False Cypresses (*Chamaecyparis formosensis*) and Taiwan False Cypresses (*C. obtusa* var. *formosana*). Above 3000 metres (9840 ft) these give way to forests of Taiwan Fir (*Abies kawakamii*) which are in turn replaced by montane azalea scrub and grassland at over 3600 metres (11,810 ft) above sea level.

ABOVE: Japanese White-eyes (*Zosterops japonica*) have close relatives throughout southern Asia and Africa. They breed in the mountain forests of southern China. RIGHT: the camphor tree *Cinnamon camphora* is one of many commercially valuable trees in these rich forests, which are home to an abundance of wildlife.

The vegetation of the southern part of the Yü mountain range consists of tropical, seasonal rainforest and tropical rainforest. The former is made up of trees that shed some, but not all, of their leaves in the dry season – such as Banyan (*Ficus microcarpa*), Chinese Cryptocarya (*Cryptocarya chinensis*) and Ivy Tree (*Schefflera octophylla*), as well as deciduous trees, namely Common Bombax (*Bombax malabaricum*) and Tall Albizzia (*Albizia procera*). The tropical rainforest consists mainly of Cagayan Nutmeg (*Myristica cagayanensis*), Taiwan Wingseedtree (*Pterospermum niveum*) and Longleaf Artocarpus (*Artocarpus lanceolatus*).

The Yü mountain range is well known in China for its dense forests, especially for its abundant tall Camphor trees. Camphor has great commercial value for furniture and for camphor oil, used on aching joints. Mothballs are made from its resin. Although this is the most commercially useful tree in the forests there are, in fact, over 200 commercially exploited species. The conifer forests include Formosan False Cypresses, Taiwan False Cypresses, Taiwan White Pines (*Pinus morrisonicola*) and Formosan Hemlocks (*Tsuga formosana*). The broad-leaved forests include Formosan Michelias (*Michelia formosana*).

There are 428 species of birds on Taiwan of which 70 are endemic, and 61 pecies of mammals, 42 of which are endemic, including Reeve's Muntjac (*Muntiacus reevesi*) – introduced into Britain at the turn of the century – and he Taiwan Macaque (*Macaca cyclopis*). There are also 135 species of reshwater fish, 90 species of reptiles, 30 species of amphibians and a pectacular array of butterflies with more than 400 species.

The Altai Mountains

The Altai range is one of the great mountain systems of central Asia, located at the intersection of China, Mongolia and the Soviet Union. The section that lies within Chinese territory is the southern side of the middle part of the range, over 3000 metres (9840 ft) above sea level. The terrain gets lower as you travel from north-west to south-east. The air temperature is low with mean annual value of 3 to 4°C (37 to 39°F), but although the mountains are far from any sea the climate is fairly humid, being wetter the higher up the mountains you are. Annual precipitation is about 250 mm (10 in.) at 1000 metres (3280 ft), 250 to 350 mm (10 to 14 in.) between 1000 and 1500 metres (3280 and 4920 ft), and 350 to 500 mm (14 to 20 in.) from 1500 to 3000 metres (4920 to 9840 ft). This creates a vertical zonation of plants: from the bottom there is mountain steppe, mountain forests, sub-alpine and alpine meadows and, finally, tundra desert.

The mountain steppe vegetation consists mainly of needle grasses and some shrubs of the wild rose *Rosa spinosissima*. The mountain forests are typical of the cold-temperate zone, with the dominant species being Siberian Pines (*Pinus sibirica*) and Siberian Larches (*Larix sibirica*), 20 to 25 metres (65 to 82 ft) high. These tree species are in the southern region of the northern coniferous forests, which in places protrude southwards along the mountains into the adjacent steppe. In general, however, they grow on gentle slopes between 1900 and 2300 metres (6230 and 7550 ft) above sea level.

Because the cones of Siberian Pines are very large they do not roll far when they fall from the trees. The seeds fall out and are eaten by birds and rats, and as a result the trees do not become widely distributed and natural regeneration is a hit-and-miss affair.

Siberian Firs grow in places on the middle and lower shady slopes of the river valleys, and clumps of honeysuckle (*Lonicera altaica* and *L. hispida*) and Blackfruited Cotoneaster (*Cotoneaster melanocarpa*) are often found in the coniferous forests.

The Kanas Lake in the north-west of the Altai Mountains was formed by a glacier during the Quaternary ice ages. Surrounding the lake is a remnant of boreal coniferous forest, the sole example of taiga landscape in China, and the sole representative of this particular type of Euro-Siberian flora. A nature reserve has been set up at Kanas to preserve the forest and the animals that live in it.

The Tien mountain range

Running from west to east for a distance of some 2500 kilometres (1553 miles), the Tien is one of the largest and most imposing mountain ranges in Asia. Its eastern part lies within Chinese territory, while the western end is in the USSR. The average altitude is 4000 metres (13,120 ft) above sea level. To the south is the Tarim Basin which is 1000 metres (3280 ft) above sea level, while to the north is the Junggar Basin, with an elevation of 500 metres (1640 ft). This means that the difference in height between the mountains and the basins is often well over 3000 metres (9840 ft). The highest mountain is Tuomuer Peak, 7435 metres (24,394 ft) high.

BELOW: extensive coniferous forests survive near Kanasi Lake in the Altai Mountains, part of one of the largest mountain systems of central Asia. BOTTOM: the 7435 metre-high (24,394 ft) Tuomuer Peak, the highest of the Tien Mountains, provides a striking contrast with its icy and formidable crags.

Precipitation on the windward side of the mountains is plentiful, with heavy snowfall. As a result there are well-developed glaciers on the mountain tops. There are 6896 glaciers on the peaks of the Tien Mountains, covering an area of 9550 square kilometres (3687 square miles). These glaciers are the sources of numerous rivers which carry away the meltwater to irrigate the oases on the plains at the foot of the mountains. The snowline lies between 3800 and 4200 metres (12,470 and 13,780 ft) above sea level.

There are about 2500 species of plants on the northern slopes of the range, which makes it the most abundant in plant species of all the desert mountain ranges. From the foothills to the peaks, the northern slopes show distinct vertical zonation. Between 800 and 1100 metres (2620 and 3610 ft) lies mountain desert, or more precisely wormwood desert, which is dominated by various wormwood species including *Artemesia borotulense* and *S. kaschgaricum*. Other plants include Prostrate Summer Cypresses (*Kochia prostrata*) and the grass *Poa bulbosa*. Short-lived plants decline in numbers gradually from west to east, and give way completely to desert in the east with only sparse shrubs such as Songory Reaumuria (*Reaumuria songorica*) and Shortleaf Anabasis (*Anabasis breuifolia*).

From 1100 to 1300 metres (3610 to 4260 ft) is a narrow, mountainous desert-steppe subzone, mainly composed of the needle grass *Stipa capillaca*, the wormwood *Artemesia borotulense*, and the graphically named Manyroot Onion (*Allium polyrhizum*). Typical steppe is found between 1300 and 1500 metres (4260 and 4920 ft) above sea level, with needle grasses and the fescue grass *Festuca sulcala*.

The slopes from 1500 to 2700 metres (4920 to 8860 ft) above sea level are covered by coniferous forest, which is dominated by Schrenk's Spruce (*Picea schrenkiana*). Schrenk's Spruce is a tall tree, which is usually about 20 to 30 metres (65 to 100 ft) in height but can grow to 70 metres (230 ft) under favourable conditions. The crown is narrow, so the tree is like a long cylinder. Fossil remains indicate that these trees were thriving in the Tertiary period as far back as 10 million years ago.

The forests are interspersed with mountain meadows, steppe and scrub. In this zone the annual rainfall is between 500 and 800 mm (20 and 30 in.) and the mean July air temperature varies from 10 to 20°C (50 to 68°F). Under the Schrenk's Spruce trees the soil is the grey-cinnamon colour characteristic of mountain coniferous forests in arid areas. It is a soil rich in accumulated lime, and covered by a thick layer of humus.

There are a few other kinds of tree mingled with the Schrenk's Spruce. The common small trees are the Tien Mountain Ash (*Sorbus tianschanica*) and the willow *Salix xerophila*, with the aspen *Populus tremula* and several species of birch.

The common shrubs are Blackfruited Cotoneaster (*Cotoneaster melanocarpa*) and wild roses such as *Rosa alberti* and *R. suavis*. The sparse forests on the rocky subalpine slopes are composed largely of Turkey Juniper (*Juniperus turkestanica*), Siberian Juniper (*Juniperus sibirica*) and Shagspine Peashrub (*Caragana jubata*). There are many species of herbaceous plants in the forests: about 300 species can be identified, among which Wood Poa (*Poa nemoralis*), American Milletgrass or Wood Millet (*Milium effusum*) and the meadowrue *Thalictrum collinum* are the most common.

The shady slopes of the Tien Mountains in the Yili area are home to Sievers's Apples (*Malus sieversii*), usually found along the river valleys. These valleys are screened from the cold, dry winds, and precipitation is fairly high owing to the effect of the humid oceanic air currents blowing in from the west. These conditions have favoured the survival of Sievers's Apples, which

The Tien Mountains in Xinjiang Province with their high, snow-clad peaks, forested upper slopes and green, grassy pastures on lower slopes.

remain from the broad-leaved forests that flourished in the temperate zone during the Tertiary period. They are deciduous trees that grow some 5 to 1, metres (16 to 43 ft) high. Growing alongside them are Ansu Apricots (*Prunu armeniaca*) and Tien Mountain Maples (*Acer semenovii*).

A few specimens of Chinese Walnut (*Juglans cathayensis*) – also remnants o the Tertiary flora – grow in Gongliu County, the sole native site for thi species in China. Another Tertiary survivor is a kind of ash, *Fraxinu sogdiana*, which, like the Sievers's Apples, can be found in the valleys of th Yili area.

From 2700 to 3500 metres (8860 to 11,480 ft) above sea level are th subalpine steppe zones. In the lower part of this zone the dominant plants ar the subalpine juniper *Juniperus sabina* ssp. *procumbens*, plus other juniper such as *J. pseudosabina*, *J. turkestanica*, *J. semiglobosa* and the Siberian Juniper These form a narrow strip just above the limit of the coniferous forests Shagspine Peashrub is found at the same altitude.

The upper part of the zone presents a landscape of flourishing grasses including the lady's mantles *Alchemilla sibirica* and *A. krylovii*. The pastures o this sub-zone are much used for summer grazing.

The zone between 3500 and 3600 metres (11,480 and 11,800 ft) is the high mountain zone, characterized by numerous low-growing plants with beautifu flowers such as Viviparous Bistort or Serpentgrass, also known as Solomon' Seal (*Polygonum viviparum*), Alpine Bistort (*P. alpinum*), the cinquefoil *Poten tilla gelida*, Snow Lotus (*Saussurea involucrata*), the gentian *Gentiana algide* and Fairy Primrose (*Primula fedtschenkoi*).

Above 3600 metres (11,800 ft) the weather is bitterly cold, and the frost shattered rocks lie across the mountains in scree slopes. Very few plant manage to survive these conditions; those that do include Snow Lotu (*Saussurea involucrata*), *Kobresia bellardii* and *K. capillifolia*, which grow t some 5 to 10 cm (2 to 4 in.) high, and ground-hugging plants.

The Himalayas

Two thousand four hundred kilometres (1490 miles) long, 200 to 300 kilometres (124 to 186 miles) wide and 6000 metres (19,680 ft) high or average, the Himalayas are the highest mountain range on earth. Stretching along the southern margin of the Qinghai-Tibet Plateau, they consist of series of parallel ranges crowned with a forest of snow peaks; the foothills (the 'Piedmont Zone') are to the south, followed (moving northwards) by the Small Himalayan mountain range and the Great Himalayan range. The latter 50 to 90 kilometres (31 to 56 miles) wide, is the main range of the mountain chain and most of it is distributed along the boundaries between China and Nepal, Sikkim, India and Bhutan.

The Himalayas are quite different on the south and north sides. The south side is precipitous, with the altitude zones following each other in rapid succession: an imposing inclined plane is formed by a sharp drop of 6000 metres (19,680 ft) from the high mountains to the flat plain below. Owing to the plentiful rainfall there is considerable water erosion, and this ha produced many deep gorges. On the north side, by contrast, is a much gentle landscape. The altitude difference between the mountains and the plateau lakes in the foothills is only 1500 metres (4920 ft); rainfall is less abundan too, and as a result the effects of river erosion are less marked.

Glaciers are very common in the Himalayas, and those within Chinese territory cover an area of 11,055 square kilometres (4268 square miles). The mountain glaciers occur in various characteristic forms, such as hanging glaciers, cirque glaciers (that sit in deep troughs they have gouged out of the mountainsides), and valley glaciers.

The glaciers on the northern side are of the valley type and join together like the branches of a tree, the longest glacier being 22 kilometres (14 miles). On the glacier surfaces stand extraordinary ice forests, which look rather like large expanses of cake-icing shaped into pyramids. They are several kilometres long and 40 to 50 metres (130 to 165 ft) high. These ice forests are the result of differential ice melting: this is caused by the combination of intense solar radiation and rapid evaporation which occurs in the dry climate found in the high mountains of low latitudes. This kind of tower-shaped ice forest has only been found here and on the Karakoram range further to the west.

In the Himalayas, vertical zonation changes are evident in almost every panorama. Snow and ice cover the mountain tops and glaciers are common, but luxuriant forests and carpets of green grassland mantle the landscape beneath the snowy peaks.

On the southern flanks of the Himalayas, rivers cut deeply into the mountains to form steep-sided valleys. The low mountains below 1000 metres (3280 ft) are clothed in seasonal rainforests of Timber Tree (*Shorea robusta*). From 1000 to 2500 metres (3280 to 8200 ft) mountain evergreen broad-leaved forests grow, dominated by trees of the beech family (Fagaceae) such as evergreen chinquapins (*Castanopsis*). The trees are 20 to 30 metres (65 to 100 ft) high and are entwined by creepers which flourish in the high rainfall of up to 2000 mm (79 in.) a year.

From 2500 to 3100 metres (8200 to 10,170 ft) are mixed forests of conifers and broad-leaved trees. These include Alpine Oak (*Quercus semicarpifolia*),

A vast, rolling system of glacier ice covers the Tanggula range in the Qinghai-Tibet Plateau, where the mountains seem to go on forever into a limitless horizon.

TOP: a waterfall cascades over limestone deposits in Jiuzhaigou, Sichuan Province. ABOVE: flora in the high mountain belt near Mount Everest is restricted to low growth such as the Cushion Rock Jasmine (*Androsace tapete*) here.

Himalayan Hemlock (*Tsuga dumosa*) and the endemic Himalayan Pine (*Pinus griffithii*). Beneath the trees, which can grow up to 25 metres (82 ft) high, are fountain bamboos (*Sinarundinaria*) and shrubs of Papery Daphne (*Daphne papyracea*).

From 3100 to 3900 metres (10,170 to 12,790 ft) the mountains are shrouded in dark coniferous forest composed mainly of Himalayan Fir (*Abies spectabilis*). It is dark and damp in the forests; Himalayan Birches (*Betula utilis*) often appear at the forest margins, but very little grows on the gloomy forest floor except mosses and lichens.

Above the forest zone, from 3900 to 4700 metres (12,790 to 15,420 ft), the mean temperature of the warmest months rarely rises above 10°C (50°F). This is too low for trees to flourish, so the vegetation consists mainly of shrubs such as rhododendrons (*Rhododendron*), willows (*Salix*) and Himalayan Cassiope (*Cassiope fastigiata*). From April to June the rhododendrons are covered with flowers of various colours – red, purple, white and yellow – transforming the mountains into a vast garden.

On the northern flank of the Himalayas the climate is drier and mountain steppe takes the place of the forests. Between 4000 and 5000 metres (13,120 and 16,400 ft) lies the herbaceous vegetation zone, consisting mainly of Purpleflower Needle Grass or Feather Grass (*Stipa purpurea*), the wormwood *Artemisia wellbyi* and Thorold's Orinus (*Orinus thoroldii*). On the upper slopes of both the southern and northern flanks the zones are roughly similar. In order from low to high, there are high-mountain meadows, ground-hugging vegetation, the high-mountain zone of frost-shattered rock and, at the top, the zone of permanent ice and snow.

The ecological conditions in the zones of mountain meadow and ground-hugging vegetation are harsh, with sub-zero air temperatures even in the

FROZEN SCULPTURES OF TIBET

The vivid blue and white scenery of the Himalayan glaciers produces some unusual sights. The climate is controlled by the opposing forces of low latitude and high altitude. This means that the air is generally cold, but the sun shines overhead with great intensity. This in turn can result in sudden partial thaws that are followed by equally sudden returns to freezing temperatures at sunset. As the exposed surfaces thaw far faster than the shady ones, the water refreezes into strange ice sculptures.

LEFT: a glacier at 5000 metres (16,000 ft) in Tibet provides a dazzling backdrop in the clear atmosphere.
ABOVE: a glacier on Mount Qomolangma (Everest) has repeatedly thawed rapidly and refrozen; a rock protecting the ice beneath it has formed this 'mushroom'.

warm season. The Alpine Kobresia (*Kobresia pygmaea*) is the dominant plant in the meadow zone, while the Shrubby Cinquefoil (*Dasyphora fruticosa*) and sandworts (*Arenaria*) are the major plants in the ground-hugging zone.

The zone of frost-shattered rock lies at altitudes of 5200 to 5500 metres (17,060 to 18,040 ft) on the southern side and 5600 to 6000 metres (18,370 to 19,680 ft) on the northern side. The average height of the snowline is 5500 metres (18,040 ft) on the southern flank and up to 6000 metres (19,680 ft) on the northern. The mean air temperature of the warmest months near the snowline is 2°C (35°F), and the annual precipitation is 600 to 700 mm (24 to 28 in.).

In these areas the bare rock is exposed to the freezing winds, and only scattered plants such as the buttercup *Ranunculus involucratus*, Alpine Gentian (*Gentiana algida*), Dwarf Willow (*Salix resetoides*) and Himalayan Rhodiola (*Rhodiola himalayensis*) grow in the cracks between the rock fragments. Gentians have been found as high as 6100 metres (20,000 ft).

These plants have special ecological and biological characteristics which suit them for their harsh environment. The plants are low, with ground-hugging foliage, and cluster tightly together. They are covered with thick, soft hairs, and their root systems are extensive. They reproduce vegetatively (non-sexually), by shoots from the stem on which new plants bud and grow, and by dropping seeds which have already sprouted.

Of these low plants, the willows are only 3 to 5 cm (1¼ to 2 in.) high. Creeping False Tamarisks (*Myricaria prostrata*) are even shorter at 1 to 3 cm (⅜ to 1¼ in.) high. Snow Lotus (*Saussurea involucrata*), which is covered with white hairs and white flowers, has roots up to a metre (3 ft) long, but these roots are five to ten times as long as the foliage above ground. These features make Snow Lotus both cold- and wind-resistant, and able to blossom and

RIGHT: the Red Goral (*Nemorhaedus cranbrooki*) here is a goat-like antelope of rocky forests.

bear fruit even when the ground is covered in snow.

The huge Himalayan range acts as a vast barrier to animals, and as a result the faunas of the south and north sides are quite different. Some very large groups of creatures are represented on only one side of the range. For example, the tree frogs (Rhacophoridae), sunbirds (Nectariniidae) and minivets (Campephagidae), civets (Viverridae) and primates (Primates) are all creatures of the south, and have failed to cross the high mountain ranges to get into the Qinghai-Tibet Plateau. The Fire-tailed Sunbird (*Aethopyga ignicauda*) is one example: it occurs in the forest zone of the southern slopes, but nowhere on the northern side. The Hanuman Langur (*Semnopithecus entellus*) is a common primate in the broad-leaved forests of the southern slopes, but quite absent from the northern.

Similarly, the creatures of the north side such as accentors (Prunellidae) and pikas (Ochotonidae) are restricted in their distribution by the great wall of the Himalayan massif.

In China, several species of birds and animals are found only in the Himalayas. They include the toad *Bufo himalayanus*, the chisel-tooth lizard *Agama himalayana*, the snail-eating snake *Pareas monticola*, birds such as the Satyr Tragopan (*Tragopan satyra*) and Himalayan Monal Pheasant (*Lophophorus impejanus*), and mammals such as the Himalayan Tahr (*Hemitragus jemlahicus*) and the Hanuman Langur.

The Hengduan Mountains

This range is composed of a series of approximately south-to-north oriented mountains in western Sichuan, western Yunnan and eastern Tibet. The range is 1200 kilometres (746 miles) long and 500 to 800 kilometres (311 to 497 miles) wide and includes the mountains of Qionglai, Daxue, Nu and Gaoligong. The terrain is higher in the north, at about 4000 metres (13,120 ft) above sea level, and descends to about 2000 metres (6560 ft) in the south. The mountain rivers run along the fault zones, cutting deep valleys. The climate, vegetation and soil all display obvious vertical zonation. Being a seismically active region, the Hengduan range experiences frequent earthquakes, and landslides and debris flows are common occurrences.

The area around the mountains of Qionglai and Daxue in the northern part of the range is at the intersection of the three major Chinese natural regions, and as a result plants and animals from all three are found there. There are some surviving species from before the Quaternary glaciations. These include the Giant Panda (*Ailuropoda melanoleuca*), Golden Monkey (*Pygathrix roxellanae*) and Dragon (Chinese) Spruce (*Picea asperata*). Most of the 600 species of rhododendron found in China grow here. The larger ones are about 10 metres (33 ft) high and shorter species grow as shrubs or cling to the trunks of Dragon Spruces or firs. When they flower they create a multihued blaze of colour.

Several nature reserves have been set up. The Wolong Nature Reserve, on the east slope of Qionglai Mountain in north-western Sichuan, was set up in 1975. It covers an area of 200,000 hectares (494,200 acres). In 1980 it was made the main study centre for protection of the Giant Panda.

Wolong is in the transition zone between the Sichuan Basin and the Qinghai-Tibet Plateau. There are high mountain peaks and deep valleys. The lowest point is 1218 metres (4000 ft) above sea level and the highest peak

Seismic activity in the Hengduan Mountains has done little to diminish the natural beauty of this deeply dissected region.

rises to 6250 metres (20,500 ft). There are a further 100 peaks that are more than 5000 metres (16,400 ft) high. Because the moist air currents from the Pacific Ocean are impeded by these high mountains, they receive a lot of rain: the annual precipitation varies from 1500 to 1800 mm (59 to 71 in.). The climate is humid and temperate.

The vertical zonation from the foothills to the top consists of evergreen broad-leaved forests, mixed forests of evergreen and deciduous broad-leaved trees, mixed forests of broad-leaved and coniferous trees, subalpine conifer forests, alpine meadows and finally a zone of ground-hugging plants. There are 4000 species of plants in all, with 55 species of mammals and over 250 species of birds.

Below 1500 metres (4920 ft) lies the subtropical evergreen broad-leaved forest, dominated by trees of the laurel (Lauraceae) and beech (Fagaceae) families. The cinnamon *Cinnamomum longepaniculatum*, Chinese Phoebe (*Phoebe chinensis*) and the oak *Quercus gracilis* form a large part of these forests. Lianas are often found climbing up the taller trees.

Mixed forests of evergreen and deciduous broad-leaved trees occupy the band from 1500 to 2100 metres (4920 to 6890 ft) above sea level. Besides evergreen species they include maples, birches and lacquertrees, as well as the Dove Tree or Handkerchief Tree (*Davidia involucrata*). Beneath the tree cover there is a flourishing shrub layer composed of various species of bamboo including fountain bamboos (*Sinarundinaria*) and Umbrella Bamboo (*Thamnocalamus spathaceus*) and the honeysuckle *Lonicera webbiana*.

From 2100 to 2600 metres (6890 to 8530 ft) are mixed forests of coniferous and broad-leaved trees. From 2600 to 3600 metres (8530 to 11,810 ft) above sea level the mountains are clothed in coniferous forests consisting mainly of firs and tall Dragon Spruces. There are also many fountain bamboos and azaleas. Fountain bamboos are distributed throughout the zone from 1500 to 3600 metres (4920 to 11,810 ft) above sea level. If the trees of the upper layer are destroyed, the bamboo grows quickly from its underground stems to form a thick bamboo jungle. Fountain bamboo is a significant element in the diet of the Giant Panda, so the areas from 2100 to 3600 metres (6890 to 11,810 ft) where it grows thickest are the panda's main habitat.

The climate becomes colder above this altitude, and the forest trees gradually give way to various kinds of mountain azaleas and Creeping Cotoneaster (*Cotoneaster adpressus*). Cold-resistant herbs emerge in vast numbers to form mountain meadows. During the flowering season both large and small flowers are profuse. A variety of blooms can be seen together, making a magnificent sight which has earned these slopes the nickname 'Five-flower Meadows'.

Above 4000 metres (13,120 ft) it is very cold and windy, and only ground-hugging plants accustomed to the conditions can survive.

DISTRIBUTION OF VEGETATION IN THE HENGDUAN MOUNTAINS	
Height above sea level	*Predominant vegetation*
Below 1500 m (4920 ft)	Evergreen broad-leaved trees
1500–2100 m (4920–6890 ft)	Evergreen and deciduous broad-leaved trees
2100–2600 m (6890–8530 ft)	Coniferous and broad-leaved trees
2600–3600 m (8530–11,810 ft)	Coniferous trees, fountain bamboos and azaleas
Above 3600 m (11,810 ft)	Mountain azaleas and Creeping Cotoneaster
Above 4000 m (13,120 ft)	Ground-hugging plants

Wildlife of the mountains

Most of the mountains of China are well covered in forests of various kinds, and it is in these forests that most of the mountain animals live – see Forests. The following mountain species are those that live on exposed rocks, in the sparse forests and above the vegetation line on the high peaks.

Mammals

Of the large mammals living in the mountains the most typical are the various goat antelopes. The Goral (*Nemorhaedus goral*) is the most common, being widespread throughout almost all the mountains of China with four local subspecies. Gorals have grey wool, short legs and narrow hooves suitable for scaling cliffs. Both males and females have horns which are short, gently curved and backswept. They usually live in cliff areas on mountain peaks, either individually or in family groups, and feed on young foliage and grass. They mate in winter and, after a gestation period of about six months, give birth to one or two young in the spring.

Ibex (*Capra ibex*) are found in the high-mountain areas in the north-west of China. They have long, backswept horns, and the males have long beards beneath their lower jaws. They live, sometimes in herds of a hundred or so, on the exposed rocky slopes above the tree line, where they eat grasses and young shoots. Like the Goral, they mate in winter and give birth to one or two young the following May or June.

The Blue Sheep (*Pseudois nayaur*) is found in mountain valleys in Shaanxi, Sichuan, Inner Mongolia and on the Qinghai-Tibet Plateau. It has back-curved horns that sweep upward a little at the end. These animals live on the exposed rock and rough mountain grassland in groups of three to ten. In winter they stay at about 2400 metres (7870 ft) above sea level, but in summer they migrate to the high-level pastures above the forest limit, 3500 to 6000 metres (11,480 to 19,680 ft) up. They are very agile, and when alarmed they can easily climb steep cliffs to escape.

The wild sheep called Argalis (*Ovis ammon*) is a species that has greatly interested Chinese researchers. In the past it was widespread in the mountains of north and north-west China, but it has become rare in recent years. It is a sturdy animal with a body length of about 1.7 metres (67 in.) and with big, strong, spiral horns up to 90 cm (35 in.) long. Argalis are characteristic of mountainous, cold desert or semi-desert areas 1000 to 3000 metres (3280 to 9840 ft) above sea level. They are adept at climbing high mountains, but cannot scale the steep cliffs inhabited by Gorals. Thus each species occupies its own ecological niche and they do not compete for food.

Argalis usually move about in large flocks or in groups of three to ten. Outside the mating season the females take care of their young while the adult males live alone or associate in 'bachelor flocks'. They graze on tender young needle grasses or feather grasses, sedges, annual blue grasses, wild onions and shrubs. The mating season is from October to December and they give birth the following April or May.

BELOW: the Argalis (*Ovis ammon*), now a very rare animal of the north-western mountains, cannot match the agility of the Goral on sheer cliffs.
BOTTOM: small groups of Blue Sheep (*Pseudois nayaur*) live in the high mountains of Sichuan and the north-west.

THE SNOW LEOPARD

The Snow Leopard (*Panthera uncia*) has the densely coated appearance of an animal that inhabits very cold regions. It is a fierce predator of hares, sheep and antelopes, and is quite capable of killing creatures three times as large as itself. Living at altitudes above 3000 metres (9840 ft) in remote mountain ranges, it is rarely seen. It hunts in isolation, and the young leave their parents to fend for themselves at a year old. The Snow Leopard has enormous paws and a long, thick tail; the size of its paws helps it regain its balance after the prodigious leaps of which it is capable. To keep warm in near-freezing temperatures it has developed a two-layer coat, with a long, tough, outer fur covering a soft and warm fur underneath. Now a protected species, the Snow Leopard is the subject of research conducted by China's Ministry of Forestry and the World Wide Fund for Nature. It lives in the mountains of Tibet, Qinghai, Xinjiang, Gansu and Sichuan.

LEFT: the characteristically patterned grey-white face of the elusive Snow Leopard (*Panthera uncia*).

BELOW: two Snow Leopards in a tree at dusk, which is the time of day when they are usually most active.

The Snow Leopard (*Panthera uncia*) is one of the most celebrated of the mountain mammals. Now rare, it is found on high mountains at altitudes of 3000 to 6000 metres (9840 to 19,680 ft). Similar to an ordinary leopard in size, it has a body length of about 1.3 metres (51 in.) and weighs some 200 kg (440 lb). It has a greyish-white coat dotted with circular clusters of black spots. The coat is in two layers with soft, wool-like fur underneath a layer of harder, longer fur, so the leopard is well protected from the cold of the exposed rocky areas where it lives. It generally makes a lair in a rock cavity which it occupies for several years. These lairs are often lined with mats of moulted fur, and in Sichuan examples have been found up to 1.5 metres (5 ft) across and 3 cm (1¼ in.) thick.

Snow Leopards prey on Gorals, Blue Sheep, Argalis, Mountain Hares (*Lepus timidus*), marmots and other rodents, and they sometimes raid domestic poultry houses when food is scarce in winter. They hunt by night, and are especially active at dusk and dawn, moving briskly and alertly. They are agile creatures and adept at jumping.

Birds

The main habitats for mountain birds are in the bushy grasslands or the bare rocks. Many of the birds fly down to the steppe in search of food, but return to nest in the mountains.

The typical birds of the mountains are snowcocks, partridges, pigeons and birds of prey. There are two species of snowcocks, the Tibetan Snowcock (*Tetraogallus tibetanus*) and the Himalayan Snowcock (*T. himalayensis*). The former occurs in the Hengduan mountain range and the Himalayas; the latter in the high mountains of Gansu, Qinghai and Xinjiang. Snowcocks are related to partridges and are very similar in build, but larger. They live in high mountains from 3000 to 6000 metres (9840 to 19,680 ft), being widely distributed throughout the mountain scrub zone above the tree line, well up into the snow-covered regions. They often gather together in flocks of ten or so. In autumn they migrate downhill to spend the winter at an altitude of between 2000 and 3000 metres (6562 and 9840 ft). They feed mainly on the tubers and seeds of plants, together with some insects and small animals. They breed from May to June, nesting on the ground below precipices. There are between six and eight eggs in a clutch, and the incubation period is about 25 days.

The Snow Partridge (*Lerwa lerwa*) is another high-mountain bird found in Tibet, Sichuan and Yunnan. It is most common on mountains 3000 to 5200 metres (9840 to 17,060 ft) above sea level, from the high-mountain shrub zone to the snow line. Similar to snowcocks in both their habits and appearance, Snow Partridges differ in their tail plumes – they have 14 tail feathers whereas snowcocks have 20 to 22.

The Chukar Partridge (*Alectoris chukar*) is a widespread partridge in mountainous, low-mountain and rocky areas in the north of China. These birds fly to the neighbouring plains to feast on the berries, buds and seeds of lowland plants, but return to the mountains to breed. They lay between nine and 20 eggs in the grass. They are a popular target for hunters because of their widespread distribution. They have been introduced into the USA and domesticated, where they are bred for food.

The Blue Hill Pigeon (*Columba rupestris*) and Rock Dove (*C. livia*) are common in the Chinese mountains. They live and breed in the cliff areas, but often fly to the plains to seek food. They feed on plant seeds, especially cereals, and will descend in groups of 30 or 40 to ravage the crops. Blue Hill Pigeons are widespread in the areas north of the Yangtze (Chang) River. Their plumage resembles that of Rock Doves, but with white feathers on the rump and at the base of the tail, so the two species can easily be distinguished in the field.

The Rock Dove is the ancestor of the familiar domestic and feral pigeons. At present there is some controversy about its distribution: some naturalists maintain that it can be found in the mountains of north and north-east China, but the research of the past decade or so suggests that those found in the north and north-east are not naturally wild, but are domestic pigeons which have escaped or been released and have established breeding flocks.

Truly wild Rock Doves inhabit central Asia, and are confined to mountains in the desert and semi-desert areas of Xinjiang, Qinghai and Gansu. Like Blue Hill Pigeons, Rock Doves can devastate fields, and in the Tien Mountains in Xinjiang they can often be seen in flocks of thousands as they descend on crops in the morning in search of food, or return from the fields to the mountains at dusk. There are no Blue Hill Pigeons in this area, suggesting that the Rock Doves occupy their ecological niche.

The large birds of prey include vultures, falcons, eagles and owls. Most of these birds will tend to nest in cliff eyries, but leave the cliffs to hover over the nearby plains and forests where they seek their prey. The Eurasian Black Vulture (*Aegypius monachus*) and Lammergeier or Bearded Vulture (*Gypaetus*

TOP: the Chukar Partridge (*Alectoris chukar*), found on exposed mountains, has been introduced into the USA and domesticated.

ABOVE CENTRE: the Daurian Partridge (*Perdix dauricae*) is not as well-known as the Chukar.

ABOVE: the Rock Pigeon or Rock Dove (*Columba livia*) is the ancestor of the domestic pigeon found worldwide.

149

ABOVE: a widely distributed species in Asia, and more rarely in parts of Europe, the Cinereous or Eurasian Black Vulture (*Aegypius monachus*) nests in trees but is basically a bird of the mountains. It is the largest of the Old World vultures and one of the biggest flying birds in the world.

OPPOSITE: the Golden Eagle (*Aquila chrysaetos*) is one of the world's more common eagles, but hard to spot in the vast mountainous regions it inhabits.

barbatus) live in the Qinghai-Tibet Plateau and the Hengduan Mountains. Eurasian Black Vultures are big birds with a wingspan of 2 metres (78 in.) and weight of 7 kg (15 lb). On the tops of their heads and on their necks there are dense, light yellow and black down feathers. They feed on the carcasses of mammals such as goats, hares and marmots, and will sometimes kill small or young animals.

The Lammergeier is much the same size and weight, but with normal feathers on its head and neck and black beard feathers below the beak. These birds often accompany Black Vultures, although they are more specialized scavengers and rarely attack live prey. They start to breed in January or February, laying one or two eggs per clutch, and the nestlings hatch in April. This is a rare species in the rest of the world – according to recent statistics, there are only about 70 to 90 pairs remaining in Europe – but the wild Lammergeier population is still comparatively large in China.

Golden Eagles (*Aquila chrysaetos*) are the most widespread of the eagles of China, living in most of the mountain areas from 1000 metres (3280 ft) above sea level in the east to 4000 metres (13,120 ft) in the west. Alone or in pairs they soar high in the sky, searching for prey such as hares and marmots. They build their eyries on the cliffs; the nests consist of large branches and may be used for years, being repaired each season. They lay one or two eggs at a time and they incubate them for about 45 days. If they produce two eggs they are laid several days apart, but incubation begins as soon as the first one appears. There is then a substantial difference in size between the two nestlings, and the smaller one often starves to death because the larger one grabs most of

TOP LEFT: Golden Eagles lay two eggs and usually both hatch, but often only one chick will survive to fledge.
TOP RIGHT: only in years with an abundant food supply will both chicks be reared successfully.
ABOVE: the young bird about to leave the nest has the large white wing and tail patches typical of immature Golden Eagles.

the food. Researchers in Shanxi Province have discovered that the larger nestling, when hungry, will often eat its smaller sibling. As a result, only one baby bird is left in the brood, but it is always the larger and stronger of the two. This slow breeding pattern partly explains why there are so few Golden eagles.

Many falcons, such as Saker Falcons (*Falco cherrug*) and Kestrels (*F. tinnunculus*), nest mainly on cliff ledges. The wings of these birds are long, narrow and pointed, and they fly at high speed, preying mainly on small birds. They lay four to six eggs to every brood and the incubation period is about 28 days. They have been seen throughout China.

The Eagle Owl (*Bubo bubo*) is one of the few species of owl which nests on cliff faces. It is the biggest owl in China, with a body length of up to 70 cm (28 in.). It occurs in most of the mountains in China and preys on hares, rodents, lizards, small birds and insects. It builds its nest of branches and lays three or four eggs which are white and roughly spherical. The nestlings are covered with white feathers. Eagle Owls are night-active birds, with a distinctive 'wang-dong-du' call. They have large eyes for seeing at night, and acute hearing for locating prey, which they hunt down on silent wings of soft feathers.

Several members of the crow family (Corvidae) and sibling species thrive in rocky areas. One of the most typical of this habitat is the Red-billed Chough (*Pyrrhocorax pyrrhocorax*), which has black plumage, a curved red bill and red feet. It occurs in most of the mountains over a wide area north of the Yangtze River, from 1000 metres (3280 ft) above sea level in the east to 4000 metres (13,120 ft) in the west. Red-billed Choughs are often seen hovering over mountains in flocks of ten or so. Their sibling species, the Alpine Chough (*P. graculus*), is found at higher altitudes in the north-west of China. The bill of this bird is yellow rather than red.

Amphibians and reptiles

In terms of numbers of species, amphibians and reptiles are few in China's mountains. The amphibians are found near streams, rivers or ponds, while the reptiles are mainly those adapted to rocky conditions.

The Siberian Salamander (*Hynobius keyserlingii*) and Chinese Giant Salamander (*Andrias davidianus*) are the two principal species of amphibian; they are found in mountain brooks in the north and south of China respectively. The Siberian Salamander inhabits the mud at the bottom of hallow swamps in the Changbai range and preys on snails, worms and aquatic insects.

The Chinese Giant Salamander is the biggest salamander alive today, at up to 180 cm (6 ft) long. It lives in the clear waters of high mountain streams at over 1000 metres (3280 ft) above sea level in central and south-west China. It is dark brown with large spots, and the aquatic young have prominent external gills. These salamanders have a ferocious disposition, hiding in rocky caves from where they leap out suddenly on fish and frogs. Their teeth are quite small, but they eat with their mandibles, which are so strong that it is very difficult to pull out your hand it it gets trapped. This makes them difficult to catch, and scientists therefore go looking for them in the early morning when the cold makes them sluggish. Because their flesh is considered a delicacy their numbers are now much depleted.

The racerunner *Eremias brenchleyi* and the Chinese Skink (*Eumeces chinensis*) are the two most common Chinese mountain lizards. The former is covered with rows of square scales, while the latter has smooth, round scales. Both of them live on exposed rocks and among grasses, preying on small animals such as insects. When the temperature falls at night and rises too high at noon they retreat to caves or crevices beneath rock fragments.

The pit viper *Agkistroden halys* is the most widespread of the poisonous snakes, and its bite will kill a human being. However, the venom also has a medical use in treating leprosy. *Agkistroden halys* is spread over an area from southern China to the Changbai Mountains and the Da Hinggan Mountains in north-eastern China, and is commonly seen moving about on exposed rocky areas in search of food in the form of small animals such as rodents. Tens of thousands of them inhabit the 'Snake Island' (Shedao) in Laotieshan of Lüshun. This island is an important staging post for migrating birds in spring and autumn, so the snakes there subsist largely on birds, climbing the small shrubs ready to ambush their victims.

ABOVE: the pretty Siberian Salamander (*Hynobius keyserlingii*) is commonly found in shallow, muddy ponds in north-eastern China.
LEFT: the flesh of the Chinese Giant Salamander (*Andrias davidianus*) is considered a great delicacy; consequently it is now severely endangered.

GRASSLANDS

草原

China is a country with rich grassland resources. The grasslands are an extension of the Eurasian grassland which crosses southern USSR, and they cover an area of some three million square kilometres (1,200,000 square miles) in the western part of the north-eastern region, the Inner Mongolian Plateau, the northern part of the Loess Plateau and the central part of the Qinghai-Tibet Plateau. In Eurasia the belt of grassland extends east to west, but the belt extends south-westwards in the North-eastern Plain of China. This is related to the climatic pattern caused by monsoon: humidity decreases from the south-eastern coast to the north-west, so the main bands of vegetation accordingly change from forest to grassland and desert in broad belts running roughly north-east to south-west.

The main groups of plants of the grassland in the grass family (Gramineae) include the needle grasses or feather grasses (*Stipa*), which are characteristic of dry steppe throughout the world, fescues (*Festuca*) and *Cleistogenes*, together with Chinese Aneurolepidium (*Aneurolepidium*), which is rare outside China; other grassland plants are wormwoods (*Artemisia* and *Seriphidium*) in the daisy family (Compositae), onions (*Allium*) in the lily family (Liliaceae) and many species of sedges (family Cyperaceae).

Grassland types

The type of grass in any region is dependent on the amount of rainfall and the temperature conditions – generally the wetter the area, the taller the grass. Four major grass types are found in China.

Meadow steppe

A transition belt of meadow steppe is on the North-eastern Plain and in Inner Mongolia, between the forest and the steppe proper, where the annual rainfall is between 350 and 500 mm (14 and 20 in.). In such conditions grasses grow luxuriantly, reaching a height of 40 to 60 cm (16 to 24 in.) or more. The majority of the plants here belong to the grass family (Gramineae) and pea family (Leguminosae). On the North-eastern Plain and in eastern Inner Mongolia, Baikal Needle Grass or Feather Grass (*Stipa baicalensis*), Chinese Aneurolepidium (*Aneurolepidium sinensis*) and Siberian Filifolium (*Filifolium sibiricum*) are the main species.

Baikal Needle Grass has leaves 30 to 40 cm (12 to 16 in.) high, overtopped by tall flower stalks. In Inner Mongolia it begins to grow in early May, and flowers in July and early August. During the growing season, the whole area becomes a splendid landscape of dark purple flowerheads waving in the breeze across the steppe. Needle grass pasture is good for grazing animals and for haymaking, because of its height and density. This kind of steppe is currently underexploited, but has great potential for animal husbandry.

Chinese Aneurolepidium is dominant in the eastern Eurasian steppe region and covers an area of 200,000 square kilometres (77,000 square miles) on the plains of the Songhua River and the Nen River. Chinese Aneurolepidium is resistant to drought, cold and trampling, yet is sufficiently nutritious to be suitable for the grazing of oxen, horses and sheep. The fragrant hay made from this grass can be stored for a long time, and is of immense value to farmers.

Siberian Filifolium is found mainly in the hilly areas of eastern Inner Mongolia where forest steppe merges into typical steppe. It grows best on dark red-brown, lime rich soils. The plants are 30 to 40 cm (12 to 16 in.) in height, but reach over 70 cm (28 in.) in more fertile areas.

The appearance of the Siberian Filifolium grassland varies with the seasons. In late May, Slender-leaved Pulsatilla (*Pulsatilla turczaninovii*), related to the anemones, *Iris ventricosa* and Dewberry-leaved Cinquefoil (*Potentilla*

PREVIOUS PAGE: the extensive Hulun Buir Grassland of Inner Mongolia.

fragarioides) flower silver-white, blue-purple and vivid yellow respectively. By mid-June, most plants have produced new leaves and the grassland turns green and provides livestock with lush grazing. Then the grassland becomes a vast flowery meadow, with the yellow flowers of Grass-leaved Daylily (*Hemerocallis minor*), rose-coloured *Stellara chamaejasme*, the snow-white *Clematis hexapetala* and silver spikes of Junegrass (*Koeleria cristata*) adding colour and variety to the windswept plains.

In July and August, high rainfall and warm temperatures (averaging 18 to 20°C, or 64 to 68°F) enable most species to flower and fruit in this period. Against the background of the golden heads of Siberian Filifolium, the blue-purple flowers of Baikal Skullcap (*Scutellaria baicalensis*), campanula (*Campanula*), Ladybell (*Adenophora gmelinii*), the Chinese Bellflower or Balloonflower (*Platycodon grandiflorum*), the paler blue flowers of Narrow-leaved Scabious (*Scabiosa comosa*) and the deep purple heads of Garden (Salad) Burnet (*Sanguisorba officinalis*) make a spectacular show. The grassland at the peak of its productivity presents a lush appearance and this is a busy season for haymakers.

Before the first frosts of early September, most plants have completed their life cycle; even the needle grass (*Stipa*), which is the latest to flower, will have ripe seeds. The sharp drop in temperature signals a change of colour on the grassland landscape. The leaves of Siberian Filifolium turn red, contrasting with the withered yellow colour of the pure grass of the grass family (Gramineae) nearby. Siberian Filifolium remains dormant from late September until the following May.

Currently, the meadow steppe is used for grazing only during a short period in the summer and autumn, so its agricultural potential is yet to be fully realized, but as a result wildlife has been little disturbed. This meadow steppe provides reliable grazing and a good hay crop, and livestock includes fine breeds such as the Sanhe Ox, Mongolian Fine-wool Sheep and Uzhumuqin Sheep are reared.

TOP: a rider surveys the arid steppe of Inner Mongolia.
ABOVE CENTRE: the edge of the Mongolian Scots Pine (*Pinus sylvestris* var. *mongolica*) forest in the foothills of the Da Hinggan Mountains.
ABOVE: the richness of the meadow steppe is apparent high in the Da Hinggan Mountains where the herb layer is deep and lush.

GRASSES OF THE MEADOW STEPPE

Meadow steppe has the richest array of grass species of any type of grassland and can be very beautiful in summer when it is thick with prettily coloured flowers. Members of the buttercup, rose, lily and sedge families can be widely found amongst the representatives of the grass and pea families which predominate.

LEFT: valley meadow in Inner Mongolia with Chinese Globeflower (*Trollius chinensis*) and Lilac Pink (*Kianthus superbus*).
RIGHT: Chinese Aneurolepidium (*Aneurolepidium chinense*) and Siberian Filofolium (*Filofolium sibiricum*).

Typical steppe

The true steppe, or arid steppe, is drier than meadow steppe; it is characteristic of the middle part of the Inner Mongolian Plateau, the south-western part of the North-eastern Plain, the northern Loess Plateau and below the forest belt in the north-western mountain areas.

True steppe is developed on the semi-arid transitional area between meadow steppe and the desert steppe where the annual rainfall is between about 250 and 400 mm (10 and 16 in.). This type of steppe is composed mainly of grasses, composites and various peas and vetches, with Greater Needle Grass or Feather Grass (*Stipa grandis*), Krylov's Needle Grass or Feather Grass (*Stipa krylovii*), *Stipa capillata, Festuca sulcata, Cleistogenes squarrose*, Junegrass (*Koeleria cristata*) and Crested Wheatgrass (*Agropyron cristatum*) being the predominant species.

Greater Needle Grass grows mainly in the eastern part of Inner Mongolia. Generally, it begins to shoot in late April; it flowers in mid August and dies back after seeding in late September. The best habitat for Greater Needle Grass is on well drained, lime rich, chestnut-coloured soils. It also can be found on sandy chestnut soils, but is then less luxuriant. It is absent from soil that is affected by ground water and becomes salty or alkaline, or turns to wet meadow soil with a relatively high degree of organic matter. Fresh, green growth is eagerly devoured by livestock, but when the seed heads mature they cause some damage, as the hard ears have sharp bristles which may hurt the tender mouths of sheep. Ripe seed heads also become entangled in the wool of sheep and reduce the quality of the fleece, so shepherds move their flocks to other pastures when the grass heads ripen.

Typical steppe has a comparatively uniform appearance, but it changes radically with the passing seasons. Between one and two thirds of the ground may be devoid of plant cover, but in places a moderately rich growth of grasses is the norm. Because of the physical conditions and the characteristics of the dominant grasses, the ratio of large livestock to small gradually decreases from meadow steppe to typical steppe, and small livestock predominates on desert steppe. Typical steppe offers suitable grazing for sheep, horses and oxen, especially for fine-wool sheep.

Desert steppe

Desert steppe characterizes the middle and western parts of Inner Mongolia and the lower levels of the north-western mountains. Broadly speaking it stretches between the true steppe, with its intermittent but sometimes considerable plant cover, and the barren desert, occurring where the climate is of an arid nature and the annual rainfall only around 150 to 250 mm (6 to 10 in.). The plants are mainly perennial herbs, accompanied by some shrubs and tough, low, bushy species, all adapted to long, dry periods and intermittent rain. The representative species are Gobi Needle Grass or Feather Grass (*Stipa gobica*) – one of the most drought-resistant species of the steppe – Short-flowered Needle Grass (*Stipa breviflora*) and Sandy Needle Grass or Feather Grass (*Stipa glareosa*).

These grasses are typically slender, wiry and tough, and root in brown soil, which has a thin layer of humus and an accumulation of lime 20 to 25 cm (8 to 10 in.) below the surface. The humus content is low, and so is the fertility of the soil. There is always a layer of grit and coarse sand on the surface, enhancing the desert-like aspect. Gobi Needle Grass plants are short, with an average height of only 10 to 20 cm (4 to 8 in.). The biomass – the total weight of plant and animal matter in a given area at a particular time – is very low, and changes greatly with the seasons and also from year to year. The landscape is impoverished in winter, but, in a good year, spring sees a considerable growth of grasses and shrubs. In a dry or cold year, the vegetation may scarcely develop even in summer.

Sandy Needle Grass, adapted to this arid climate, can form a vast area of almost uniform desert-steppe vegetation on sandy and gritty soils. Though short and sparse, its pasture is of fairly high quality, good enough for grazing sheep and camels, like Gobi Needle Grass steppe. Dwarf, often thorny, wiry undershrubs dot the sand and gravel, typical species being Frigid Hippolytia (*Hippolytia frigida*) and Shrubby Ajania (*Ajania achilleoides*), with Manyroot Onion (*Allium polyrhizum*) on low and flat alkaline land. However, the growing season is relatively brief; by mid- to late September, the grasses have withered away and the ground becomes almost bare for the next eight months.

On desert steppe, the vegetation is sparse. The height of the grasses is generally in the range of 10 to 20 cm (4 to 8 in.) with a coverage of 20 to 40 per cent. Compared with the 2000 to 4500 kg of green grass per hectare per year (1800 to 4000 lb/acre/year) of the true steppe, the average green production of the desert steppe is very low, only 1000 to 2000 kg/ha/year (900 to 1800 lb/acre/year). However, the grass quality is quite high, so there are quite a number of good pastures on this type of grassland for goats and camels.

Although typically sustaining Greater Needle Grass or Feather Grass (*Stipa grandis*) this steppe is in a relatively humid region and has a more luxuriant appearance than most of the 'true steppe'.

Highland steppe

Common Cranes (*Grus grus*) cross an extensive grassland in the shadow of the magnificent peaks bordering the Qinghai-Tibet Plateau.

The last type of grassland is that found at high altitudes, with low temperatures and little rain, in areas of above 4000 metres (13,000 ft) on the Qinghai-Tibet Plateau, above 3000 metres (9800 ft) in north-western Sichuan, and in the zone above the forest in the north-western mountains. The plants there are drought-resistant and withstand the very low temperatures of most of the year. These are low tussocks of grasses, sedges and dwarf alpine shrubs, with the most widely distributed species being Purple-flowered Needle Grass (*Stipa purpurea*), *Stipa subsessiliflora*, *Festuca krylovii* and *Carex moorcroftii*.

Purple-flowered Needle Grass grows over large areas at 4500 to 5100 metres (14,800 to 16,700 ft) on the Qinghai-Tibet Plateau and the Pamir Mountains. It is very short (about 20 cm, or 8 in.) and sparse, and grows in almost uniform tracts. In the short summer growing season, the grassland briefly assumes a yellow-green colour. Generally, Purple-flowered Needle Grass germinates in middle and late May, and grows quickly until, at the end of August, the fully mature steppe vegetation is at its most beautiful. The ripening spikes sparkle in the sunshine and flicker in the almost constant breeze in an extraordinary, lovely landscape dominated by spectacular peaks. Purple-flowered Needle Grass grassland makes surprisingly good pasture with tender, nutritious leaves.

Krylov's Fescue (*Festuca kryloviana*) is found on submountain and mountain zones above the alpine forest. It grows thickly to a height of 20 to 25 cm (8 to 10 in.). In summer, it is yellow-green, and it provides high level pasture in summer and early autumn.

Moorcroft's Sedge (*Carex moorcroftii*) is an endemic species of the Qinghai-Tibet Plateau. With its strongly developed root system, it is a plant of great vitality. The growing season is very short, and even during July and August the plant may be damaged by frost. The tips of the leaves are mostly withered, and the grassland takes on a dry, yellow appearance. The height of the plants is only about 10 to 15 cm (4 to 6 in.) and, although sometimes used as summer pasture, the grassland is of low productivity and the plants are coarse, wiry, and unpalatable for livestock.

The few species of plants on this type of steppe are uniformly short and sparse. Ground coverage averages only 20 to 25 per cent, and the yield is very low, with dry grass producing only 400 to 500 kg/ha/year (350 to 450

Yaks (*Bos grunniens*) in the Tibetan grasslands.

b/acre/year); the grazing season is rather short. However, the long hours of intense sunshine give some of the species, like Purple-flowered Needle Grass, an unusually high crude protein and crude fat content, with a low content of crude fibre. The nutritional value of the forage grasses is therefore surprisingly high. The cold highland steppe serves as an important pasture for Tibetan yaks, Tibetan sheep and Tibetan goats, all highly adapted to the hard, spartan life at high altitudes.

Wildlife of the steppes

The grassland animal communities are simpler than those of the forest, where the availability of food and the physical nature of the habitat are so much more diverse. Rodents that eat the green parts of the grasses are especially numerous. Many of them live in large groups, making complex networks of burrows under the open grasslands. There are few species of larger grazing animals, and gazelles live in quite large numbers. They are nimble and fleet of foot, as they need to be to avoid the attacks of carnivorous animals and birds of prey. Few birds live on the grasslands, and the numbers and variety of amphibians and reptiles are equally restricted by the paucity and uniformity of the environment.

Several species of pikas inhabit the Chinese grasslands, including the Moupin Pika (*Ochotona thibetana*), shown above in the Qinghai-Tibet Plateau steppe.

The climate of the grassland has a marked effect on the biology of the animals of the steppes. The short growth period, the relatively long cold season, and the dryness in spring combine to create a short breeding season and, in many cases, the necessity for hibernation and winter food storage. Furthermore, the temperature changes abruptly, and the annual rainfall is erratic, with years of drought and sudden downpours which cause flash floods. In their turn, these variable factors mean that the quality and quantity of the food plants are highly unpredictable, and the rodents and ungulates have to cope with years of hardship as well as enjoying years of plenty.

Gazelles adapt by moving long distances in a nomadic life on the steppes, but small rodents spread rapidly in the good years, reaching high population densities, and survive only in greatly reduced numbers in the intervening years. The birds and mammals that prey on them are also subject to fluctuations related to the cycles of the rodent population. In poor years, they may die, or rear fewer young.

Mammals

Rodents and lagomorphs are the main types of grassland mammals found in China. Lagomorphs include the Daurian Pika (*Ochotona daurica*) and Pallas's Pika (*O. pallasi*), which are typical grassland animals, living in areas of sandy hills and flat grassland. On the Fringed Sagebrush (*Artemisia frigida*) grassland that has deteriorated through overgrazing they have thrived and their density is at its highest, reaching more than 50 pikas per hectare (20 per acre) in years of high numbers. Pikas look like small squirrels or rabbits without a tail; the length of their bodies is about 15 to 20 cm (6 to 8 in.), and they have large, round ears. The body fur is mainly grey and cinnamon coloured. They eat fresh green grass in summer, and in winter they do not hibernate, surviving instead on the dry grass collected in autumn and stored for their winter food. While they are carrying out this harvest, large piles of grass stems can be seen near the mouths of the burrows, where they are left to dry before being dragged into the tunnels for storage underground. The pikas live in groups in the burrows, breeding twice a year from April to October. When disturbed they stand on their hind legs and give a high-pitched whoop as a warning to the others.

Their distribution and numbers are to some extent related to the effects of overgrazing and the natural productivity of the grassland. They do not favour

A stocky form and broad head characterize the Bobak Marmot (*Marmota bobak*), a gregarious rodent of the grassy steppes.

grassland on fertile soil, with moderate moisture and abundant grass, and the number of pikas will be small in such conditions. Higher densities are found in drier regions with sparse, wiry grasses.

Brown Hares (*Lepus capensis*) are widely distributed from the lowland to the grasslands of mountain slopes. Normally, they nest in a simple 'form' shaped in the grasses, but sometimes they use the abandoned hole of a marmot. Their breeding season is from February to September, and two to three litters of three to six young are born each year. Marmots often carry fleas which transmit tularemia virus (*Bacterium tularense*) and hares will frequently pick up the fleas and act as carriers of the disease, infecting new groups of other animals as they come into contact with them and spreading tularemia widely over the steppe.

The Bobak Marmot (*Marmota bobak*) is a large rodent with a body length of about 50 cm (20 in.). It lives off green grass in spring and summer and dry grass in autumn and winter. Bobak Marmots mainly inhabit low mountains and hills where Chinese Aneurolepidium (*Aneurolepidium sinensis*) dominates the steppe vegetation. They live in family groups of ten to twenty members and are most active at dawn and dusk, when the temperature is moderate. In daytime, an adult marmot stands guard, standing up on high ground to scan the surrounding terrain. When there is any disturbance, the 'guard' begins to call with a high, dog-like bark, whereupon the other marmots run to mounds of earth by the entrances to burrows, and also bark to spread the alarm. If danger threatens, they quickly hide in the burrows. In late autumn, marmots begin to block the mouths of the burrows with stones and soil, in preparation for their long winter hibernation. In the following April their hibernation comes to an end, and they emerge into the spring sunshine. Their breeding season is from May to July.

Marmots are hunted for their fur, and they are also sometimes eaten by nomads. However, this can be a dangerous practice, because of the disease they carry.

Just as marmots are the main carriers of tularemia near the mountains, so ground squirrels are the major carriers on the plains. In fact, the squirrels are the more dangerous to human beings as they live in closer contact with them. Ground squirrels (*Citellus*) are medium-sized rodents of a yellow-cinnamon colour, with rather large heads and eyes, insignificant ears and short tails, with a long, distinct white tuft at the end. *Citellus erythrogenys* and the Daurian Ground Squirrel (*Citellus dauricus*) are commonly seen species. The former is a typical squirrel of the desert steppe, found in the northern part of Inner Mongolia, and the latter is more widely distributed over most of the steppe types. Either species will devour any green plants, but their favourite plants are Manyroot Onion (*Allium polyrhizum*), Mongolian Onion (*Allium mongolicum*), *Aster altaicus* and Common Russian Thistle (*Salsola collina*), a beet-like plant adapted to the saline conditions of arid steppe. These squirrels hibernate in winter and a few even have a short-term hibernation in summer. Ground squirrels breed once a year with two to ten young in a litter. Their appetite and numbers make them pests in terms of agriculture, animal husbandry and forestry, and for this reason, and because they are hosts of tularemia, large sums of money are spent on controlling their numbers. They may also spread brucellosis and other diseases.

The other common rodents in the grasslands are hamsters (*Cricetulus*) and voles (*Microtus*), both of which are characterized by a fat, rounded body and a very short tail. The most important species include the Greater Long-tailed Hamster (*Cricetulus triton*), the Striped Hamster (*Cricetulus barabensis*), the Common Vole (*Microtus arvalis*), Brandt's Vole (*M. brandti*), the Mandarin Vole (*M. mandarinus*) and Reed Vole (*M. fortis*). All of them are small, nocturnal animals. The burrows that they make are complex and well organized, with different areas for storing grain, for sleeping and for excreting. Different types of grain will be stored in different tunnels; in large burrows there will be as much as 10 kg (22 lb) of grain stored. The voles carry it to their burrows in pouches in their cheeks, which means that it arrives ready cleaned for storage. Voles also eat grass, but the large numbers that have decimated cereal crops have caused them to be viewed as pests. In addition, Common Voles and Reed Voles nibble the tender bark and seeds of trees, with harmful consequences elsewhere for forestry.

There is another special group of rodents which burrow underground, namely the zokors (*Myospalax*), which include two commonly seen species, the Common Chinese Zokor (*Myospalax fontanieri*) and the Manchurian Zokor (*Myospalax psilurus*). They have short, fat bodies, small eyes, ears hidden away in their fur, and short, thin tails. The fur on the body is dense and soft and does not naturally lie in any particular direction, which is helpful for going forward and backward in the narrow tunnels of the burrows! The claws of the front feet are especially large and are used for tunnelling; the longest one, the third claw, is as long as 20 mm (¾ in.). As they burrow through the ground they dig the earth with their front paws and kick it behind them with their back legs. They live permanently underground, burrowing through the earth. For food they pull grasses down into the burrows by their roots, preferring grasses with long roots and short stems. Being subterranean they have only tiny eyes, and rely mainly on their sense of smell.

The structure of the tunnels is rather complicated, occupying from about 30 to 1000 or more square metres (323 to 10,764 square ft) for each pair of zokors. On the surface, many mounds of soil, about 50 cm (20 in.) across and

ABOVE: zokors are densely-furred, bulky rodents with tiny ears and eyes.
LEFT: Common Chinese Zokors (*Myospalax fontanieri*) leave distinctive mounds of soil where they burrow.

10 cm (4 in.) high, can be seen piled up when the zokors dig their underground pathways.

The Mongolian Gazelle (*Procapra gutturosa*) is the typical ungulate of the eastern grassland of China. It is delicately proportioned, with slender limbs, narrow hoofs and a short tail. The body is yellow-brown, and there is a prominent white rump patch around the tail. In favoured areas, which vary according to the season and the quality of the grazing, they may form large groups of tens to hundreds. Mongolian Gazelles eat *Agropyron pseudogropyron*, a grass closely related to wheat, barley and rye, and other forage grasses. Late autumn to early winter is their mating season and there may be up to three calves born together. Mongolian Gazelles migrate seasonally, covering long distances to reach good feeding grounds and a reliable supply of water. They run rapidly, at speeds up to 90 kilometres (55 miles) per hour; such speeds were necessary in the past to escape the large wolf packs which once roamed the steppe.

Birds

The most common birds of the grassy steppe are various species of larks (family Alaudidae). These are rather small, mostly pale brown and sand coloured with fine darker markings. They have fairly short, thick but pointed bills with which they can take both seeds and insects. Their legs are strong and the hind claw is long and straight, typical of many small ground-living birds. They spend most of their time on the ground, and several species run well, but their most notable characteristic is their song flight of spring and summer. In the wide, treeless landscape, the larks sing in mid-air, some, such as the Skylark (*Alauda arvensis*), soaring upwards while singing a beautiful, continuous song. This is their downfall in China, as many thousands are trapped and kept in tiny cages.

Larks nest on the ground, lining a shallow depression with fine grass stems. They lay a clutch of four or five eggs, which are blotched or speckled

ABOVE: Tibetan Gazelles (*Procapra picticaudata*) live in the grasslands of Gansu on the Qinghai-Tibet Plateau.

BELOW: a magnificent Great Bustard (*Otis tarda*) reaches back to preen its fanned tail; it is a bird of undisturbed stretches of steppe in Asia and Europe.

LARKS OF THE GRASSLAND

Larks are well adapted to life on the open spaces of the grassland plateaux where they are widely distributed. They make distinctive song flights to advertise their territories in these largely featureless country areas. They nest in the open ground, which leaves them susceptible to predators, but the eggs are camouflaged in their surroundings. The most common species of lark on the Qinghai-Tibet Plateau is the Shore Lark (*Eremophila alpestris*).

ABOVE RIGHT AND RIGHT: *Eremophila alpestris* nests at over 5200 metres.
ABOVE: the eggs of the Lesser, or Oriental, Skylark (*Alauda gulgula*).

with brown and grey to give excellent camouflage. The Skylark, the Crested Lark (*Galerida cristata*) and the Eastern Short-toed Lark (*Calandrella cinerea*), are widely distributed on grassy plains. The Shore (Horned) Lark (*Eremophila alpestris*), which has a facial pattern of yellow and black, with tiny feathery 'horns' each side of the crown, is the dominant species on the highest and most desolate steppe of the Qinghai-Tibet Plateau; the Long-billed Calandra (*Melanocorypha maxima*) and Oriental (Small) Skylark (*Alauda gulgula*) are other typical larks of the plateau steppe. The Yellow Wagtail (*Motacilla flava*), Robin Accentor (*Prunella rubeculoides*), Twite (*Carduelis flavirostris*) and Przevalski's Rosefinch (*Urocynchramus pylzowi*) are also typical species of birds in this region.

The Great Bustard (*Otis tarda*) is a huge bird, now scarce, found mainly in Inner Mongolia. At 10 to 15 kg (22 to 33 lb), it has the heaviest body of all flying birds. It looks somewhat like an ostrich, with much shorter, strong legs, a large, brown body and an upright neck. In flight it shows large areas of white on the wing.

Great Bustards make crude nests on mounds of dry grass, and lay two to three eggs in each clutch. The eggs are grey-green with cinnamon streaks and blotches and the incubation period is 21 to 28 days. In the breeding season they live in pairs, but at other times they gather in small groups. In winter they migrate to the Yangtze (Chang) River. Females mature in three to four years, and males in five to six years.

Sandgrouse are characteristic birds of steppe and semi-desert, although their numbers and distribution vary with local conditions. They gather in large flocks to fly long distances each day to drink. Pallas's Sandgrouse (*Syrrhaptes paradoxus*) is widespread in sandy semi-desert and open steppe. Its plumage is a mixture of grey, white, orange, black and fawn, and it has long tail streamers and long, pointed wings. Sandgrouse are rather dove- or partridge-like, but with longer wings and tail. Their legs are short, the three broad toes covered with feathers for ease of walking rapidly in the tufted grass and loose sandy ground. They line shallow scrapes in the ground with grass stems to make simple nests; each clutch is of two or three elliptical brown-spotted eggs.

The Lapwing (*Vanellus vanellus*) and Grey-headed Lapwing (*Vanellus cinereus*) are members of the family Charadriidae, which breed in grassland areas and migrate to wetter areas in winter. The Lapwing is found widely on the steppe in the northern part of China, while the Grey-headed Lapwing is more common in the eastern part of Inner Mongolia.

A typical bird of prey is the magnificent Steppe (Tawny) Eagle (*Aquila rapax*). This large, dark brown eagle, with a 2 metre (6½ ft) wingspan, is widely, but sparsely, distributed. It nests in rocks, trees or in marmots' empty burrows. The clutch is of two to three white eggs with brown spots, which hatch after 45 days. Rodents are its main food, but it also takes some birds and lizards. In autumn all the Steppe Eagles migrate to Africa.

Rooks (*Corvus frugilegus*) and Magpies (*Pica pica*) often nest in windbreak forests in the grasslands. They make untidy stick nests, and a number of small birds, such as Tree Sparrows (*Passer montanus*), nest within the structure of them. Red-footed Falcons (*Falco vespertinus*) will fight Rooks and Magpies to take over their nests but are unconcerned by the sparrows, which continue to inhabit the nests peacefully, hatching their eggs and feeding their young under the protection given by their new hosts.

Reptiles and insects

Generally speaking, other grassland animal species are relatively few, but among them there are some unusual creatures. Several species of viviparous lizards live in the alpine steppe of the Qinghai-Tibet Plateau. The females of these unusual reptiles hatch their eggs in their bodies and then give birth. About 25 species of snakes also inhabit the Qinghai-Tibet Plateau, the Mongolia-Xinjiang Plateau and the higher part of the Da Hinggan Mountains. Among these species, Orsini's Viper (*Vipera ursinii*), which is also viviparous, is an endemic race of a snake species that is widely distributed on the Mongolia-Xinjiang Plateau. Unlike other vipers its venom is relatively weak. Like many reptiles it is short-sighted and judges the approach of its prey by feeling the vibrations on the ground. However, this does not help it locate its prey if the animal has stopped moving, so it has special receptors between its eyes and nose which sense by registering infra-red radiation. The pit viper *Agkistrodon strauchii*, which is a species endemic to the Qinghai-Tibet Plateau, also has these special sensors.

Among the major pests as far as herdsmen are concerned are grasshoppers. Species found in great numbers include the Common Field Grasshopper (*Chorthippus brunneus*), *C. dubius*, *C. fallax*, *C. hammas* and *C. dorsatus*.

RIGHT: the impressive Steppe Eagle (*Aquila rapax*) is widespread on dry grasslands, but its numbers have been reduced by the effects of pesticides which it may encounter elsewhere in its range. It spends the winter in Africa, feeding extensively on termites, as well as on a wide variety of larger prey – in addition to scavenging carrion and robbing other birds of prey and storks of their food. It migrates to Africa via the eastern edge of the Black Sea and down through Israel and Jordan.

DESERTS 荒漠

Throughout recorded time, deserts have impeded human settlement, trade and mobility, their harsh, uncompromising conditions presenting too great a challenge to all but a few nomadic tribes. The domestication of the camel opened up trade routes for the great caravans which could then cross from oasis to oasis instead of making enormous diversions around the desert boundaries, but the desert nevertheless remained a hostile place to be crossed as speedily as possible, and there was no thought of long-term exploitation. In recent years, however, human ingenuity has developed ways of utilizing desert resources, including oil, salt, ground water and mineral deposits; large-scale irrigation projects, coupled with the use of the boundless energy of the sun, have created agricultural possibilities which had hitherto been undreamt of. Cultivation of arable crops and ranching, using special breeds of livestock, have begun to make an impact and turn areas of desert green.

This is a reversal of an all too frequent process – the mismanagement of dry lands which turns vast areas of previously productive land into desert or semi-desert. At the same time the fragile ecosystem of the desert itself is at risk from human interference.

The desert area of China is vast. The arid north-west has 1,095,000 square kilometres (422,800 square miles). Some 637,000 square kilometres (246,000 square miles) are sandy desert; 458,000 square kilometres (176,800 square miles) are stony desert. Altogether, deserts occupy about 11.3 per cent of the total land area of the country.

Parched landscapes

In the deserts of China the average annual precipitation is lower than 200 mm (8 in.). There is nowhere in China that does not receive some rain each year but in the driest areas, such as the centres of the Tarim Basin and Qaidam Basin, the rainfall is less than 50 mm (2 in.), and Toksun, in the Turfan Depression, just south of the Tien Mountains, has an annual average of a mere 5.9 mm (¼ in.) – the 0.5 mm (¹⁄₄₈ in.) there in 1958 is the lowest recorded in China. Rainfall is erratic in these deserts. There is usually a long period without any at all – the longest on record being 290 days in the Turfan Depression and Tarim Basin. The wind here is strong and adds a further element to the harshness of the desert – the sandstorm. High speed winds of 117 kilometres (73 miles) per hour or more – force 12 – are not uncommon. The long periods of complete aridity and the almost constant wind make the sandy deserts unstable and mobile, with extensive dunes.

Most of the deserts are in inland basins and plateaux at an elevation of 500 to 1500 metres (1650 to 5000 ft) and are surrounded by high mountains. The surface of the deserts is loose sand and bare rock with high concentrations of salt and gypsum, which limit plant growth.

There are no permanent rivers, only some intermittent streams and a few larger rivers which flow when ice and snow melt on surrounding mountains in spring. The amount of ground water varies greatly from area to area. In general, abundant water exists at the foot of the mountains or near the meltwater streams, and oases often form in such places in spectacular contrast to the barren and parched landscapes which stretch for miles.

Vegetation is sparse and short and the variety of plants is small. Most plants are bushes or low shrubs and almost nowhere do plants achieve more than 30 per cent coverage of the ground. There are large areas that are completely devoid of vegetation. However, on the banks of a river, or where underground streams reach the surface, some kinds of plants, such as the poplar *Populus diversifolia*, Branched Tamarisk (*Tamarix ramosissima*) and Common Reed (*Phragmites australis*), grow densely to form natural oases.

PREVIOUS PAGE: the Gobi, in Gansu Province, is China's most famous desert.
ABOVE: there are great sandy wastes in the Turfan Depression in Xinjiang Province.
OPPOSITE ABOVE: the edge of the desert makes an abrupt contrast with the woodland of the Tien Mountains where trees are planted to reduce erosion and the spread of loose sand.
OPPOSITE BELOW: beautiful and colourful rock formations in the Turfan Depression.

Annual and daily fluctuations in temperature are significant and place extra stress on the plants and animals that live in the desert. The land surface temperature in the afternoon in summer can reach 60 to 70°C (140 to 160°F). On a sandy surface in the Junggar Basin it can be as hot as 84°C (183°F), but the temperature in winter at Fuvun in Xinjiang has dropped to an astonishingly low −51.5°C (−60.7°F), which is the second lowest temperature recorded in China. It is difficult for plants and animals to live in an environment with such large fluctuations in temperature.

Tarim Basin

Located between the Tien Mountains and the Kunlun Mountains, the Tarim Basin is the biggest desert in China. The climate here is extremely arid. The basin consists of three rings: at the foot of the mountain slopes at the edge of the basin is a mixture of stone and sand; inside that is a band of stone desert with oases like islands or green ribbons; and at the centre of the basin is the Taklimakan Desert with an area of 327,000 square kilometres (126,250 square miles), making up 43 per cent of the desert area in China. Eighty-five per cent of Taklimakan is made up of mobile sand dunes which, under the effect of prevailing north-east and north-west winds, drift mainly southwards. As a result of the wind, the few roads which cross this desert are often blocked by moving sand. Dunes stabilized and semi-stabilized by tamarisk (*Tamarix*) bushes, covering about 15 per cent of the whole desert, are scattered at the edges of the desert and along the banks of the few rivers which flow from the mountains. The other huge dunes are so unstable as to be utterly devoid of vegetation. However, on the river banks in the centre or around the edges of the deserts, poplars, tamarisks and other plants form the distinctive oasis landscape. These are potentially good land areas for growing cereals and cotton, and such development has started in places.

The Lop Lake lowland, in the east of the Tarim Basin, is its lowest point. Originally, there was a great deal of water in the lake, but it has dried up because of irrigation in the lower and middle reaches of the river, which has had dramatic effects on the special and unusual natural history of the desert lake. The evaporation of water flowing into the lake has created significant deposits of salt, alkali and gypsum. Wind eroded mesas and extraordinary features created by the effects of blown sand on these deposits and on harder rocks can be seen over a wide area, especially in the 2600 square kilometres (1000 square miles) of the north-western quarter.

Junggar Basin

The Junggar Basin lies between the Tien Mountains and the Altai Mountains, occupies about 47,300 square kilometres (18,250 square miles), and is the second largest of China's deserts. Although this is true arid desert, it is quite different from the Tarim Basin Desert. The annual rainfall here is higher, at 70 to 150 mm (2¾ to 6 in.), because a comparatively humid western wind reaches here through many mountain passes in the west and north-west of the basin. Even this meagre supply of moisture is sufficient to allow the growth of some plants. Up to half of the stable dunes and 15 to 25 per cent of the semi-stable dunes can support plants which can then be used for winter grazing. The mobile dunes occupy less than five per cent of the total area of the basin.

At the edge of the basin, especially in the eastern part, is gravel and stony desert. The strong wind from the mountains in the western part of the basin

The rock formations in the east of Lop Nur Lake, now dry, reflect its recent history as a shallow desert lake and create a landscape of striking appearance. A new system of irrigation in the middle and lower reaches of the Lop River was responsible for robbing the lake of its water, leaving only salt, alkali and gypsum deposits.

173

The eroded landscape of the northern Junggar Basin is not entirely barren, as there is a little rainfall in this vast region. It is the second largest desert in China.

creates a region of fascinating natural rock sculptures of endless variety, especially in Urho, Xinjiang, known as 'Wind City', where, from a distance, the eroded forms look like castles.

Alxa Desert

This region of western Inner Mongolia is surrounded by the Helan Mountains in the east, the Qilian Mountains in the south and the Ruoshui River in the west. It includes the Badain Jaran Desert, the Tengger Desert and the Ulan Buh Desert. In the Badain Jaran Desert, 83 per cent of the area is covered by mobile dunes, usually 200 to 300 metres (650 to 1000 ft) high, but the highest reach 500 metres (1650 ft). Among these high dunes there are a number of small lakes, but they are of little use for sustaining life as the rapid rate of evaporation has made the salt content of the water very high. However, where springs appear, the surrounding areas support abundant grasses and can be used as grazing land. In the Tengger Desert there are more lakes with fresh water, and these can be put to good use to irrigate areas of the desert.

Under the influence of a prevailing north-west wind, the deserts are gradually expanding to the south-east and sand has approached the Yellow (Huang) River, where it has affected the traffic and the agriculture along the riverbank. The Baotou-Lanzhou railway, built in 1958, is kept open by reducing the movement of dunes through the planting of trees and grass. This has effectively put a grassy barrier along the whole of the 40 kilometre (25 mile) route through the desert.

Ordos Desert

This region is south of the great bend of the Yellow River in the Inner Mongolian Autonomous Region and north of the Great Wall. It is a large transition zone from true arid desert to semi-desert conditions. The Hobq Desert, along the south bank of the Yellow River, is composed mainly of mobile dunes which reach 10 to 15 metres (33 to 50 ft) high. The Mu Us Desert in the south of Ordos has a good supply of ground water, so there are fewer mobile dunes and the area of stable and semi-stable dunes is large. However, the vegetation has been destroyed by misuse of the natural resources and the extent of unstable dunes has thus been increased.

Deserts of the Qaidam Basin

This area is about 2500 to 3000 metres (8250 to 10,000 ft) above sea level in the north-west of Qinghai Province. In the north-west of the basin the effects of wind erosion are very clear and severely eroded 'badland' topography has developed. The plain at the foot of the mountains in the south of the basin is largely covered by dunes.

Gobi

The desert, or 'gobi', of China is very extensive and can be divided into two main classifications according to its surface: stony desert, which is characterized by rocky detritus and angular boulders, and sand and gravel desert.

Stony desert

This type of gobi is located in the east of the Xinjiang Autonomous Region and the western part of Gansu Province. Erosion over a vast period of time has created a surface that is flat and almost bare with the bedrock exposed or with only 1 metre (3 ft) of detritus. The surface of the rocks is a shiny black colour almost like oil in appearance; it is called 'desert varnish'. Here, both surface water and ground water are rare; rainfall is less than 50 mm (2 in.) per year and in places it is almost non-existent. Vegetation is scarce and most of this desert is entirely devoid of plant cover.

Sand and gravel desert

This category of desert is located mainly at the foot of the Tien Mountains, the Kunlun Mountains and the Qilian Mountains. The processes of erosion create vast amounts of rocky material in the mountains which is broken into smaller fragments and transported by water over long distances. The material is deposited at the foot of the mountains to form plains of graded sand and gravel. Scoured by wind and water, the fine material has been carried away, leaving only the comparatively large, coarse pebbles.

Plants of the deserts
Stony deserts

The extremely dry nature and temperature fluctuations of the desert climate and the poor, salty soil restrict the growth of plants. Few species can survive, let alone thrive, in these conditions, and the plant communities lack variety and are simple in structure. Those that prosper have adopted special characteristics.

A typical adaptation is a small leaf area; species of Peashrub (*Caragana*) that survive here are tough and xerophytic (drought-resistant) with small leaves, and many species of wormwood (*Seriphidium* and *Artemisia*) have deeply divided and fingered leaves. Many species of the broom-like shrubs of

A stretch of the wormwood *Artemesia ordosica* scrub in the Mu Us desert, where there is sufficient ground water for the surface to be stabilized and vegetation to become established; the area is, however, threatened by overgrazing.

175

the genus *Calligonum* and the salt-tolerant *Anabasis* have leaves that are slender and stiff, rather like stems. The leaves of some xerophytic plants are needle-like or almost non-existent; for instance Common Horaninowia (*Horaninowia ulicina*), Little Nanophyton (*Nanophyton erinaceum*) and Leafless Anabasis (*Anabasis aphylla*) are almost leafless, and are dependent upon their annual green branches to conduct the process of photosynthesis that is the usual role of leaves. The leaves of another group of xerophytes roll up at noon in summer to restrict water loss through transpiration, as do the leaves of some kinds of fescue grasses (*Festuca*) and the feather grasses or needle grasses (*Stipa*), for example.

Many plants exhibit other adaptations to life in deserts: a covering of fine hair, thickening of the cuticle layers of the leaves and a reduction in the number of stoma to reduce transpiration. Some kinds of Goosefoot (*Chenopodium*) and Orache (*Atriplex*) have fine hairs growing thickly on both leaves and stems. Because there is a high concentration of salt in the soil of arid areas, most of the plants have developed salt tolerance and many have linear leaves with a sticky sap which is capable of absorbing large quantities of soluble salts. The most notable examples are the genus *Anabasis* and some goosefoots such as Fat Hen (*Chenopodium album*).

DESERT VEGETATION

Plants which thrive in deserts have developed special means of coping with the arid conditions. The herb saussurea (*Saussurea*) and some species of wormwood (*Artemisia*) have dense, fine hair on their leaves which reduces transpiration. Some plants have almost no leaves at all; the process of photosynthesis is conducted by their branches. Others have leaves that roll up at the hottest time of the day in summer, to minimize water loss through transpiration. The leaves of certain grasses, such as needle grasses, do the same.

Some kinds of flowering shrubs such as reaumuria (*Reaumuria*) and the closely related tamarisk (*Tamarix*) expel surplus salt through their stoma. Their leaves and stems have a waxy layer to reduce water loss in the dry wind, and during extremely hot and arid periods they will preserve moisture by shedding leaves, or even branches, and becoming dormant until the next rainfall.

TOP: wormwood desert on the Inner Mongolian Plateau.
ABOVE: Tamarisk (*Tamarix*) grows well on saline, alkaline soils, and helps bind dunes together.
ABOVE LEFT: Saline Saussurea (*Saussurea salsa*) growing in the Tarim Basin.

Sand and gravel deserts

Apart from highly specialized shrubs and small bushes, little can survive in sand and gravel deserts. There are no grasses and very little herbaceous vegetation, and ground cover is always extremely sparse; the plant community is a very simple one. The few species that do grow are all bushes and small shrubs that are xerophytic; they include broom-like calligonum bushes and saxauls (*Haloxylon*). On the mobile and semi-mobile dunes in the Alxa Desert, Mongolian Calligonum (*Calligonum mongolicum*) grows more than 1.5 metres (5 ft) high, accompanied by Squarrose Agriophyllum (*Agriophyllum arenarium*), Milkvetch (*Astragalus*) and other related species. In addition, Junceous Calligonum (*C. flavidum*) grows on dunes of the Junggar Basin, to form stable and semi-stable dunes 10 to 30 per cent covered by vegetation. Of the *Haloxylon* species of small, low trees or bushes, the dominant species are the saxaul *Haloxylon ammodendron* and Persian Saxaul (*H. persicum*). Scattered over the Alxa Desert and the Junggar Basin Desert, saxaul grows 1 to 3 metres (3 to 10 ft) high with dense branches, and often stabilizes or partially stabilizes the dunes on which it grows. Plants which grow with it in profusion are calligonum, Golden Sea Lavender (*Limonium aureum*), Mongolian Ephedra (*Ephedra equisetaina*), a strange, tall tree with whorls of leaves from jointed stems, Agriophyllum (*Agriophyllum lateriforum*) and Beancaper (*Zygophyllum fabago*), a shrub related to the tropical timber tree *lignum vitae*. The Persian Saxaul is limited to the Junggar Basin Desert. It grows to 1.5 to 3 metres (5 to 10 ft) on the stable dunes. Once the semi-stable dunes have 10 to 20 per cent plant cover, they become stable and other plants take over. The Persian Saxaul then declines to less than 5 per cent of the vegetation cover. Its main associated plants are calligonum, *Ammodendro argenteum*, Three-awn Grass (*Aristida pennata*), Common Horaninoria (*Horaninoria ulicina*) and Sand-loving Ceratocapnos (*Ceratocapnos arenarius*).

The Beancaper (*Zygophyllum fabago*) is a tough bush with a strong resistance to drought. It grows amongst saxaul (*Haloxylon*) in sandy deserts.

Detritus areas

These areas of sand and gravel are situated in the fan-shaped mass of deposits left by rivers at the foot of mountains; they also form on some bare, stony hills. The dryness of the surface, thick layers of gypsum and salt and the rocky or stony terrain in places create an almost totally barren landscape. A few small bushes and shrubs manage to find a hold in cracks or fissures. As the water passes through in the brief and irregular rainy period, the salt in the soil will be diluted and germination becomes possible.

The main plants that grow in these conditions are Kaschgar Ephedra (*Ephedra przewalskii*), Siberian Nitraria (*Nitraria sphaerocarpa*), Yellow-flowered Reaumuria (*Reaumuria trigyna*), Kashgar Reaumuria (*R. kaschgarica*), Short-leaved Anabasis (*Anabis brevifolia*), Leafless Anabasis (*A. aphylla*) and Woolly Anabasis (*A. eriopoda*). The plants are nearly all very short, under 40 cm (16 in.) high, and the ground cover is extremely sparse.

Loess deserts

Loess material is fine, wind-blown dust which builds up on vegetation to create a loose, light soil. It has accumulated over alluvial plains and mountain slopes, where dwarf shrubs have adapted to the aridity and about 10 to 30 per cent of the ground can be covered by vegetation. Songory Reaumuria (*Reaumuria soongorica*) is the dominant plant.

Saline deserts

On strongly saline soil or saline-alkaline soil there may be no lack of water at times, but the landscape is still desert due to the toxic effects of high concentrations of salt in the soil. The plants that can survive are necessarily tolerant of both salt and aridity, and are mostly dense shrubs with fleshy leaves such as Slender-branched Kalidium (*Kalidium gracile*), which is widely distributed around ancient lake basins and salt lakes where the ground wate[r] can be 2 to 4 metres (6 to 12 ft) below the surface. The salt content of th[e] surface soil is more than 3 to 5 per cent.

Slender-branched Kalidium is 40 to 50 cm (16 to 20 in.) high and forms u[p] to 15 per cent of the vegetation cover. Its associated plants are all salty-so[il] species. They include *Suaeda* species, Blackfruit Wolfberry (*Lycium rutheni*[-] *cum*) – which is a shrub of the large potato family – Caspian Halostachy[s] (*Halostachys belangeriana*), Marshfire Glasswort (*Salicornia herbacea*) an[d] various others.

BELOW: an area of salty desert with Kalidium (*Kalidium*); this plant is eaten by camels only when it is dead and withered.
BOTTOM: the valleys of the Helan Mountains, west of the Yellow (Huang) River, have a sparse cover of Siberian Elm (*Ulmus pumila*).

Oases

The arid desert landscapes are occasionally broken by *Populus diversifolia* forests growing along river banks and at the edge of alluvial desert fans. Where the water is sufficiently abundant the woods also contain Siberian Elm (*Ulmus pumila*), and make striking features in the landscape. These poplar forests can be found north and south of the Tien Mountains, in the Yumin Gobi, the Alxa Desert, the Qaidam Basin and especially in the Tarim Basin, where they are the most fully developed. Along the Tarim River the trees grow 7 to 15 metres (25 to 50 ft) tall (the tallest more than 20 metres, or 65 ft) and cover 20 to 40 per cent of the ground.

Another poplar, *Populus pruinosa*, also forms forests along the banks of the upper and middle reaches of the river, but its salt tolerance and drought resistance are poor so it does not thrive elsewhere. In suitable areas its height is 4 to 8 metres (13 to 25 ft) and it has various uses; the timber is taken as building material, the leaves for fodder. Poplar is also a source of alkali as an industrial material; but arguably the greatest advantage of the poplar forests is that they provide windbreaks and stabilize the sand dunes, thus exerting an important influence on the overall ecology of the desert.

TOP: an oasis at Lü Zhou Lieh. Oases create remarkable scenes of greenery in the most barren settings imaginable.
ABOVE: forests of David's Poplar (*Populus davidiana*) on the banks of the Ejin River are important resources within the desert.

179

Wildlife of the deserts

The wide open landscapes, arid climate and lack of vegetation for food or for cover are a great challenge to the survival of insects, mammals, birds and reptiles alike. Herbivorous rodents and ungulates can only thrive in areas where there is suitable vegetation. Of the two, the rodents are more common and more varied, since they can avoid predators by burrowing and, because they are nocturnal, suffer less from the extremes of temperature which make deserts such hostile environments. The ungulates, especially gazelles, avoid predators by running and have to brave the extremes of heat and cold as best they can.

Birds also find desert conditions difficult, but they have ways of adapting to overcome the problems. Many are countershaded – darker above and paler below to 'cancel out' the shadows cast by the sun which could give away their whereabouts to predators. They are also mostly pale and sandy in colour to blend in with the background, but often have striking wing patterns which show as warning colours when they fly or display. Sandgrouse fly very long distances to drink at a regular time of day; the males also wet their absorbent belly feathers and transport water to cool their chicks and quench their thirst. Birds do not perspire, but pant like dogs to reduce body temperatures; they can ruffle their feathers to take advantage of a cooling breeze. In the heat of the desert day, rather than sitting on their eggs to warm them, they may stand over them to cast a cooling shade.

The breeding seasons of desert animals are related to the short spells of rain and the consequent sudden emergence, flowering and seeding of plants, rather than to the calendar. Rodents hibernate through the long winter and also store food in their burrows, but gazelles roam widely, with no home territory, and go wherever the vegetation happens to be in good condition at the time. Even though the grazing varies from place to place and from year to year, depending on the unpredictable rains, the gazelles are thus able to maintain a stable population. In contrast, rodents, which have a small territory and have to make do with the vegetation of that area, decrease in numbers in bad years. When it rains their numbers boom; when it is dry populations decline through higher mortality and a reduced birth rate. However, they rarely drink and can survive on the little moisture contained in the plants that they eat, and in times of extreme drought their metabolism

BELOW: the Ring-tailed Gecko (*Cyrtodactylus louisiadensis*) is a nocturnal desert reptile. It has no eyelids: at night there is little wind to blow sand in its eyes. OPPOSITE: wild populations of Bactrian Camels (*Camelus bactrianus*) of remote desert areas have not been seen for many years. They are the epitome of desert-adapted mammals.

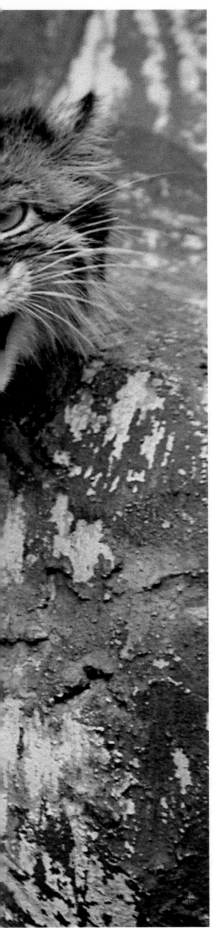

changes to reduce their moisture needs still further.

The desert is such a demanding environment that the mammal adaptations there are among the most remarkable on earth. It is a testament to the vitality of the living world that life has evolved there at all.

Mammals

China's desert mammals include two beautiful small carnivores, the Chinese Desert Cat (*Felis bieti*) and Pallas's Cat (*F. manul*). The former is an endemic species and manages to survive in the burning hot summers, freezing winters and dry winds which make one of the most difficult environments for any cat in the world. Both species look like domesticated cats with a fur of sandy brown; the Chinese Desert Cat is sandy yellow, with quite red ears which are set more closely together than those of Pallas's Cat, which are very short and rounded, and set widely apart on either side of the head.

Pallas's Cat is well adapted to very cold weather, being thick coated, with a short nose and very short legs almost hidden in long fur. Shorter fur on the back allows the heat of the sun to penetrate to the skin, while the fur on the underside is longer to give insulation against cold ground and snow. This rare animal hunts the high plateaux, where vegetation is sparse, looking for small mammals, but often makes its home in desert grassland and stony desert, and sometimes can be seen in forests. It makes its lair in cracks of rocks or in the abandoned holes of Bobak Marmots (*Marmota bobak*), and lives singly, the young being raised by the female on her own. She gives birth to kittens from April to early May, three to four at a time.

The most interesting mammal of the deserts and semi-deserts is the two-humped Bactrian Camel (*Camelus bactrianus*). Although it is the ancestor of Asia's domesticated camel, wild populations used to be found in some parts of Xinjiang, Gansu and Qinghai, taking the leaves of saxauls (*Haloxylon*), tamarisks (*Tamarix*), Yellow-flowered Onion (*Allium chrysantum*), *Populus diversifolia* and other trees and bushes as food. Their current existence is disputed. They can live for a month without water and in autumn and winter used to migrate to valleys where food and water were plentiful, and where they gathered in large groups of about 30 animals. Sexual maturity comes at the age of four to five and the gestation period is very long, about 13 months. Bactrian Camels have a lifespan of 30 to 50 years.

Two gazelles, Przewalski's Gazelle (*Procapra przewalskii*) and the Goitred Gazelle (*Gazella subgutturosa*), inhabit desert areas. They are small hoofed mammals, widely distributed in the north-western area. They usually live in low, relatively flat regions on the plains, in low hills and in stony desert and gather in groups of ten to several hundred animals, leading a nomadic existence in search of food. They eat tender leaves and shoots of desert plants. In recent years their numbers have declined due to both hunting and the deterioration of the grasslands.

The dominant mammals in deserts are rodents, with a large number of species and a wide distribution. The predominant ones are jerboas and gerbils. China's jerboas include no fewer than 11 species, such as the Northern Three-toed Jerboa (*Dipus sagitta*), Mongolian Five-toed Jerboa (*Allactaga sibirica*), Thick-tailed Three-toed Jerboa (*Stylodipus telum*) and the Long-eared Jerboa (*Euchoreutes naso*). Their hind legs are twice to four times as long as the front ones and they jump forwards in powerful bounds. They have a well camouflaged, sandy yellow coloured back, with a white belly and a long, whip-like tail. They movement of the tail aids balance when they

Pallas's Cat (*Felis manul*) is a rare and beautiful predator of high plateaux, adapted to very cold conditions. The fur on its legs and underside is long to protect it from the snow, while on the back it is shorter to take advantage of the sun's heat. It lives in rock hollows or in the abandoned burrows of marmots.

ABOVE: the Clawed Jird (*Meriones unguiculatus*) is one of the most common desert gerbils.

jump. They are active at night, when they forage for plants and insects. Jerboas are unpopular with man in the semi-desert steppe as they destroy the grass and any crops and seedlings planted in oases, and they are also carriers of plague.

Seven or eight species of gerbils live in the deserts. The most common are the Clawed Jird or Mongolian Gerbil (*Meriones unguiculatus*), which has black claws, Midday Gerbil (*M. meridianus*), which has yellow claws, and the Great Gerbil (*Rhombomys opimus*), which is markedly larger than the others. Cheng's Gerbil (*M. chengi*), found only in the Turfan Depression of Xinjiang, was discovered by the biologist after whom it is named as recently as 1964. Gerbils have sandy backs and white bellies. Their burrows, which they dig near bushes, are complex affairs with many exits and a network of passages. Individual chambers are assigned specific functions such as storeroom or latrine. They breed very rapidly, two to three times a year with six to nine babies in a litter. They do not hibernate in winter, but often migrate from their feeding ground to a wintering place a short distance away.

Birds

Large birds are seldom seen in deserts and semi-deserts, as there is insufficient food for them. The Long-legged Buzzard (*Buteo rufinus*) and Booted Eagle (*Hieraaetus pennatus*) are the only birds of prey seen with any frequency. They move about alone or in pairs, hunting rabbits and rodents.

The European or Blue Roller (*Coracias garrulus*) is a much more common desert bird and is also the most beautiful, with its brilliant plumage of chestnut, blue and turquoise. There are a few telephone cables across the deserts and European Rollers can often be seen perching on them looking for a chance to catch insects.

There are three species of sandgrouse (Pteroclidae) in China, including Pallas's Sandgrouse (*Syrrhaptes paradoxus*), the Tibetan Sandgrouse (*S. tibeta-*

nus) and the Black-bellied Sandgrouse (*Pterocles orientalis*). They do not breed only in deserts, but cover vast areas, ranging from desert to grassland, and each species has very specific requirements. Their nests are simple hollows scooped out of the ground in which they lay three or four eggs per clutch. The males of all species except the Tibetan Sandgrouse bring back water to their chicks from afar by immersing themselves in it and then carrying it back in their specially absorbent belly feathers. Sandgrouse can be seen in autumn gathering in large groups, hundreds or thousands strong, in preparation for migration south. Their routes are irregular, being determined by the prevailing climatic conditions.

Three species of ground jays are found in China: Henderson's Ground Jay (*Podoces hendersoni*), Biddulph's Ground Jay (*P. biddulphi*) and Hume's Ground Jay (*Pseudopodoces humilis*). They feed on ground insects and lizards or seek seeds and fruits. When disturbed they fly close to the ground for a short distance, but are otherwise terrestrial birds, except they build their nests low down in trees.

Both the Isabelline Wheatear (*Oenanthe isabellina*) and the Desert Wheatear (*O. deserti*) are representatives of the thrushes and chats (subfamily Turdinae) in deserts and semi-deserts; they are also common in the stony deserts. They nest in the abandoned burrows of marmots or ground squirrels or in branches of burrows still in use. Among the shrike family (Laniidae), the Isabelline Shrike (*Lanius isabellinus*) and Great Grey Shrike (*L. excubitor*) are common.

Larks (family Alaudidae) are very well adapted to the desert, having the widest distribution of the desert birds and species specific to arid areas. The dominant species are the Short-toed Lark (*Calandrella brachydactyla*), Hume's Short-toed Lark (*C. acutirostris*), the Lesser Short-toed Lark (*C. rufescens*), the Crested Lark (*Galerida cristata*) and the Skylark (*Alauda arvensis*).

BELOW: Henderson's Ground Jay (*Podoces hendersoni*) breeds in semi-desert in Qinghai and Xinjiang.
BOTTOM: Pallas's Sandgrouse (*Syrrhaptes paradoxus*) breeds in the deserts of the Inner Mongolian Autonomous Region. Occasionally the population becomes so large that the species 'erupts' and spreads westwards to Europe. One such eruption even led to nesting in Britain.

Reptiles and insects

Reptiles, as a group, are better suited to desert conditions than mammals. They have evolved a variety of different biological adaptations in response to the arid environment.

Only one representative species of tortoise (family Testudinata), Horsfield's Tortoise (*Testudo horsfieldi*), lives in China's deserts, in the north-western part of Xinjiang. Its front limbs each have four claws, unlike those of the other two species of tortoises in China, which have five claws. The desert vegetation which Horsfield's Tortoise feeds on also supplies its chief source of moisture; in summer the shortage of water may force it to hibernate underground. Horsfield's Tortoises lay two to four eggs at a time in a small, shallow hole, and there may be three clutches in a season. They may not reach sexual maturity until ten to 20 years old.

The most common desert and semi-desert reptiles are lizards, the main kinds in China being species of the genera *Phrynocephalus* and *Agama* of the family Agamidae and of the genus *Eremias* of the family Lacertidae. Ten species of toad-headed agamid lizards (*Phrynocephalus*) live in the deserts; they are *P. mystaceus* in the north-western part of Xinjiang, *P. helioscopus*, *P. grumgrizimaloi*, *P. forsythi*, *P. axillaris* and *P. albolineatus* from Dunhuang to the middle part of Xinjiang, *P. przewalskii* and again *P. forsythi* in the western part of the Yellow (Huang) River Basin and the western part of Inner Mongolia to the Hexi Corridor in Gansu Province, *P. vlangalii* in the Qaidam Basin in Qinghai Province, and, finally, *P. phrynocephalus* and *P. frontalis*. All of them have flat backs with prominent scales. Unlike snakes, they have

An agamid lizard (*Agama*) in Tibet; lizards of this genus are mostly large and strong, with prominent scales.

ABOVE LEFT: Horsfield's Tortoise (*Testudo horsfieldi*) inhabits north-western Xinjiang. It sometimes buries itself underground during the dry summer period.
ABOVE: the Sand Boa (*Eryx miliaris*) is only 50 cm (20 in.) long. Little is known of its habits.

eyelids which close to protect their eyes from the wind and blowing sand, and they can also close their nostrils for the same purpose. Their strong limbs support the body clear of the hot sand and their long tails often curl upward as they run. They emerge from hibernation in early April; their mating season is from May to June and they lay just two to three eggs. When danger threatens they often lie on the sandy surface, shake their bodies rapidly, rake the ground with their back limbs to kick up the sand and shuffle down in it to hide.

A. *stoliczkana* and A. *tarimensis* are two particularly interesting species of agamid lizards and have been seen only in Xinjiang. Their body length can be as much as 30 cm (12 in.) and they have long tails. There are nine species of *Eremias* in China and all of them are found in this habitat, including *E. argus* and *E. velox* in the north-west of Xinjiang and *E. przewalskii* and *E. vermiculata* in Inner Mongolia. They are of small or medium size, with large, symmetrical scales on the top of the head, bead-shaped scales on the back and horizontal, square scales on the belly. Their tails are long and thin and they are predominantly sandy in colour, with darker stripes and spots and a variety of ornamental patterns according to species.

There are some special species of geckos (Gekkoninae) in deserts and semi-deserts, the dominant ones being in the genera *Alsophylax*, *Cyrtodactylus* and *Teratoscincus*. All are small with bead-shaped scales on the head and the back. They have no eyelids and prefer to be active at night when there is usually little wind to blow sand into their eyes. These reptiles live on insects.

Desert snakes include one of the sand boas, *Eryx miliaris*, and the Arrow Snake (*Psammophis lineolatus*), the only representatives of the genera *Eryx* and *Psammophis* in China. *Eryx miliaris* is small, being about 50 cm (20 in.) long, and is light brown with dark horizontal stripes. Not much is known of its habits as it has been little studied. The Arrow Snake, which is also found in semi-deserts, is, as its name suggests, extremely swift; it eats lizards and is an excellent tree climber.

Grasshoppers are the commonest insects in deserts and semi-deserts, living on the sparsely growing grasses. The dominant and endemic species in the southern part of Xinjiang is *Duroniella angustata*, while the dominant species in the northern part of Xinjiang include *Dociostaurus kraussi*, *Ramburilla turcomann*, *Stauroderus scalaris*, *Calliptamus italicus* and the Siberian Grasshopper (*Gomphocerus sibiricus*). The species found in stony deserts is *Bryodema gebleri*. The next most common insects in the deserts, as they can live off most of the desert plants, are the beetles (order coleoptera). China's many endemic species include *Polyphylla schestakovi*, *Melolontha tarimensis*, *Lasiexis duchoni* and *L. kuldzhensis*.

CONSERVATION AND NATURE PROTECTION

自然与环境保护

自
然
与
环
境
保
护

Protecting the environment in a developing country like China, with its vast population, is exceptionally important. It is necessary for the continuing development of agriculture and industrial output, for preserving the beauty of the planet and for the benefit of future generations.

In recent years much effort has been put into nature conservation by the government and the people of China. A series of measures has been taken to protect the environment and improve environmental quality, although clearly it is difficult to put right much of the extensive damage caused by years of misuse. Some of the activities that have been denuding landscapes, deforesting mountains and spreading desertification have been stopped or reversed and there is a greater awareness of the need to protect rare plants and animals before they disappear. Nevertheless, the outstanding problems are huge, and many species, some of which are endemic to China, hover on the brink of extinction.

Conservation problems

The forerunners of the modern Chinese nation first founded an agricultural civilization 5000 years ago. This formed the basis for the development of the nation over its long recorded history and enabled the population to increase, which in turn led to greater cultivation and exploitation of the land. Inevitably, the point had to come where the load placed on the land by the dramatic increase of the population would create considerable problems of nature conservation. Careless exploitation of China's natural resources and the devastations of the wars of the first half of this century considerably exacerbated these problems. The main problems China faces are those of soil erosion, desertification, deforestation and pollution, which in turn contribute to a decline in the numbers and variety of wildlife species.

Soil erosion and water loss

About a sixth of China, or 1.53 million square kilometres (590,000 square miles), faces problems of soil erosion. The amount of soil washed away by water annually reaches about 50 billion tonnes, which is equivalent to a centimetre (⁶⁄₁₆ in.) of soil from over the whole of the country's cultivated land. The situation is especially serious on the Loess Plateau, where 80 per cent of the total area is subjected to soil erosion due to the nature of the landscape and the climate. The land has been folded by tectonic movements, and the landforms are characterized by steep slopes and deep valleys. Rainfall is variable from year to year and periods of heavy rain sweep away the porous, silty, friable loess soil, which is easily broken down. Loess has well-developed vertical cracks, known as jointing, and a weak resistance to erosion, having been formed by loose, wind-blown particles settling around plant stems. Furthermore, the careless and ill-considered use of land and the clearance of natural vegetation – such as destruction of forests to increase areas of open land for growing crops, reclamation on steep slopes and over-utilization of the woods and grasses as fuels – all leave the fragile soils exposed to the action of wind and water, and are frequently the direct causes of serious erosion.

Land degradation and desertification

In the arid and semi-arid regions of northern China, there are several provinces or autonomous regions influenced by desertification – the gradual desiccation of the environment, loss of vegetation and therefore loss of humus in the soil, and a change to a looser, sandier soil structure, and ever more arid conditions. Of a total area of 3 million square kilometres (1.2 million square miles) of grassland, some 500,000 square kilometres (200,000

PREVIOUS PAGE: one of the many lakes in Jiuzhaigou Nature Reserve in Sichuan Province. Jiuzhaigou was the first reserve set up to preserve outstanding scenery rather than specific animals or plants.

ABOVE: desertification is a major problem in those areas of northern and north-western China that already suffer from a dry climate. This lake in Xinjiang was once abundantly supplied by the Peacock River, but the fall in the water flow means that it is now shrinking, and the lack of ground water is evident from the sparseness of the poplar *Populus diversifolia*.

LEFT: a change in a river course has destroyed the oasis in Xinjiang completely.

square miles) have been degraded. Even today, despite identification of the problem and moves to arrest it, the area of desertification is still increasing at the rate of 6660 square kilometres (2570 square miles) per year. Most of this has been caused by reclamation, overgrazing and the destruction of vegetation for use as fuel. Due to the degradation of the grassland, the grasses become low and sparse, the biological productivity is reduced and the quality of the grasses deteriorates. All these have adverse effects on the livestock, and dramatic effects on wildlife; the beautiful balance of the grassland has to some extent been destroyed.

The ground water beneath the plains of northern China is comparatively high in salt and in places where the irrigation has not been properly carried out to allow for this, salinization of the soil has occurred. On the other hand, in some places in the north-eastern and southern regions, the soil has become waterlogged and the crops are starved of oxygen, which is another cause of reduction of land quality.

Deforestation

A large part of China was once covered in forests, and this is reflected in the great variety of tree species that still exist in the country. However, the forest cover has been contracting constantly through recorded history, and it now accounts for only 13 per cent of the total area of China. Moreover, the distribution of the forest is uneven, and most of the remaining woodland is now found in mountainous regions. The destruction of forests to create agricultural land, forest fires, plant disease and insect pests are all causes of the reduction of forest coverage, but the first factor, related so directly to population growth, has long been the major one.

Pollution

Environmental pollution is primarily a result of the improper discharge of waste water, waste gas and industrial residues and the noise, vibration and smoke from industrial centres. Excessive use of chemical fertilizers and pesticides in agricultural areas also contributes to the pollution of the environment. China's main fuel is coal, and this also creates air pollution and acid rain; the latter is especially a problem in the south, where there is higher natural acidity in some areas.

Declining wildlife

In China all the factors already mentioned – desertification, loss of forest cover, soil erosion, pollution from agriculture and industry and the steady drainage of wetlands in the search for more fertile arable land – disturbed the natural environment of the wild animals and plants. Lakes, rivers and marshes are, in themselves, rich in wildlife and also have great influence on the animals, plants and climatic conditions of their surroundings. The drainage of a swamp or lake produces flat and, for a time, fertile ground which can help to feed the growing population, but has a hugely adverse effect on all wildlife.

In addition, China had a culture in which the collection of plants, the trapping of birds for the caged bird trade, and the hunting of birds and animals were popular and, in many areas, excessive. Animal skins, including those of protected species such as tigers, leopards and even pandas, were traded daily in the market in Jiangxi Province as recently as 1987. Nevertheless, the earliest decree in China to protect birds was as long ago as 63 BC, when Emperor Xuan Di of the Han Dynasty issued an edict outlawing the killing of birds and the destruction of their eggs.

All these activities have contributed to a decline in the numbers of animals and plants and a contraction in their ranges, with the result that a disturbing number have been reduced to the level of endangered species. For example, Père David's Deer (*Elaphurus davidianus*), a large, impressive animal whose numbers dwindled to nil, has had to be reintroduced from captive stocks in Europe. The huge, ox-like Gaur (*Bos gaurus*) has become practically extinct because of hunting and the disappearance of forests. The loss of forest in the eastern monsoon regions has also accounted for the decline of the Giant Panda (*Ailuropoda melanoleuca*), which has become a symbol of the fight to preserve endangered species worldwide, the Rhesus Macaque (*Macaca mulatta*), the Golden Monkey (*Pygathrix roxellanae*), the Sika Deer (*Cervus nippon*) and the Chinese Water Deer (*Hydropotes inermis*). In the north-western arid region and the Qinghai-Tibet Plateau, the Mongolian Gazelle (*Procapra gutturosa*), Asiatic Wild Ass (*Equus hemionus*), Bactrian Camel

(*Camelus bactrianus*) and Siberian Musk Deer (*Moschus moschiferus*) have been hunted in large numbers, and these animals have sadly decreased to near extinction. Some precious and rare plants, such as Cathay Silver Fir (*Cathaya argyrophylla*), Dove Tree (*Davidia involucrata*), Chinese Parashorea (*Parashorea chinensis*), Chinese Rhoiptelea (*Rhoiptelea chiliantha*), a primitive relative of the walnuts and hickories, *Camellia chrysantha*, Beshanzu Fir (*Abies beshanzuensis*), Puto Hornbeam (*Carpinus putoensis*), hopeas (*Hopea* spp.), which are lofty trees of rainforests, and Common Mesua (*Mesua ferrea*), which produces valuable drugs and cosmetics, have been destroyed to a greater or lesser degree by the onslaught against the forests.

The Asiatic Wild Ass (*Equus hemionus*) was once abundant on the desert steppe of Asia but is now only found in the wild in China in the Kalamaili Mountains Nature Reserve in Xinjiang.

Conservation measures

A series of conservation measures has been instigated, aimed at preventing further degradation and contamination of the natural environment and protecting the rare species of plants and animals.

Environmental legislation

The Constitution of the People's Republic of China, which was promulgated in 1982, stipulates that the nation protects and improves the living environment and the ecosystem, prevents pollution and other calamities to the public, guarantees the proper utilization of natural resources and protects precious animals and plants. With this, the basis for the future development of nature protection was formed. In the Law of Environmental Protection (implemented for a trial period), concrete regulations for the protection of various types of natural environment were set down and nature protection organizations have been established at both national and local levels. In order

to co-ordinate the proper exploitation of natural resources and the protection of the natural environment with the modernization of industry and agriculture, a series of laws and regulations has been drawn up.

These important proposals include The Law for Forests of the People's Republic of China, The Law for Protection of the Oceanic Environment of the People's Republic of China and similar laws for prevention of water pollution, the protection of precious, rare and endangered wild plants, the management of national nature reserves, the prevention of atmospheric pollution and several other regulations. Moreover, there are some additional provincial regulations for conservation. With these laws and regulations, enforced by practical management and supervisory work, nature conservation has at last been given priority, and a framework for long-term progress has been created. Some measures are already taking effect, although pollution remains a long-term problem.

Land management

Since 1949, a great deal of work has been done in the land management sphere, including the construction of hydrological projects, afforestation and the protection of grassland. The area of irrigated agricultural land has now reached 440,000 square kilometres (170,000 square miles) which accounts for one third of the total cultivated area. Some 33,000 square kilometres (12,750 square miles) of salt-affected ground has been brought back into cultivation. Rivers like the Hai, that used to flood regularly, have been dammed to prevent this and to store water for irrigation, but the consequent loss of seasonal floods may have reduced many wetland species. Forests have been planted to provide windbreaks to improve the ecosystems of semi-desert areas. On the Loess Plateau, various measures for controlling soil erosion and water loss have been carried out. According to the needs of different conditions, the proportions of cultivation, animal husbandry and forestry have been adjusted to give the most efficient land use system. The cultivation of steep slopes, which was difficult, inefficient and liable to lead to soil erosion, has been replaced by afforestation. Improved farming methods elsewhere have compensated for the loss of production. Other slopes have been terraced to reduce erosion and dams and irrigation canals have been constructed so as to manage the flow of water. Although the main purpose of these particular measures is to improve the land for human use, the numbers of some small animals and birds have increased because the habitats have improved for them.

In the semi-arid and arid areas of northern China, the efficient use of land, based on a proper understanding of the environment, is vital in order to prevent the degradation of the grassland. Protection of the natural vegetation and the avoidance of overgrazing is also important. On land already damaged, trees, bushes and grasses with strong resistance to the severe natural conditions are grown on semi-mobile dunes to stabilize the sandy surface. Moreover, shelter belts and extensive pastures have been established to increase the vegetation cover, to reduce the effects of the constant wind and to relieve the pressure of grazing on the natural vegetation.

On the largest plain of China, the North China Plain, the reclamation of saline soil has been carried out successfully. Some areas of soil damaged by salt have been turned into cotton, fruit or other suitable crop fields.

Much effort has been expended on afforestation. Since 1949, the total area afforested has been 310,000 square kilometres (120,000 square miles). Forests that are cut down for commercial uses are being replanted, belatedly

Bayanbulak Nature Reserve in the Tien Mountains in Xinjiang is famous for its swans. It is the largest breeding centre in China for the Whooper Swan (*Cygnus cygnus*); other species of swans are also to be found here.

introducing a simple system of forest management into Chinese forestry policy. In order to reduce desertification in the northern part of China, in 1978 the State Council approved the planting of a huge belt of almost continuous shelter forest from Bin County in Heilongjiang Province to Uzbel Pass in the Xinjiang Autonomous Region, over a length of 7000 kilometres (4350 miles). This has proved to be a great success, protecting large areas of agricultural fields, reducing soil erosion and preventing desertification to some degree.

Environmental protection

In an effort to reduce or, where possible, prevent environmental pollution, research has been carried out to reform China's industrial technology. Environmental pollution and destruction in China are closely related to the inefficient use of resources and energy, so industries are therefore encouraged to adopt advanced techniques and equipment, to reduce the drain on natural resources and energy, to seek raw materials from other types of factory that might produce them as waste by-products, and to treat wastes properly before disposal. Pollution caused by the burning of coal is being tackled on a pilot scale by encouraging factories to fit converters into their chimneys, by treating the coal to remove or fix sulphur before it is burnt, and by an increase in the use of gas.

Experimental agricultural units are being developed to obtain the best possible results with the least damage to the environment. Agricultural production is more closely tailored to the environmental conditions, and natural resources are properly used in a sustainable system. Better agricultural management, the treatment of soils to increase fertility and reduce erosion and new ways of producing energy are all involved. Solar power and the use of methane from refuse tips and composted vegetation are widely exploited. Liumin Ying village, in the suburbs of Beijing, has achieved outstanding success in these areas, and in future the use of renewable energy sources must replace exploitation of fossil fuels to an increasing extent.

In any country with such a large population, the protection of crops is bound to be a priority, and that in turn leads to the use of pesticides. However, pesticides stay in the ecosystem, so attempts are being made in various regions to exploit the pests' natural enemies. Biological methods have been applied in place of pesticides in a total area which increased from 33,000 square kilometres (12,750 square miles) in 1976 to 167,000 square kilometres (64,500 square miles) in 1984. Furthermore, the national government decided to stop production of two pesticides, DDT and BHC (benzene hexachloride), in 1983. The need to assess the quality of pesticides, their persistence in the environment and safe methods of use have been given greater prominence in the drive to achieve higher production with less environmental damage.

Since the promulgation of the Environmental Protection Law of China, enterprises, institutions and factories that cause pollution to the environment are no longer allowed to be built in residential areas of cities and towns, in reservoir catchment areas, designated scenic spots, historical sites and areas of beautiful landscape, or within nature reserves. Those that have already been sited there are to be brought under strict control, and their emissions reduced, or moved to less sensitive areas. On the basis of this and the other principles, factories are no longer constructed in the upper reaches of water catchments or windward of a city, or in other environmentally unsound locations. These legal controls on industrial development give some hope for a future free of the worst pollutions of past decades.

Comprehensive programmes to prevent pollution have been developed for various regions. Environmental standards and permitted capacities for both water and air have been established step by step and these fixed limits serve

The Dadaeishui waterfall in Yunnan Province. China has abundant supplies of water in the monsoon regions of the southeast, but the demands of industry have made river pollution a problem.

as the basis for environmental quality evaluation and environmental impact assessment. A network of more than 4000 monitoring institutions at various levels has been established to record the levels of pollutants in the atmosphere and to check if the permitted emission levels are exceeded. Environmental management has been strengthened so that problems can be solved at both national and local levels and long-term programmes can be drawn up.

Protection of rare species

Various lists of precious, rare and endangered species have been compiled, in an attempt to protect biological resources and save endangered species. The first such list of plants was published in 1984 and included 354 species; 206 wildlife species have been specially protected since 1987. It is illegal to kill or destroy any species on the lists.

Besides the establishment of various types of nature reserves, several species have been helped by introductions and captive breeding programmes. In 1980, the Ministry of Forestry and the World Wide Fund for Nature co-operated to establish the Research Centre for Giant Pandas in Wolong Nature Reserve. In 1983, large areas of fountain bamboo (*Sinarundinaria*) blossomed and died. This cycle is typical of bamboos, but the restricted area of bamboo groves which survived meant that many pandas died. This posed a serious danger to the Giant Panda, and a series of measures was taken to try to save them. By 1986, 64 Giant Pandas had been taken into captivity, and 46 of them were saved. The zoos in Beijing and in Chengdu have succeeded in breeding Giant Pandas, using artificial insemination. However, no attempt has yet been made to introduce them into the wild. In 1985, a breeding centre for Giant Pandas was established in the nature reserve at Baishui River.

Père David's Deer (*Elaphurus davidianus*) is an endemic Chinese species which declined to the point that only a few were left at the end of the nineteenth century. These were taken to the grounds of Woburn Abbey in England, where a herd was successfully established. In recent years, deer have been sent back to China from Britain.

The Chinese River Dolphin (*Lipotes vexillifer*) is recognized as a symbol of the health of the aquatic environment. Only about 200 of them survive. In 1987, a breeding centre was established in Tongling County, Anhui Province, and at the same time, a reserve area was defined in the middle and lower reaches of the Yangtze (Chang) River. Captive breeding programmes are planned at the Institute of Aquatic Organisms at Wuhan and artificial insemination experiments are currently under way. Although the wild populations are still at a critically low level, there is now hope that this rare and endemic species can survive.

In 1986, a captive breeding centre for the Blue Eared-Pheasant (*Crossoptilon auritum*) was set up in Zhangye Prefecture, Gansu Province. The breeding of the Black-necked Crane (*Grus nigricollis*) and the beautiful Snow Leopard (*Felis uncia*) has proved possible in the zoo at Xining city, Qinghai Province. Nevertheless, there is still a very long way to go before their survival in the wild is secure.

There are 1186 species of birds in China, no less than 13.5 per cent of the total in the world. Since 1982, more than 20 provinces, autonomous regions and municipalities have taken part in the special activities of 'Bird Week' and 'Bird Month' which aim to increase public awareness of the importance of wild birds. Many schools have begun nest box schemes in their grounds. There has already been a measure of success in bird conservation. Nature reserves, mainly for protecting cranes, have been increased to 18, with an area of 5542 square kilometres (2140 square miles). In the famous bird reserve at Poyang Lake, Jiangxi Province, and in the Yancheng tidal nature reserve in

The Asiatic Elephant (*Elephas maximus*) used to be widespread in southern China, but is now found only in small numbers in Xishuangbanna Nature Reserve in Yunnan Province and in zoos.

Jiangsu Province, thousands of Siberian White Cranes (*Grus leucogeranus*), 500 to 600 Japanese Cranes (*Grus japonensis*) and other rare birds spend the winter, now relatively safe from human persecution, although they still face destruction in summer and on their long migrations. In Yancheng Nature Reserve and in Zhalong Nature Reserve of Heilongjiang Province, breeding centres for cranes have been established. The cranes breed in open enclosures, which are visited by extra birds in winter, but some of the young cranes reared in the reserve tend to remain all year, instead of migrating north.

In some provinces, a series of measures has been taken to protect rare plants. For example, in Fangcheng, Guangxi Autonomous Region, a reserve for *Camellia chrysantha* has been established and attempts at introducing and propagating fine varieties have been successful. In Chishi, Guizhou Province, a nature reserve for *Cyathea spinulosa* has been established. In the nature reserve at Baokang, Hubei Province, the Wintersweet (*Chimonanthus*) has been successfully introduced and cultivated. At many Chinese reserves such as these, not only is the habitat managed, but wildlife species are themselves artificially bred and released in a way that is not familiar in nature reserves in the west, and once released they do not fully adapt to the wild. Animals on the reserves are partially domesticated.

In recent years, quite a number of botanical gardens and forestry centres have carried out the propagation of rare and precious plants. For example, in Hangzhou botanical gardens 56 rare and endangered plants have been introduced and, among these, 48 species have been reintroduced to the wild. The Plant Research Institute in southern China, located in Guangzhou, has grown 90 species of plants of the magnolia family (Magnoliaceae), which accounts for 70 per cent of the total number of species. This institute and others have created gene pools, and they store a wide variety of species selected from their native regions.

BELOW: Whistling Swans (*Cygnus columbianus*) on the lake of Bayanbulak Nature Reserve in Xinjiang.
BELOW RIGHT: *Auricularia auricula-judae*, the Jew's Ear fungus, growing in Linzhi Nature Reserve.

Nature reserves

The increase of nature reserves has been rapid in recent years. There were about 70 in 1980; by 1987 there were 468, covering a total of 237,497 square kilometres (91,700 square miles), 2.47 per cent of the total area of China. There are 31 national reserves, another 300 at provincial level, 21 are municipal reserves and 116 are administered by counties. Their management is improving and important contributions to conservation have been made by many of them. Public access is strictly limited in these reserves, and the use of land for farming or commercial purposes is banned or restricted. The reserves at the Changbai Mountains, Wolong, Dinghu Mountain, Xilin Gol, Fanjing Mountain and Wuyi Mountain have participated in the United Nations network of reserves under the 'Man and Biosphere' programmes.

The nature reserves can be classified into six types according to their aims and objectives. Firstly, there are nature reserves aimed at protecting the overall natural ecosystem which are intended to keep whole environments intact. The main ones are in the Changbai Mountains, for protecting the mountain ecosystem and natural landscape in the temperate zone; at Taibai Mountain, for preserving the typical warm-temperate ecosystem; and at Xishuangbanna in Yunnan Province, for protecting the tropical environment and its wildlife.

Secondly, nature reserves for protecting rare animals have been established with much narrower aims, with particular species in mind. Besides the famous Zhalong and Wolong reserves which will be described in detail, there are the Xianghai and Momoge nature reserves in Jilin Province, mainly for the protection of Japanese Cranes, Wanglang Nature Reserve in Sichuan Province for the protection of Giant Pandas (*Ailuropoda melanoleuca*), and Tiebu Nature Reserve in Sichuan Province for the protection of the Sika Deer (*Cervus nippon*).

Other nature reserves are specifically for the protection of rare, precious and relict plants or special types of vegetation. Examples of this type are the Huaping Nature Reserve in Guangxi, where the subtropical forests are dominated by Cathay Silver Fir (*Cathaya argyrophylla*); the Fenglin and Liangshui nature reserves in Heilongjiang Province, for protecting the primeval forests of Korean Pine (*Pinus koraiensis*); and splendid nature

BELOW: Tibet has large numbers of endemic species of mountain plants, several of them rare, but many now widely cultivated in other parts of the world. These azaleas are in the Yigong Nature Reserve.

BOTTOM: Jiuzhaigou is one of the most beautiful spots in China, with its combination of mountains, rivers and lush warm-temperate vegetation.

The geology of the entire Himalayas is worth a huge reserve just to itself. This forbidding glacier is in the Bomi Nature Reserve in Tibet.

reserves at Dongdai Mountain, Changeen Mountain and Shoulu Mountain of Gansu Province, mainly created for protecting the forests of Thickleaf Spruce (*Picea crassifolia*).

Fourthly, there is also a rather different category of nature reserves established to protect natural scenery and national gardens. Some of them may have only marginal value for wildlife. Examples of this category are Xianren Cave and Fenghuang Mountain nature reserves in Liaoning Province, the Lu Mountain Nature Reserve in Jiangxi Province and Yu Mountain in Taiwan Province.

Special geological profiles and noteworthy landforms are also catered for in reserves. The Wudailianchi reserve in Heilongjiang Province protects volcanic landscape. The Dailuge reserve in Taiwan Province has a wonderful series of marble gorges, and Shanwang Wnajuan reserve in Shandong Province is important for its extraordinary range of fossils.

Finally, coastal nature reserves include the tidal zones of Dongzhai and Qinglan harbours on Hainan Dao Island for the protection of mangroves, and others at the mouth of the Danshui River and on the shores of Lanyang and Suhui in Taiwan Province.

These broad categories, which lay down the criteria for selection, are not, of course, necessarily exclusive and there are a number of reserves which combine several functions.

Changbai

This nature reserve is typical of the mountain ecosystem of northern Eurasia. An area of primeval forest surrounding the Tianchi (Heaven) Lake at the top of the Changbai Mountains is a humid-temperate woodland preserved in a perfectly natural state, complete with its typical bird and plant life. The reserve covers 1898 square kilometres (733 square miles) and the flora is wonderfully varied. There are ancient, relict species such as Korean Pine (*Pinus koraiensis*), Amur Cork Tree (*Phellodendron amurense*), Manchurian Ash (*Fraxinus mandschurica*) and Manchurian Walnut (*Juglans mandschurica*). Rare and endangered species include Manchurian Fir (*Abies holophylla*), Khingan Fir (*Abies nephrolepis*), Korean Spruce (*Picea pumila*), Little-beaked Leontice (*Leontice microrryncha*) and Chinese Magnolia Vine (*Schisandra chinensis*).

In this mountainous, dense forest, there are more than 300 species of wild animals. Among these, the main species which require protection include the magnificent Tiger (*Panthera tigris*), Sika Deer (*Cervus nippon*), Lynx (*Felis lynx*), Leopard (*Panthera pardus*), Siberian Musk Deer (*Moschus moschiferus*), Sable (*Martes zibellina*), Goral (*Nemorhaedus goral*) and Eurasian Badger (*Meles meles*). There are over 200 species of birds in this area. The Red-rumped Swallow (*Hirundo daurica*) and Great Tit (*Parus major*) are among the ones that can be most frequently seen.

Wuyi

This reserve is situated in the highest section of Wuyi Mountain in Fujian Province in south-east China where the average elevation is about 1200 metres (4000 ft) and the height of the highest peak is 2158 metres (7080 ft), forming a natural barrier which blocks the cold northern airstream in winter. In summer, because of the warm, humid, easterly winds from the sea, the reserve has abundant rainfall. The average annual precipitation is about 2000 mm (80 in.) and the annual average temperature is 13 to 14°C (55 to 57°F). The landscape here is a spectacular and varied one, characterized by towering mountains, deep valleys and basins, with a great range in altitude which allows a similarly wide range of habitats and species. It is an exceptionally rich area biologically, because of this extraordinary diversity within a relatively small space. Many new species have been discovered within its boundaries, especially at Guadun and Daizhulan.

There are more than 1800 species of angiosperms in the reserve, and the plant communities are many and varied. Subtropical evergreen broad-leaved forest is the most stable and widely distributed vegetation. Dominant species within this forest include species of beech (Fagaceae), which are common in the temperate zone, and laurels (Lauraceae), species of the tea family (Theaceae), magnolias (Magnoliaceae) and the silverbell and snowbell trees (Styracaceae) which are widely distributed in the subtropical zone. The ancient 'living fossil', Maidenhair Tree or ginkgo *Ginkgo biloba* also grows in this area. This is a remarkable tree. Fossil evidence shows that it has survived unchanged for around 200 million years, giving it a truly ancient pedigree, unmatched by almost any other living organism. The species was once common worldwide, but declined before the ice ages and eventually retreated to its present relict stronghold in China. Whether it still exists in a truly wild state is questionable, but it has long been planted by the Chinese as an ornamental tree. Its Chinese name, *Yin-Xing*, means 'silver fruit'.

There are many economically valuable plants here; for example, the fruits and leaves of most species in the laurel family can be used to extract aromatic oil; most plants of the magnolia family are of ornamental value, and their petals can be used to produce perfume for cosmetics. Phoebe (*Phoebe*) and Hupeh Rosewood (*Dalbergia hupeana*) make good timber, although none of the trees that grow in the reserve is used commercially. Rare species include Shining-leaf Beech (*Fagus lucida*), Chinese Yew (*Taxus chinensis*), the ever-green relative of the magnolia, Manglietia (*Manglietia fordiana*), and the

TOP: the sun sets over the mangrove swamps in Hainan Dao Island. Mangrove fruit drops into the water and takes root in the muddy margin.
ABOVE: the high mountain reserve of Wuyi.

201

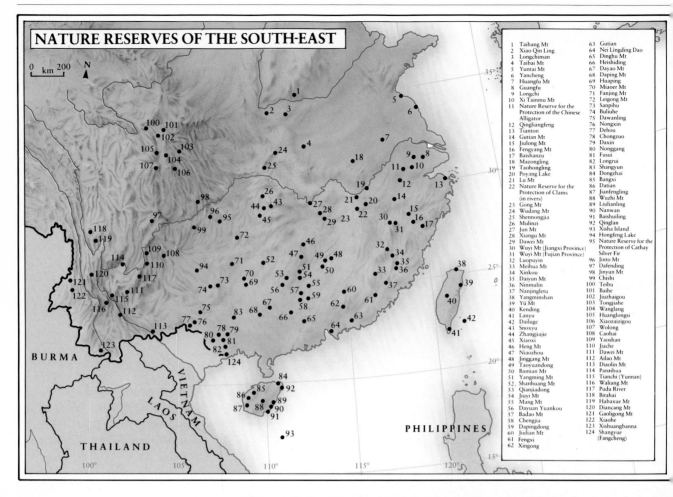

NATURE RESERVES OF THE SOUTH-EAST

1	Taihang Mt	63	Gutian
2	Xiao Qin Ling	64	Nei Lingding Dao
3	Longchiman	65	Dinghu Mt
4	Taibai Mt	66	Heishiding
5	Yuntai Mt	67	Dayao Mt
6	Yancheng	68	Daping Mt
7	Huangfu Mt	69	Huaping
8	Guangfu	70	Miaoer Mt
9	Longchi	71	Fanjing Mt
10	Xi Tainmu Mt	72	Leigong Mt
11	Nature Reserve for the	73	Sanpihu
	Protection of the Chinese	74	Buliuhe
	Alligator	75	Dawanling
12	Qingliangfeng	76	Nongxin
13	Tianton	77	Dehou
14	Gutian Mt	78	Chongzuo
15	Jiulong Mt	79	Daxin
16	Fengyang Mt	80	Nonggang
17	Baishanzu	81	Fusui
18	Mazongling	82	Longrui
19	Taohongling	83	Shangyun
20	Poyang Lake	84	Dongzhai
21	Lu Mt	85	Bangxi
22	Nature Reserve for the	86	Datian
	Protection of Clams	87	Jianfengling
	(in rivers)	88	Wuzhi Mt
23	Gong Mt	89	Liulianling
24	Wudang Mt	90	Nanwan
25	Shennongjia	91	Baishuiling
26	Mulinzi	92	Qinglan
27	Jun Mt	93	Xisha Island
28	Xiangu Mt	94	Hongfeng Lake
29	Dawei Mt	95	Nature Reserve for the
30	Wuyi Mt (Jiangxi Province)		Protection of Cathay
31	Wuyi Mt (Fujian Province)		Silver Fir
32	Luopuyin	96	Jinto Mt
33	Meihua Mt	97	Dafending
34	Xinkou	98	Jinyun Mt
35	Daiyun Mt	99	Chishi
36	Ninmulin	100	Teibu
37	Nanjingletu	101	Baihe
38	Yangminshan	102	Jiuzhaigou
39	Yü Mt	103	Tongjiahe
40	Kending	104	Wanglang
41	Lanyu	105	Huanglongsi
42	Dailuge	106	Xiaozaizigou
43	Snoxyu	107	Wolong
44	Zhangjiajie	108	Caohai
45	Xiaoxi	109	Yaoshan
46	Heng Mt	110	Jiache
47	Niaozhou	111	Dawei Mt
48	Jinggang Mt	112	Ailao Mt
49	Taoyuandong	113	Diaolin Mt
50	Bamian Mt	114	Panzihua
51	Yangming Mt	115	Tianchi (Yunnan)
52	Shanhuang Mt	116	Waliang Mt
53	Qianjiadong	117	Pudu River
54	Jiuyi Mt	118	Bitahai
55	Mang Mt	119	Habaxue Mt
56	Dayuan Yuankou	120	Diancang Mt
57	Badao Mt	121	Gaoligong Mt
58	Chengjia	122	Xiaohe
59	Dapingdong	123	Xishuangbanna
60	Jiulian Mt	124	Shangyue
61	Fengxi		(Fangcheng)
62	Xingong		

Chinese Cedar (*Cryptomeria fortunei*), making this whole region a very special one. The large number of different forest communities encourages the growth of a wide variety of lower plants.

There are hundreds of species of fungi. Jew's Ear (*Auricularia auricula-judae*) is one such edible, nutritious and delicious fungi. Glossy Ganoderma (*Ganoderma lucidum*), Fuling (*Poria cocos*) and Chinese Caterpillar Fungus (*Cordyceps sinensis*) are used as medicines. There are also various fungi that poison insects which are harmful to trees or crops, and which thereby act as a natural pest control with none of the secondary pollution caused by artificial pesticides.

The Wuyi Mountain reserve alone supports more than 100 species of mammals and more than 400 species of birds. Many species have been discovered in this area, including the Silver Pheasant (*Lophura nycthemera*), Pale-headed (Bamboo) Woodpecker (*Gecinulus grantia*) and Collared Hill-Partridge (*Arborophila gingica*). The White-backed Woodpecker (*Picoides leucotos*), Black-throated Parrotbill (*Paradoxornis nipalensis*), Red-tailed Laughing Thrush (*Garrulax milnei*) and Green Shrike-Babbler (*Pteruthius xanthochlorus*) are notable bird species found at Guadun.

About 100 species of amphibians and reptiles inhabit the reserve. One of the Asiatic salamanders, *Vibrissaphora liu* (family Hynobiidae), the tree frog *Hyla sanchiangensis*, the agamid lizard *Acanthosaura lepidogaster* and horned toad *Megophrys kuatunensis* are endemic species. It has a wide range of particularly rare species given special protection: the Tiger (*Panthera tigris*), the Large Indian Civet (*Viverra zibetha*), the Small Indian Civet (*Viverricula indica*), pangolins (*Manis* spp.), the Rhesus Macaque (*Macaca mulatta*) and other monkeys, Elliot's Pheasant (*Syrmaticus ellioti*) and the beautiful Chinese Tragopan (*Tragopan caboti*) among others.

Dinghu

Dinghu Mountain Nature Reserve is located on the north-eastern edge of Zhaoqing city, Guangdong Province, at a latitude of 23°10′, which is very close to the Tropic of Cancer. It is in the transition zone between subtropical and tropical and is a wonderful example of subtropical monsoon evergreen broad-leaved forest that has been preserved intact. Due to its geographical position and the preservation of the ecosystem, this reserve has been designated part of the worldwide network of nature reserves for 'Man and the Biosphere' through the United Nations.

The reserve was set up in 1956, making it the first nature reserve in China. The area of the reserve is not very large, being about 11 square kilometres (4 square miles), but it contains more than 2000 species of angiosperms. Some 20 species are especially rare, including Wild Lychee (*Litchi chinensis*), Ford's Erythrophleum (*Erythrophleum fordii*) and Tsoong's Tree (*Tsoongiodendron odorum*), the only member of its genus in the magnolia family. Relict plants include *Cyathea spinulosa* and *Cycas revoluta*. Ford's Erythrophleum is a tree with a tall and straight trunk, and wood that is so hard that it is difficult to drive a nail into it; it has excellent resistance to rot and damage. Dinghu has more than 300 species of trees that can be used for timber or for industry, and about 900 species of medicinal plants. One that falls into both categories is Climbing Entada (*Entada phaseoloides*), a kind of large woody vine, with a 1 metre (3 ft) long seed pod containing seeds 4 to 6 cm (1½ to 2¼ in.) in diameter with an oval or egg shape, generally known as 'Glass Legumes'. The woody vine and the seeds are used as medicine to cure rheumatism, to invigorate the blood and to heal bruises, and the sap can be used as a laxative. The fibre is used as raw material for paper and staple rayon production, and industrial oil is extracted from the seeds. In short, it is a versatile and valuable plant.

In recent years, abundant fungi have been discovered in the Dinghu Mountain Nature Reserve. There are more than 400 species of large fungi, some of which are edible and some medicinal. Some of these species of fungi have only recently been discovered in China and several were new to science when first found in this reserve. The steep mountainside setting of the reserve introduces distinct vertical zoning of the dominant vegetation types, from the valley floor to high peaks.

Wildlife in the forest includes 32 species of mammals, 27 species of reptiles and 11 species of amphibians. Among these, the Leopard (*Panthera pardus*) and the goat-like Mainland Serow (*Capricornis sumatrensis*) are rare animals which receive special protection under Chinese law.

Xishuangbanna

The Xishuangbanna Nature Reserve is situated in Yunnan Province on the northern boundary of the tropical zone. It is a very large reserve of 2000 square kilometres (770 square miles).

There are more than 4000 species of angiosperms in this reserve. Among them are 200 species of edible plants, 300 species which are of medicinal use, more than 100 species from which vegetable oils can be extracted, and over 100 species of valuable timber trees. No fewer than 50 per cent of the plants which are given legal protection in China can be found within the boundaries of this vast reserve.

Tropical monsoon rainforest is the predominant vegetation type here, and is what makes the reserve so exceptionally valuable in international terms. The rainforest is characterized by its dense, luxuriant growth, with an abundance of lianas and parasitic plants. In some places, the Lofty Fig (*Ficus altissima*), which is a relative of the banyan trees but found at higher altitudes, grows well. The crown of the tree is very large and the trunk thick and strong. The mature tree takes on a most remarkable appearance. It has narrow,

Typical woodland in Xishuangbanna, Yunnan Province. This reserve covers a vast area and encompasses over 4000 plant species, most of them typical of tropical monsoon rainforest.

plank-like buttress roots at the base, and in addition many aerial roots grow out from the branches and penetrate the soil, forming a network of free-standing pillars, which look like a cluster of separate tree trunks that soar up into the leafy canopy. The trees are often also festooned with creepers. The people who live in Xishuangbanna like to plant this tree close to villages, for the cool shade within the network of stems and because this kind of tree is a symbol of good luck.

Another remarkable tree in the reserve is the Chinese Parashorea (*Parashorea chinensis*) which is a member of the gurjun oiltree family (Dipterocarpaceae) and which was only discovered, to a considerable degree of excitement in the international scientific community, in the 1970s. Its tall, straight trunks tower over the dense, closed canopy, and it is impossible to see the tree top from the base. Chinese Parashorea grows very quickly, and the height of a 70-year-old tree is more than 50 metres (165 ft) which is about 20 metres (65 ft) higher than the other trees that surround it. This gives the impression that the tree penetrates the sky so it is known as the 'look at the sky' tree in Chinese. The importance of this truly magnificent tree can be judged by looking at its close relatives, the other members of the family Dipterocarpaceae. Many of these are very lofty trees, and they dominate the lowland forests of Asia; they are among the most splendid trees of the tropics and, to the misfortune of the rainforest, are now the major source of all the world's hardwood. In the tropical monsoon forests vast areas are dominated by one species. They have buttressed trunks which rise smooth and unbranched to the great, billowing canopy. Tragically, these forests seem doomed to rapid extinction unless the appallingly profligate exploitation and ruination by timber interests can be stopped. The trees are popular with timber merchants because the narrow, even width of their trunks and

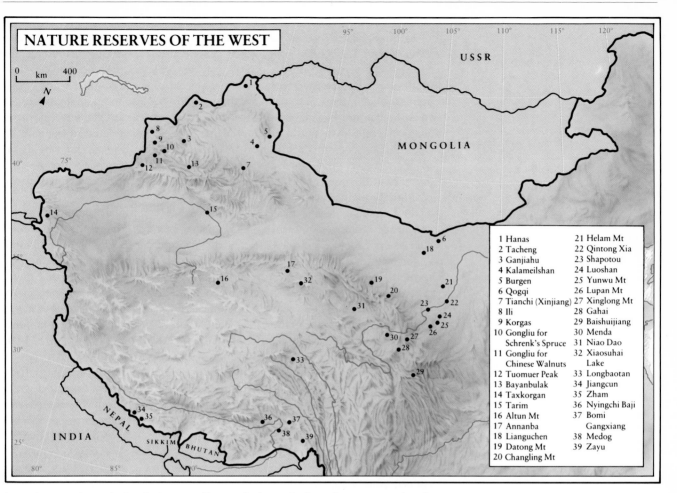

NATURE RESERVES OF THE WEST

1 Hanas	21 Helam Mt
2 Tacheng	22 Qintong Xia
3 Ganjiahu	23 Shapotou
4 Kalameilshan	24 Luoshan
5 Burgen	25 Yunwu Mt
6 Qogqi	26 Lupan Mt
7 Tianchi (Xinjiang)	27 Xinglong Mt
8 Ili	28 Gahai
9 Korgas	29 Baishuijiang
10 Gongliu for Schrenk's Spruce	30 Menda
11 Gongliu for Chinese Walnuts	31 Niao Dao
12 Tuomuer Peak	32 Xiaosuhai Lake
13 Bayanbulak	33 Longbaotan
14 Taxkorgan	34 Jiangcun
15 Tarim	35 Zham
16 Altun Mt	36 Nyingchi Baji
17 Annanba	37 Bomi Gangxiang
18 Lianguchen	38 Medog
19 Datong Mt	39 Zayu
20 Changling Mt	

branches makes their timber easily graded, and therefore more simply marketed. Moreover, the strength of the wood and its light, pale colour put it in great demand.

The main trunk of the Chinese Parashorea may produce 10.5 cubic metres (370 cubic ft) of timber, and it can be planted in large areas to give a considerable, immensely valuable yield within a relatively short time. Now a protected species, it is also a symbol of the rainforests and, in a reserve such as the Xishuangbanna Nature Reserve, may sadly become a relict to remind the future generations how wonderful tropical monsoon forest and its wildlife was, before man destroyed it.

Parts of the Xishuangbanna reserve show remarkable limestone rock formations featuring spiny pinnacles and watery caves. Remarkably, trees grow on these exposed rocks, either by putting down roots into the fissures between them, or by encircling boulders with their networks of roots. The monsoon forest is of a kind unique to the limestone mountains, and is dominated by species quite different from those of the tropical monsoon rainforest elsewhere. One of its individual characteristics is the presence of large deciduous trees which constitute the upper layer of the forest and which shed leaves in the dry season, such as the Chinese Semiliquidambar (*Semiliquidambar cathayensis*) and the Woolly Sterculia (*Sterculia pexa*). A common deciduous tree in this reserve is the dragon tree *Dracaena draco*, a member of the dragon tree family (Dracaenaceae). Although the height of the tree is only about 10 metres (30 ft), the diameter of the trunk can be as much as a metre (3 ft); the leaves are long and strap-like in shape and the trees are highly prized as ornamental specimens. When the trunk of the dragon tree is damaged a special kind of resin flows out and the damaged wood becomes a purple red colour. The purple wood is made into a kind of medicine called

205

'dragon's blood', which is used to stop wounds bleeding.

Xishuangbanna boasts several other famous medicinal plants. Yunnan Devilpepper (*Rauvolfia yunnanensis*) can be used to produce medicine for curing hypertension; it is a relative of the leanders and periwinkles and produces the alkaloids reserpine and rescinnamine. Many-leaf Paris (*Paris polyphylla*) can be used to produce the 'baiyao', a white medicinal powder for treating haemorrhages, wounds and bruises. Hooker's Mayten (*Maytenus hookeri*) is one of several medicinal plants in its genus, related to the spindle trees; it produces medicine used in treating cancer. Among the various oil plants, a woody vine, the Large-fruited Hodgsonia (*Hodgsonia macrocarpa*), a member of the gourd family (Cucurbitaceae), is valued for its seed, because it is about 75 per cent edible oil.

The Xishuangbanna reserve has an extremely abundant fauna: about 62 species of mammals, more than 400 species of birds (one third of the total species in China), some 100 species of fish and 32 species of amphibians. Among these, 250 are rare and protected animals, and Xishuangbanna is aptly termed 'the kingdom of plants and animals'. Scientists consider that many species originally evolved in this region, which accordingly has been given another nickname: 'the cradle for animals and plants'. The most striking of the birds in the reserve is the Great Pied Hornbill (*Buceros bicornis*), a national rarity which has a large bill and long tail, with a total length of 1 metre (3 ft). During incubation, the female hornbill seals herself in the nest cavity inside a hollow trunk, plastering up the entrance with mud and droppings from within. A small hole is left so that the male bird can pass food in for the female until the young birds are hatched. This typical hornbill behaviour is a protection against predators. The Green Peafowl (*Pavo muticus*) is another rare and remarkably beautiful bird. Among the mammals, the Hoolock Gibbon (*Hylobates hoolock*), Asiatic Elephant (*Elephas maximus*), Gaur (*Bos gaurus*) and Slow Loris (*Nycticebus coucang*) are now rare species and require special protection.

Wolong

In the mountainous region of China where the provinces of Sichuan, Gansu and Shaanxi meet, a specially important reserve has been established. The humid climate provides an ideal habitat for China's most famous and attractive mammal – the Giant Panda (*Ailuropoda melanoleuca*), a critically endangered species. Nine nature reserves have been established chiefly for its protection in the western part of the Qin Ling Mountains, Min Mountains,

The numbers of the endemic Thorold's Deer (*Cervus albirostris*) are in severe decline and it is now an endangered species. A few can still be found in southern China.

Qionglai Mountains, Daliang Mountain and Xiaoliang Mountain. Wolong is the most important of these reserves and has become the main centre for research into the behavioural patterns and environmental needs of the Giant Panda. Unfortunately, only about 1000 pandas still remain in the wild; not for nothing has this appealing and unique creature been adopted as the familiar symbol of the World Wide Fund for Nature. Wolong Nature Reserve is situated on the western edge of Sichuan Province, on the eastern slopes of Qionglai Mountain. It covers an area of 2000 square kilometres (770 square miles) and ranges across a wide variety of altitudes. As well as being one of the homes of the Giant Panda, the reserve also houses various protected species of trees, the most notable of these being the Tetracentron (*Tetracentron sinense*), the Chinese Yew (*Taxus chinensis*) and the Chinese Katsura (*Cercidiphyllum japonicum* var. *sinense*). This latter tree is in a single-species (monotypic) genus and has leaves of two distinct types as well as strange, unisexual flowers without petals, making it quite unlike any other broad-leaved tree.

The reserve is a paradise for naturalists as many of the rare animals that are protected by law in China can be found here in a wonderful range of rare species that includes the Golden Monkey (*Pygathrix roxellanae*), Red Panda (*Ailurus fulgens*), Thorold's Deer (*Cervus albirostris*), Snow Leopard (*Panthera uncia*), the Chinese Monal Pheasant (*Lophophorus lhuysii*) and Temminck's Tragopan (*Tragopan temminckii*).

Wolong Nature Reserve is situated in mid-southern China, where the climate is warm and wet. It is the home of many of China's rare and endangered animal species, including the Giant Panda (*Ailuropoda melanoleuca*). Several of China's most interesting trees, such as the Chinese Yew (*Taxus chinensis*), thrive in the conditions there too.

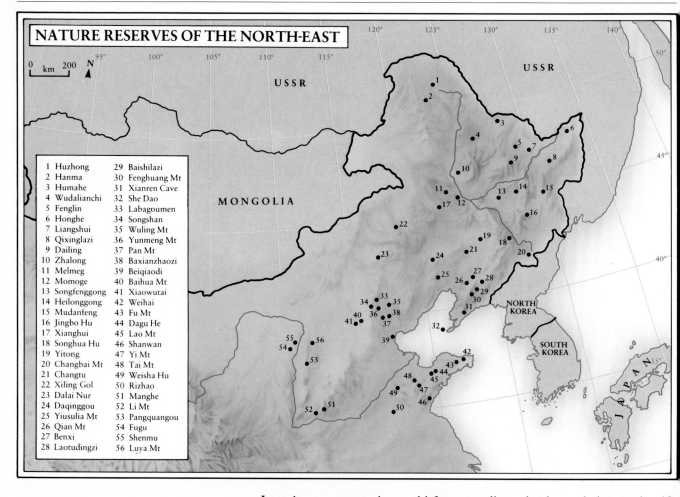

NATURE RESERVES OF THE NORTH-EAST

1	Huzhong	29	Baishilazi
2	Hanma	30	Fenghuang Mt
3	Humahe	31	Xianren Cave
4	Wudalianchi	32	She Dao
5	Fenglin	33	Labagoumen
6	Honghe	34	Songshan
7	Liangshui	35	Wuling Mt
8	Qixinglazi	36	Yunmeng Mt
9	Dailing	37	Pan Mt
10	Zhalong	38	Baxianzhaozi
11	Melmeg	39	Beiqiaodi
12	Momoge	40	Baihua Mt
13	Songfenggong	41	Xiaowutai
14	Heilonggong	42	Weihai
15	Mudanfeng	43	Fu Mt
16	Jingbo Hu	44	Dagu He
17	Xianghui	45	Lao Mt
18	Songhua Hu	46	Shanwan
19	Yitong	47	Yi Mt
20	Changbai Mt	48	Tai Mt
21	Changtu	49	Weisha Hu
22	Xiling Gol	50	Rizhao
23	Dalai Nur	51	Manghe
24	Daqinggou	52	Li Mt
25	Yiusulia Mt	53	Pangquangou
26	Qian Mt	54	Fugu
27	Benxi	55	Shenmu
28	Laotudingzi	56	Luya Mt

In order to protect the world-famous relict animal populations, scientific research is being developed with the co-operation of the World Wide Fund for Nature. Giant Pandas have been studied and tracked by radio telemetry in their natural environment. The biology of the pandas – their habitats, social behaviour, food and reproductive behaviour – has been studied in depth, so that the need for habitat management can be assessed and new techniques developed. With this knowledge and practical experience, it is hoped that optimum conditions for the Giant Panda can be created here and elsewhere, and the future survival of this animal assured.

Zhalong

Zhalong Nature Reserve is located in Heilongjiang Province. It covers an area of 420 square kilometres (165 square miles), and has an average elevation of 143 metres (470 ft). The climate is of the temperate monsoon type. Swamps and lakes are widely scattered all over the reserve. Common Reed (*Phragmites australis*) and other aquatic plants dominate large areas in an exciting landscape of reed beds and glittering water. Plankton, aquatic insects, molluscs, frogs and fishes are abundant and provide food for great numbers of water birds. The nature reserve was established with the main aim of protecting Japanese Cranes (*Grus japonensis*) and other large water birds in a prime example of the virgin Chinese wetland ecosystem. The breeding period for birds here is from April to June, when the hours of daylight are long and night is short; the daily sunshine record may be more than 14 hours. In these conditions birds can make full use of the abundance of food.

More than 200 species of birds enjoy the unique conditions here and cranes are especially numerous. Of the 15 species of cranes in the world, nine are found in China, and six species are regularly found in Zhalong: in addition to the Japanese Crane they include White-necked Crane (*Grus vipio*), the endangered Siberian Crane (*G. leucogeranus*), the Common Crane (*G. grus*) and the Demoiselle Crane (*Anthropoides virgo*). Other rare water birds include both White Stork (*Ciconia ciconia*) and Black Stork (*C. nigra*), Oriental White Ibis (*Threskiornis aethiopicus melanocephalus*), Mandarin Duck (*Aix galericulata*), Swans (*Cygnus* spp.) and the White Spoonbill (*Platalea leucorodia*).

Special research is underway in Zhalong to help combine the building of dams and reservoirs with biological measures to protect rare birds. Cranes and other species are bred in captivity as part of a research programme into the ecology of large water birds and the wetland ecosystem, making Zhalong Nature Reserve the principal centre for research on cranes in China.

Huaping

This reserve lies in the north-eastern part of the Zhuang Autonomous Region of Guangxi. It covers an area of 67 square kilometres (26 square miles), and is 1200 to 1600 metres (4000 to 5000 ft) above sea level. Large areas of primitive forest can still be seen here.

The climate is warm and humid with 2000 mm (80 in.) of rain each year, and an average temperature of 16 to 20°C (61 to 68°F). This abundant rainfall and comparatively high temperature produces luxuriant plant growth of the middle subtropical evergreen broad-leaved forest type below about 1300 metres (4300 ft). Species of evergreen chinquapin (*Castanopsis*), which are trees of the beech family (Fagaceae), predominate in this type of forest. Marked changes of vegetation with increasing altitude are very evident here, as well as typical subtropical evergreen forest. One of the main reasons for the establishment of the reserve is that it is a home for Cathay Silver Fir (*Cathaya argyrophylla*), a 'living fossil'. This is a relict evergreen conifer which dates back to the Tertiary Period. The tree reaches a height of about 20 metres (65 ft) while the diameter of the trunk is over 40 cm (16 in.). The leaves are arranged around the branches in a spiral, getting closer together as they get nearer the top of the tree. The leaves of the shorter branches are less than 2.5 cm (1 in.) long, but the larger branches have leaves up to 6 cm (2¼ in.) in

The White Spoonbill (*Platalea leucorodia*) is one of the many endangered birds that breed in Zhalong, in the north-eastern province of Heilongjiang. This beautiful long-beaked bird is also found in lesser numbers to the west, in Xinjiang.

length. On the back of the green leaves, at either side of the central vein, a belt of attractive, pinky white spots can be seen, which give the Cathay Silver Fir its name, as one sees the underside of the leaves from the ground.

There are some ten endemic plant species in the reserve, such as Lungsheng Maple (*Acer lungshengense*), species of rhododendron, Wrinkled-fruit Camellia (*Camellia rhytidocarpa*) and Late-flowered Enkianthus (*Enkianthus serotina*), which is a relative of the rhododendrons.

A number of specially protected species exist in the reserve, such as the Mainland Serow (*Capricornis sumatrensis*), the Rhesus Macaque (*Macaca mulatta*), and the Chinese Bamboo Rat (*Rhizomys sinensis*) among the mammals, and Temminck's Tragopan (*Tragopan temminckii*), Chinese Tragopan (*Tragopan caboti*), Silver Pheasant (*Lophura nycthemera*), Red Junglefowl (*Gallus gallus*) and Elliot's Pheasant (*Syrmaticus ellioti*) among the birds.

Jiuzhaigou

Jiuzhaigou Nature Reserve is located at the southern foot of the Min Mountains in Sichuan Province. Established in 1978, it was the first reserve in China for the protection of beautiful natural scenery. It is said that in the past there were nine villages here inhabited by Tibetans, and the name of the reserve means 'nine village gully' in Chinese. The area of the reserve is about 600 square kilometres (230 square miles) and the length of the valley is about 60 kilometres (37 miles). Numerous lakes, waterfalls and forests enliven the attractive scenery.

Along the valley there are no fewer than 108 lakes of various shapes and sizes; the largest, with a length of more than 7 kilometres (4⅓ miles) and a width of several hundred metres, is at the top of the mountain. Because the lakes are positioned at various elevations in the valley, water flowing down from the highest lake drops from lake to lake in a succession of waterfalls, connecting the lakes like a giant silver chain.

The scenery changes markedly with the seasons and is never less than beautiful. The leaves of the Common Smoketree (*Cotinus coggygria*), a member of the cashew family (Anacardiaceae), and the various maples (*Acer* spp.) form an especially attractive picture when they turn red in autumn. Several protected mammals inhabit the dense forest: Giant Pandas (*Ailuropoda melanoleuca*), Red Pandas (*Ailurus fulgens*), Golden Monkeys (*Pygathrix roxellanae*), Takin (*Budorcas taxicolor*), Chinese Water Deer (*Hydropotes inermis*) and Gaur (*Bos gaurus*); and birds include swans (*Cygnus*) and Blue Eared-Pheasants (*Crossoptilon auritum*).

Conclusion

Today, keeping the balance between resources, environment, population and economic development in the face of a dramatic increase in population and a rapidly expanding economy is an important issue. In China, in order to protect the natural environment, a series of laws and regulations has been promulgated, more than 400 nature reserves have been established, and propaganda and education promote the cause of nature conservation. Great progress has been made in this respect, but further work must still be carried out. There are abundant resources of wild plants and animals in China, including many world-famous rare and precious species. It is important for China, and for the rest of the world, that they are preserved by the efficient management of nature reserves and the protection of natural resources.

The first signs of autumn in Jiuzhaigou Nature Reserve, situated at the foot of the Min Mountains in Sichuan Province. It was the first reserve established solely for its beautiful scenery, which encompasses many hundreds of lakes.

PRONUNCIATION GUIDE

The Pinyin system of transcribing Chinese names has been adopted in the book. This is the official Chinese method, which is now used in publications and on signs in China, and is increasingly accepted throughout the rest of the world. It was devised to represent Mandarin Chinese sounds phonetically in the Roman alphabet, but as there is some variety in the sounds given to different letters by the cultures that use the Roman alphabet, the pronunciation of letters in Pinyin is not always the same as in modern English.

The main variations are as follows:
ai = 'y', as in 'my'
e = 'u', as in 'run'
ei = 'ay', as in 'day'
i = 'ee' as in 'green', except when it follows c, ch, r, s, sh, z or zh, when it is scarcely sounded
c = 'ts', as in 'tsar'
q = 'ch', as in 'chin'
x = 'sc', as in 'science'
z = 'dz', as in 'adze'
zh = 'j', as in 'jam'.

In accordance with this system, modern forms of Chinese names have been adopted throughout the text, such as Beijing rather than the older Peking, or Guangdong, instead of Canton. An exception is Tibet, which is not known in the West by, or recognizable from, its Chinese name of Xizang. The old names of China's two longest rivers – the Yangtze and the Yellow – are also used, together with their modern forms, as in some cases either name is still used in China, such as 'Chang' for 'Yangtze'.

APPENDICES

The following tables list the most typical animals of each major natural region of China. Latin names given in parentheses are those preferred by many biologists in the West.

TYPICAL MAMMALS OF THE FORESTS

Common name	Latin name	Northern Monsoon Region	Southern Monsoon Region	Mongolia-Xinjiang Plateau	Qinghai-Tibet Plateau
Common Tree Shrew	Tupaia glis		•		
European Hedgehog	Erinaceus europaeus	•	•		
Short-faced Mole	Talpa moschata	•	•	•	
Large Japanese Mole	T. robusta	•			
Eurasian Pygmy Shrew	Sorex minutus			•	•
Eurasian Common Shrew	S. araneus	•	•		•
House Shrew	Suncus murinus		•		
Lesser White-toothed Shrew	Crocidura suaveolens	•	•	•	•
Leschenault's Rousette (Fulvous Fruit Bat)	Rousettus leschenaulti		•		
Indian Flying Fox	Pteropus giganteus				•
Short-nosed Fruit Bat	Cynopterus sphinx		•		
Lesser Dog-faced Fruit Bat	C. brachyotis		•		
Greater Horseshoe Bat	Rhinolophus ferrumequinum	•	•		
Woolly Horseshoe Bat	R. luctus		•		
Himalayan Leaf-nosed Bat	Hipposideros armiger		•		•
Large Mouse-eared Bat	Myotis myotis		•		
mouse-eared bat	M. fimbriatus		•		
Rhesus Macaque (Rhesus Monkey)	Macaca mulatta		•		
Golden Monkey	Rhinopithecus (Pygathrix) roxellanae		•		
Francois's Leaf Monkey	Presbytis francoisi		•		
leaf monkey	P. leucocephalus		•		
Lar Gibbon (Common Gibbon, White-headed Gibbon)	Hylobates lar		•		
Hoolock Gibbon (White-browed Gibbon)	H. hoolock		•		
Concolor Gibbon (Crested Gibbon, White-cheeked Gibbon)	Hylobates concolor		•		

Common name	Latin name	Northern Monsoon Region	Southern Monsoon Region	Mongolia-Xinjiang Plateau	Qinghai-Tibet Plateau
Chinese Pangolin	Manis pentadactyla		•		
Wolf (Grey Wolf)	Canis lupus	•	•	•	•
Red Fox	Vulpes vulpes	•			•
Corsac Fox	V. corsac			•	
Raccoon-dog	Nyctereutes nyctereutes (procyonoides)	•	•		
Red Dog (Asian Wild Dog, Dhole)	Cuon alpinus		•		•
Brown Bear (Eurasian Brown Bear, Grizzly Bear)	Ursus arctos	•			•
Asiatic Black Bear (Himalayan Black Bear)	Selenarctos thibetanus		•		•
Sun Bear (Malayan Sun Bear)	Helarctos malayanus		•		
Red Panda (Lesser Panda)	Ailurus fulgens		•		
Giant Panda	Ailuropoda melanoleuca		•		
Beech Marten (Stone Marten, House Marten)	Martes foina				•
Sable	M. zibellina			•	
Yellow-throated Marten	M. flavigula		•	•	
Stoat (Ermine, Short-tailed Weasel)	Mustela erminea				
Weasel (Eurasian Common Weasel, Least Weasel)	M. nivalis	•		•	•
Chinese Ferret-badger	Melogale moschata			•	
Eurasian Badger	Meles meles	•	•	•	
Large Indian Civet	Viverra zibetha		•		
Common Palm Civet	Paradoxurus hermaphroditus		•		
Masked Palm Civet	Paguma larvata	•	•		
Crab-eating Mongoose	Herpestes urva		•		
Lynx (Northern Lynx)	Felis lynx	•		•	•
Leopard Cat (Bengal Cat)	F. bengalensis	•	•		•
Asiatic Golden Cat (Temminck's Golden Cat)	F. temmincki		•		
Clouded Leopard	Neofelis nebulosa		•		•
Leopard	Panthera pardus	•	•		
Tiger	P. tigris	•	•		•
Asiatic Elephant (Asian Elephant, Indian Elephant)	Elephas maximus		•		

Common name	Latin name	Northern Monsoon Region	Southern Monsoon Region	Mongolia-Xinjiang Plateau	Qinghai-Tibet Plateau
...plex-toothed ...ng Squirrel	*Trogopterus xanthipes*	●	●		
...Giant Flying ...irrel	*Petaurista petaurista*		●		
...erian Flying Squirrel ...ssian Flying ...irrel)	*Pteromys volans*	●	●		
...asian Red Squirrel ...d Squirrel)	*Sciurus vulgaris*	●	●	●	
...y-banded Squirrel ...ountain Red-bellied ...irrel)	*Callosciurus flavimanus*		●		
...nhoe's Striped ...irrel	*C. (Tamiops) swinhoei*		●		
...ny's Long-nosed ...irrel	*Dremomys pernyi*		●		
...e David's Rock ...irrel	*Sciurotamis davidianus*	●	●		
...nese Porcupine ...malayan Porcupine)	*Hystrix hodgsoni*		●		
...ary Bamboo Rat	*Rhizomys pruinosus*		●		
...nese Bamboo Rat	*R. sinensis*		●		
...ge Bamboo Rat	*R. sumatrensis*		●		
...rvest Mouse	*Micromys minutus*	●	●		
...ped Field Mouse	*Apodemus agrarius*	●	●	●	
...ge Japanese Field ...use	*A. speciosus*	●	●	●	●
...od Mouse (Long- ...ed Field Mouse)	*A. sylvaticus*	●	●	●	
...estnut Rat	*R. (Niviventer) fulvescens*		●		
...inese White-bellied ...t	*R. (Niviventer) confucianus*		●		
...wards' Rat	*R. (Leopoldamys) edwardsi*		●		
...eater Bandicoot-Rat	*Bandicota indica*		●		
...ey Red-backed Vole	*Clethrionomys rufocanus*	●		●	
...rthern Red-backed ...le (Ruddy Red- ...cked Vole)	*C. rutilus*	●		●	
...tt's Oriental Vole	*Eothenomys chinensis*		●		
...yle's Mountain Vole	*Alticola roylei*				●
...iped Hamster	*Cricetulus barabensis*	●	●	●	
...eater Long-tailed ...mster (Korean Grey ...mster)	*C. triton*	●	●	●	
...ld Boar	*Sus scrofa*	●	●	●	●
...erian Musk Deer ...usk Deer)	*Moschus moschiferus*	●	●		●
...pine Musk Deer	*M. sifanicus*		●		●
...rest Musk Deer	*M. berezovskii*		●		
...inese Muntjac ...eeves's Muntjac)	*Muntiacus reevesi*		●		
...ack Muntjac (Hairy- ...nted Muntjac)	*M. crinifrons*		●		
...fted Deer	*Elaphodus cephalophus*		●		●
...d Deer (Wapiti, Elk)	*Cervus elaphus*	●		●	●
...orold's Deer (White- ...ped Deer)	*C. albirostris*		●		
...ka Deer (Japanese ...er)	*C. nippon*	●	●		
...e Deer	*Capreolus capreolus*	●	●	●	●
...k (Moose)	*Alces alces*	●			
...aur	*Bos gaurus*		●		
...kin (Golden-fleeced ...ow)	*Budorcas taxicolor*		●		
...ainland Serow	*Capricornis sumatrensis*		●		●

TYPICAL MAMMALS OF THE RIVERS AND WETLANDS

Common name	Latin name	Northern Monsoon Region	Southern Monsoon Region	Mongolia-Xinjiang Plateau	Qinghai-Tibet Plateau
Eurasian Shrew (Water Shrew)	*Neomys fodiens*	●			
European Otter	*Lutra lutra*	●	●		●
Crab-eating Mongoose	*Herpestes urva*		●		
Eurasian Beaver	*Castor fiber*			●	
European Water Vole (Water Vole)	*Arvicola terrestris*			●	
Muskrat	*Ondatra zibethicus*	●	●	●	●
Reed Vole	*Microtus fortis*	●		●	
vole	*M. maximowiczi*	●		●	
Common Vole (Field Vole)	*M. arvalis*			●	
Lesser Mouse Deer (Lesser Malay Chevrotain)	*Tragulus javanicus*		●		
Chinese Water Deer (Water Deer)	*Hydropotes inermis*	●			
Elk (Moose)	*Alces alces*	●			
Chinese River Dolphin (Whitefin Dolphin, Yangtze River Dolphin, Baiji)	*Lipotes vexillifer*		●		

TYPICAL MAMMALS OF THE MOUNTAINS

Common name	Latin name	Northern Monsoon Region	Southern Monsoon Region	Mongolia-Xinjiang Plateau	Qinghai-Tibet Plateau
Greater Horeshoe Bat	*Rhinolophus ferrumequinum*	●	●		
Woolly Horseshoe Bat (Great Eastern Horseshoe Bat)	*R. luctus*		●		
Himalyan Leaf-nosed Bat (Great Leaf-nosed Bat)	*Hipposideros armiger*		●		●
Large Mouse-eared Bat	*Myotis myotis*		●		
mouse-eared bat	*M. fimbriatus*		●		
Common Noctule (Noctule)	*Nyctalus noctula*	●	●		
Indian Pipistrelle	*Pipistrellus coromandra*		●		
Schreiber's Bent-winged Bat (Schreiber's Long-fingered Bat)	*Miniopterus schreibersi*	●	●		
Slow Loris	*Nycticebus coucang*		●		
Rhesus Macaque (Rhesus Monkey)	*Macaca mulatta*		●		
Assam Macaque (Assamese Macaque)	*M. assamensis*		●		●
Stump-tailed Macaque (Stump-tailed Monkey)	*M. speciosa*		●		●
Taiwan Macaque (Formosan Rock Macaque)	*M. cyclopis*		●		
Mountain Weasel	*Mustela altaica*	●	●	●	●
Siberian Weasel (Kolinsky)	*M. sibirica*	●	●		●
Polecat	*M. putorius*	●	●	●	●
Hog badger	*Arctonyx collaris*	●	●		●
Clouded Leopard	*Neofelis nebulosa*		●		
Leopard	*Panthera pardus*	●	●		●
Snow Leopard (Ounce)	*P. uncia*			●	●
Père David's Rock Squirrel	*Sciurotamias davidianus*	●	●		

Common name	Latin name	Northern Monsoon Region	Southern Monsoon Region	Mongolia-Xinjiang Plateau	Qinghai-Tibet Plateau
Royle's Mountain Vole	Alticola roylei				•
Yak	Bos grunniens (mutus)				•
Takin (Golden-fleeced Cow)	Budorcas taxicolor		•		
Goral (Common Goral)	Nemorhaedus goral	•	•	•	•
Ibex	Capra ibex			•	
Blue Sheep (Bharal)	Pseudois nayaur			•	•
Argalis (Argali, Nayan)	Ovis ammon			•	•
Saiga	Saiga tatarica			•	

Common name	Latin name	Northern Monsoon Region	Southern Monsoon Region	Mongolia-Xinjiang Plateau	Qinghai-Tibet Plateau
Greater Long-tailed Hamster (Korean Grey Hamster)	C. triton	•	•	•	
Roburowsky's Dwarf Hamster	Phodopus roborovskii	•		•	•
Mongolian Gerbil (Clawed Jird)	Meriones unguiculatus	•		•	
Midday Gerbil	M. meridianus	•			•
Great Gerbil	Rhombomys opimus			•	
Przewalski's Horse (Asiatic Horse, Wild Horse)	Equus ferus (przewalskii)			•	
Asiatic Wild Ass	E. hemionus			•	•
Thorold's Deer (White-lipped Deer)	Cervus albirostris			•	
Yak	Bos grunniens				•
Tibetan Gazelle	Procapra picticaudata				•
Mongolian Gazelle	P. gutturosa	•		•	
Tibetan Antelope (Chiru)	Pantholops hodgsoni				•

TYPICAL MAMMALS OF THE STEPPES

Common name	Latin name	Northern Monsoon Region	Southern Monsoon Region	Mongolia-Xinjiang Plateau	Qinghai-Tibet Plateau
European Hedgehog	Erinaceus europaeus	•	•		
Long-eared Desert Hedgehog (Long-eared Hedgehog)	Hemiechinus auritus			•	
Wolf (Grey Wolf)	Canis lupus	•	•	•	•
Red Fox	Vulpes vulpes	•	•	•	•
Corsac Fox	V. corsac			•	•
Siberian Weasel (Kolinsky)	Mustela sibirica	•	•	•	•
European Polecat (Steppe Polecat)	M. putorius (M. eversmanni)	•		•	
Eurasian Badger (European Badger)	Meles meles	•	•	•	•
Hog Badger	Arctonyx collaris	•	•		•
Brown Hare (European Hare)	Lepus capensis (europaeus)	•	•	•	•
Arctic Hare	L. timidus	•			
Chinese Hare	L. sinensis		•		
Yarkand Hare	L. yarkandensis			•	
Moupin Pika	Ochotona thibetana		•		•
Daurian Pika	O. daurica	•		•	•
Altai Pika (Alpine Pika)	O. alpina	•		•	
Daurian Ground Squirrel (Daurian Suslik)	Citellus (Spermophilus) dauricus	•		•	•
Bobak Marmot	Marmota bobak			•	•
Long-tailed Marmot	M. caudata			•	
Mongolian Five-toed Jerboa	Allactaga sibirica	•		•	•
Northern Three-toed Jerboa	Dipus sagitta			•	•
Harvest Mouse	Micromys minutus	•	•		
Striped Field Mouse	Apodemus agrarius	•	•		
Common Chinese Zokor	Myospalax fontanieri	•	•		
West Siberian Zokor	M. myospalax	•			
Steppe Lemming	Lagurus lagurus	•			
Reed Vole	Microtus fortis	•	•		
vole	M. maximowiczii	•	•		
Narrow-headed Vole (Narrow-skulled Vole)	M. gregalis	•	•		
Common Vole (Field Vole)	M. arvalis	•	•		
Striped Hamster	Cricetulus barabensis	•	•	•	
Long-tailed Hamster	C. longicaudatus	•		•	•
Tibetan Hamster	C. kamensis			•	•

TYPICAL MAMMALS OF THE SEMI-DESERTS

Common name	Latin name	Northern Monsoon Region	Southern Monsoon Region	Mongolia-Xinjiang Plateau	Qinghai-Tibet
Chinese Desert Cat	Felis bieti			•	•
Pallas's Cat (Manul)	F. manul			•	•
Daurian Ground Squirrel (Daurian Suslik)	Citellus (Spermophilus) dauricus	•		•	•
Bobak Marmot	Marmota bobak			•	•
Long-tailed Marmot	M. caudata			•	
Mongolian Five-toed Jerboa	Allactaga sibirica	•		•	
Northern Three-toed Jerboa	Dipus sagitta			•	•
Roborowsky's Dwarf Hamster	Phodopus roborovskii	•		•	
Mongolian Gerbil (Clawed Jird)	Meriones unguiculatus	•		•	
Midday Gerbil	M. meridianus	•		•	
Great Gerbil	Rhombomys opimus			•	
Przewalski's Horse (Asiatic Horse, Wild Horse)	Equus ferus (przewalskii)			•	
Asiatic Wild Ass	E. hemionus			•	•
Bactrian Camel	Camelus bactrianus (ferus)			•	
Goitred Gazelle	Gazella subgutturosa			•	•
Tibetan Antelope (Chiru)	Pantholops hodgsoni				•

TYPICAL BIRDS OF THE FORESTS

Common name	Latin name	Northern Monsoon Region	Southern Monsoon Region	Mongolia-Xinjiang Plateau	Qinghai-Tibet
Black Baza	Aviceda leuphotes		•		
Crested Honey Buzzard	Pernis ptilorhynchus	•	•		
Black Kite	Milvus migrans	•	•	•	
Crested Goshawk	Accipiter trivirgatus		•		
Sparrowhawk (Northern Sparrowhawk)	A. nisus	•		•	
Crested Serpent-Eagle	Spilornis cheela		•		

Common Name	Scientific Name	1	2	3	4	5
Pied Falconet (White-legged Falconet)	Microhierax melanoleucos		•			
Saker Falcon	Falco cherrug			•	•	
Hobby (Northern Hobby)	F. subbuteo	•	•	•	•	
Kestrel (Common Kestrel, Eurasian Kestrel)	F. tinnunculus	•	•	•	•	
Black-billed Capercaillie	Tetrao parvirostris	•				
Black Grouse	Lyrurus (Tetrao) tetrix	•		•		
Hazel Grouse	Tetrastes (Bonasa) bonasia	•				
Chinese Hazel Grouse (Severtzov's Hazel Grouse, Black-breasted Hazel Grouse)	T. sewerzowi				•	
Chinese Francolin	Francolinus pintadeanus		•			
White-cheeked Hill-Partridge	Arborophila atrogularis		•			
Sichuan Hill-Partridge (Boulton's Hill-Partridge)	A. rufipectus		•			
Collared Hill-Partridge (Rickett's Hill-Partridge)	A. gingica		•			
Hainan Hill-Partridge (White-eared Hill-Partridge)	A. ardens		•			
Taiwan Hill-Partridge (White-throated Hill-Partridge)	A. crudigularis		•			
Chinese Bamboo-Partridge	Bambusicola thoracica		•			
Blood Pheasant	Ithaginis cruentus				•	
Temminck's Tragopan	Tragopan temminckii		•		•	
Cabot's Tragopan (Chinese Tragopan)	T. caboti		•			
Himalayan Monal Pheasant	Lophophorus impejanus				•	
Chinese Monal Pheasant	L. lhuysii				•	
Tibetan Eared-Pheasant (White Eared-Pheasant)	Crossoptilon crossoptilon				•	
Blue Eared-Pheasant	C. auritum				•	
Brown Eared-Pheasant	C. mantchuricum	•				
Kalij Pheasant	Lophura leucomelana				•	
Silver Pheasant	L. nycthemera		•			
Red Junglefowl	Gallus gallus		•			
Koklass Pheasant	Pucrasia macrolopha	•	•			
Common Pheasant	Phasianus colchicus	•	•	•	•	
Reeves's Pheasant (White-crowned Long-tailed Pheasant)	Syrmaticus reevesii	•	•			
Elliot's Pheasant (White-necked Long-tailed Pheasant)	S. ellioti		•			
Mikado Pheasant (Taiwan Long-tailed Pheasant)	S. mikado		•			
Lady Amherst's Pheasant	Chrysolophus amherstiae		•		•	
Golden Pheasant	C. pictus		•		•	
Grey Peacock-Pheasant (Burmese Peacock-Pheasant)	Polyplectron bicalcaratum		•			
Green Peafowl	Pavo muticus		•			
White-bellied Wedge-tailed Green Pigeon (Siebold's Green Pigeon)	Treron sieboldii		•			
Green Imperial Pigeon	Ducula aenea		•			
Eastern Rock Pigeon (Eastern Rock Dove, Blue Hill Pigeon)	Columba rupestris	•		•	•	
Rock Pigeon (Rock Dove)	C. livia			•		
Speckled Wood Pigeon	C. hodgsonii				•	
Bar-tailed Cuckoo Dove	Macropygia unchall		•			

Common Name	Scientific Name	1	2	3	4	5
Turtle Dove (Common Turtle Dove)	Streptopelia turtur					•
Rufous Turtle Dove	S. orientalis	•	•		•	•
Spotted Dove	S. chinensis		•			
Emerald Dove	Chalcophaps indica		•			
Red-breasted Parakeet (Moustached Parakeet)	Psittacula alexandri		•			
Lord Derby's Parakeet (Derbyan Parakeet)	P. derbiana				•	
Vernal Hanging Parrot	Loriculus vernalis		•			
Red-winged Crested Cuckoo	Clamator coromandus		•			
Indian Cuckoo (Short-winged Cuckoo)	Cuculus micropterus	•				
Common Cuckoo (Cuckoo)	C. canorus	•	•		•	•
Plaintive Cuckoo (Grey-breasted Brush-Cuckoo)	C. (Cacomantis) merulinus		•			
Drongo-Cuckoo	Surniculus lugubris		•			
Koel (Common Koel)	Eudynamys scolopacea		•			
Greater Coucal (Common Crow-Pheasant)	Centropus sinensis		•			
Lesser Coucal (Black Coucal, Lesser Crow-Pheasant)	C. toulou		•			
Grass Owl (Eastern Grass Owl)	Tyto capensis (T. longimembris)		•			
European Scops Owl (includes Oriental Scops Owl)	Otus scops (includes O. sunia)	•	•			
Collared Scops Owl	O. bakkamoena	•	•			
Collared Owlet (Collared Pygmy Owl)	Glaucidium brodiei		•			
Little Owl	Athene noctua	•	•		•	•
Brown Wood Owl	Strix leptogrammica		•			
Long-eared Owl	Asio otus		•			
Jungle Nightjar (Grey Nightjar)	Caprimulgus indicus	•	•			
European Nightjar (Nightjar)	C. europaeus		•			
Red-headed Trogon	Harpactes erythrocephalus		•			
Blue-throated Bee-eater (Chestnut-headed Bee-eater)	Merops viridis		•			
European Roller (Roller)	Coracias garrulus				•	
Eastern Broad-billed Roller (Dollarbird)	Eurystomus orientalis	•	•			
Hoopoe	Upupa epops	•	•		•	•
Rufous-necked Hornbill	Aceros nipalensis		•			
Oriental Pied Hornbill (Malabar Pied Hornbill)	Anthracoceros coronatus		•			
Great Pied Hornbill	Buceros bicornis		•			
Great Hill Barbet	Megalaima virens		•			
Speckled Piculet	Picumnus innominatus		•			
Rufous Woodpecker	Micropternus brachyurus		•			
Grey-headed Woodpecker	Picus canus	•	•		•	
Black Woodpecker	Dryocopus martius	•	•		•	
Great Spotted Woodpecker	Dendrocopos (Picoides) major	•	•		•	
Three-toed Woodpecker	Picoides tridactylus	•			•	•
Long-tailed Broadbill	Psarisomus dalhousiae		•			
Lesser Blue-winged Pitta (Indian Pitta, Fairy Pitta)	Pitta brachyura (P. nympha)		•			
Black-winged Cuckoo-Shrike (Dark-grey Cuckoo-Shrike)	Coracina melaschistos		•			
Grey-throated Minivet	Pericrocotus solaris		•			
Chinese Bulbul	Pycnonotus sinensis		•			
Ashy Bulbul (Chestnut-backed Bulbul, Oriental Brown-eared Bulbul)	Hypsipetes flavala		•			
Brown Shrike	Lanius cristatus	•	•			

Common name	Latin name	Northern Monsoon Region	Southern Monsoon Region	Mongolia-Xinjiang Plateau	Qinghai-Tibet Plateau
Long-tailed Shrike (Rufous-backed Shrike)	L. schach		•		
Grey-backed Shrike* (Tibetan Shrike, Long-tailed Shrike)	L. tephronotus (L. schach)				•
Golden Oriole	Oriolus oriolus			•	
Black-naped Oriole	O. chinensis	•	•	•	
Maroon Oriole	O. traillii		•		
Black Drongo	Dicrurus macrocercus	•	•		
Lesser Racquet-tailed Drongo	D. remifer		•		
Rose-coloured Starling	Sturnus roseus			•	
European Starling (Common Starling)	S. vulgaris			•	
Silky Starling (Red-billed Starling)	S. sericeus	•			
Grey Starling (Ashy Starling, White-cheeked Starling)	S. cineraceus	•			
Crested Mynah	Acridotheres cristatellus		•		
Hill Mynah	Gracula religiosa		•		
Eurasian Jay (Jay)	Garrulus glandarius	•	•	•	•
Red-billed Blue Magpie	Cissa (Urocissa) erythrorhyncha		•	•	
Azure-winged Magpie	Cyanopica cyana	•	•		
Magpie (Common Magpie, Black-billed Magpie)	Pica pica	•	•	•	•
Nutcracker	Nucifraga carycatactes	•	•	•	•
Collared Crow	Corvus torquatus		•		
Brown Accentor	Prunella fulvescens			•	•
Siberian Blue Robin	Luscinia (Erithacus) cyane	•			
Magpie-Robin	Copsychus saularis		•		
Black Redstart	Phoenicurus ochruros			•	•
Blackbird	Turdus merula	•		•	•
Rusty-cheeked Scimitar Babbler	Pomatorhinus erythrogenys		•		
Rufous-necked Scimitar Babbler (Streak-breasted Scimitar Babbler)	P. ruficollis		•		
Chinese Babax	Babax lanceolatus		•		•
Ashy Laughing-Thrush (Moustached Laughing-thrush)	Garrulax cineraceus		•		•
Hwamei	G. canorus		•		
Red-billed Leiothrix (Pekin Robin)	Leiothrix lutea		•		
Vinous-throated Parrotbill (Rufous-headed Crowtit)	Paradoxornis webbianus	•	•		
Mountain Bush Warbler (Strong-footed Bush Warbler)	Cettia fortipes		•		•
Milne Edwards' Willow Warbler (Buff-browed Willow Warbler, Yellow-streaked Willow Warbler)	Phylloscopus armandii	•			•
Yellow-browed Warbler (Inornate Warbler)	P. inornatus	•		•	•
Yellow-breasted Willow Warbler (Sulphur-breasted Warbler)	P. cantator (P. ricketti)		•		
Yellow-eyed Flycatcher-Warbler	Seicercus burkii		•		
Common Tailorbird (Long-tailed Tailorbird)	Orthotomus sutorius		•		
Yellow-rumped Flycatcher (Tricolor Flycatcher)	Ficedula zanthopygia	•			

Common name	Latin name	Northern Monsoon Region	Southern Monsoon Region	Mongolia-Xinjiang Plateau	Qinghai-Tibet Plateau
Brown Flycatcher	Muscicapa latirostris	•	•		
Verditer Flycatcher	M. thalassina		•		
Asian Paradise-Flycatcher	Terpsiphone paradisi	•	•		
Great Tit	Parus major	•	•	•	•
Turkestan Tit	P. bokharensis				•
Black Crested Tit (Rufous-vented Tit)	P. rubidiventris			•	•
Eurasian Nuthatch (Nuthatch)	Sitta europaea	•	•	•	
Giant Nuthatch	S. magna		•		
Common Treecreeper (Treecreeper)	Certhia familiaris	•		•	•
Fire-breasted Flowerpecker	Dicaeum ignipectus		•		
Crimson Sunbird (Yellow-backed Sunbird)	Aethopyga siparaja		•		
Fork-tailed Sunbird	A. christinae		•		
Japanese White-eye	Zosterops japonica		•		
Cinnamon Sparrow	Passer rutilans		•		•
Baya Weaver	Ploceus philippinus		•		
White-backed Munia	Lonchura striata		•		
Oriental Greenfinch (Grey-capped Greenfinch)	Carduelis sinica	•	•		
Tibetan Siskin	C. (Serinus) thibetana				•
Red-breasted Rosefinch	Carpodacus puniceus			•	•
Common Rosefinch (Scarlet Rosefinch, Scarlet Grosbeak)	C. erythrinus			•	•
Red Crossbill (Common Crossbill, Crossbill)	Loxia curvirostra	•		•	•
Crested Bunting	Melophus lathami		•		•

*Many ornithologists consider the Grey-backed Shrike to be merely a subspecies of the Long-tailed Shrike (Larius Schach).

TYPICAL BIRDS OF THE RIVERS AND WETLANDS OF CHINA

Common name	Latin name	Northern Monsoon Region	Southern Monsoon Region	Mongolia-Xinjiang Plateau	Qinghai-Tibet
Little Grebe	Podiceps ruficollis	•	•	•	
Slavonian Grebe (Horned Grebe)	P. auritus			•	
Black-necked Grebe (Eared Grebe)	P. nigricollis	•		•	
Great Crested Grebe	P. cristatus	•		•	
Spot-billed Pelican	Pelecanus philippensis			•	
Common Cormorant (Great Cormorant)	Phalacrocorax carbo			•	
Little Cormorant* (Javanese Cormorant)	P. niger		•		
Grey Heron	Ardea cinerea	•	•	•	•
Purple Heron	A. purpurea	•	•	•	
Green Heron (Green-backed Heron, Striated Heron)	Butorides striatus	•	•		
Chinese Pond Heron	Ardeola bacchus	•	•		
Cattle Egret	Bubulcus ibis		•		
Great White Egret (Great Egret)	Egretta alba	•	•		
Little Egret	E. garzetta		•		
Chinese Egret (Swinhoe's Egret)	E. eulophotes		•		
Eastern Reef Heron	E. sacra		•		
Intermediate Egret	E. intermedia		•		
Black-crowned Night Heron (Night Heron)	Nycticorax nycticorax	•	•		
Little Bittern	Ixobrychus minutus	•			
Yellow Bittern (Chinese Little Bittern)	I. sinensis	•	•		

Common name	Latin name				
Schrenck's Bittern	*I. eurhythmus*	•	•		
Cinnamon Bittern (Chestnut Bittern)	*I. cinnamomeus*	•	•		
Black Bittern (Yellow-necked Bittern)	*Dupetor (Ixobrychus) flavicollis*		•		
Eurasian Bittern (Bittern)	*Botaurus stellaris*	•		•	
White Stork	*Ciconia ciconia*	•		•	
Black Stork	*C. nigra*	•	•		
Sacred Ibis (Oriental White Ibis)	*Threskiornis aethiopicus (T. melanocephalus)†*	•			
Crested Ibis (Japanese Ibis, Japanese Crested Ibis)	*Nipponia nippon*				
White Spoonbill (Eurasian Spoonbill, Spoonbill)	*Platalea leucorodia*	•		•	
Swan Goose	*Anser cygnoides*	•			
Greylag Goose	*A. anser*	•	•		
Bar-headed Goose	*A. indicus*		•	•	
Whooper Swan	*Cygnus cygnus*		•	•	
Mute Swan	*C. olor*		•	•	
Lesser Whistling Duck (Lesser Whistling Teal, Lesser Tree Duck)	*Dendrocygna javanica*		•		
Ruddy Shelduck	*Tadorna ferruginea*				
Common Shelduck (Northern Shelduck, Shelduck)	*T. tadorna*			•	
Northern Pintail (Pintail)	*Anas acuta*			•	
Teal (Green-winged Teal, Common Teal)	*A. crecca*	•			
Falcated Teal	*A. falcata*	•			
Mallard	*A. platyrhynchos*	•			
Spot-billed Duck (Spotbill)	*A. poecilorhyncha*	•	•		
Gadwall	*A. strepera*	•	•		
Garganey	*A. querquedula*	•		•	
Northern Shoveler (Shoveler)	*A. clypeata*	•			
Red-crested Pochard	*Netta rufina*			•	
Ferruginous Duck (White-eyed Pochard)	*Aythya nyroca*	•			•
Baer's Pochard	*A. baeri*	•			
Tufted Duck	*A. fuligula*	•			
Mandarin Duck (Mandarin)	*Aix galericulata*	•			
Cotton Pygmy-Goose (Cotton Teal)	*Nettapus coromandelianus*		•		
Chinese Merganser (Scaly-sided Merganser)	*Mergus squamatus*	•			
Red-breasted Merganser	*M. serrator*	•			
Hen Harrier (Northern Harrier, Marsh Hawk)	*Circus cyaneus*	•		•	
Marsh Harrier	*C. aeruginosus*	•			
Osprey	*Pandion haliaetus*	•	•		
Yellow-legged Button-quail	*Turnix tanki*	•			
Common Crane	*Grus grus*			•	•
Black-necked Crane	*G. nigricollis*				•
Hooded Crane	*G. monacha*	•			
Japanese Crane (Red-crowned Crane)	*G. japonensis*	•			
White-naped Crane	*G. vipio*	•			
Demoiselle Crane	*Anthropoides virgo*	•			
Water Rail	*Rallus aquaticus*	•			
Blue-breasted Banded Rail (Slaty-breasted Rail)	*R. striatus*		•		
Baillon's Crake	*Porzana pusilla*	•			
Ruddy-breasted Crake (Ruddy Crake)	*P. fusca*	•	•		
White-breasted Waterhen	*Amaurornis phoenicurus*		•		
Watercock	*Gallicrex cinerea*	•	•		

Common name	Latin name				
Common Moorhen (Moorhen, Common Gallinule)	*Gallinula chloropus*	•		•	
Eurasian Coot (Coot)	*Fulica atra*	•		•	
Pheasant-tailed Jacana	*Hydrophasianus chirurgus*		•		
Painted Snipe	*Rostratula benghalensis*	•	•		
Oystercatcher (Eurasian Oystercatcher)	*Haematopus ostralegus*	•			
Ringed Plover (Common Ringed Plover)	*Charadrius hiaticula*	•		•	
Little Ringed Plover	*C. dubius*	•		•	•
Kentish Plover (Snowy Plover)	*C. alexandrinus*			•	
Common Redshank (Redshank)	*Tringa totanus*			•	•
Common Sandpiper	*T. (Actitis) hypoleucos*	•			
Common Snipe (Snipe, Wilson's Snipe)	*Capella (Gallinago) gallinago*		•		
Ibisbill	*Ibidorhyncha struthersii*			•	•
Black-winged Stilt	*Himantopus himantopus*			•	•
Black-headed Gull (Common Black-headed Gull)	*Larus ridibundus*			•	•
Brown-headed Gull	*L. brunnicephalus*			•	•
Saunders's Gull (Chinese Black-headed Gull)	*L. saundersi*		•		
Whiskered Tern	*Chlidonias hybrida*	•		•	
White-winged Black Tern (White-winged Tern)	*C. leucoptera*	•		•	
Common Tern	*Sterna hirundo*	•		•	•
Little Tern	*S. albifrons*	•	•		
Pied Kingfisher	*Ceryle lugubris*		•		
Lesser Pied Kingfisher	*C. rudis*		•		
Common Kingfisher (Eurasian Kingfisher, Kingfisher)	*Alcedo atthis*	•	•		
White-breasted Kingfisher	*Halcyon smyrnensis*				
Black-capped Kingfisher	*H. pileata*	•	•		
Pied Wagtail	*Motacilla alba*	•	•	•	•
Great Reed Warbler	*Acrocephalus arundinaceus*	•	•	•	
Paddy-field Warbler	*A. agricola*	•			
Thick-billed Reed Warbler	*Phragmaticola (Acrocephalus) aedon*	•			
Penduline Tit (Masked Penduline Tit)	*Remiz pendulinus*	•		•	

*Some ornithologists regard this as the same species as the Pygmy Cormorant (*P. pygmaeus*).
†The four subspecies of this bird are often regarded as being closely related species, including the Oriental White Ibis (*Threskiornis aethiopicus melanocephalus*) whose range in SE Asia includes China.

TYPICAL BIRDS OF THE MOUNTAINS

Common name	Latin name	Northern Monsoon Region	Southern Monsoon Region	Mongolia-Xinjiang Plateau	Qinghai-Tibet Plateau
Golden Eagle	*Aquila chrysaetos*	•	•	•	•
Bonelli's Eagle	*A. fasciata (Hieraaetus fasciatus)*		•		
Pallas's Sea Eagle	*Haliaeetus leucoryphus*	•		•	
White-tailed Sea Eagle	*H. albicilla*	•		•	
Cinereous Vulture (Eurasian Black Vulture)	*Aegypius monachus*			•	•
Griffon Vulture	*Gyps fulvus*				•

Common name	Latin name	Northern Monsoon Region	Southern Monsoon Region	Mongolia-Xinjiang Plateau	Qinghai-Tibet Plateau
Lammergeier (Bearded Vulture)	Gypaetus barbatus			●	●
Crested Serpent-Eagle	Spilornis cheela		●		
Snow Partridge	Lerwa lerwa				●
Tibetan Snowcock	Tetraogallus tibetanus				●
Himalayan Snowcock	T. himalayensis			●	●
Verreaux's Monal-Partridge (Verraux's Pheasant-Grouse)	Tetraophasis obscurus				●
Chukar Partridge	Alectoris chukar	●		●	●
Daurian Partridge	Perdix dauricae	●		●	
Tibetan Partridge	P. hodgsoniae				●
Eagle Owl (Eurasian Eagle Owl)	Bubo bubo	●	●	●	
Himalayan Swiftlet	Collocalia (Aerodramus) brevirostris		●		●
Common Swift (Swift)	Apus apus	●		●	
Pacific Swift (White-rumped Swift)	A. pacificus	●	●	●	
Crag Martin	Ptyonoprogne (Hirundo) rupestris			●	●
House Martin	Delichon urbica	●	●		●
Red-billed Chough (Chough)	Pyrrhocorax pyrrhocorax	●			●
Alpine Chough (Yellow-billed Chough)	P. graculus			●	●
Raven	Corvus corax			●	●
Jungle Crow (Thick-billed Crow)	C. macrorhynchos	●	●		●
Blue Rock Thrush	Monticola solitaria	●	●		

TYPICAL BIRDS OF THE STEPPES

Common name	Latin name	Northern Monsoon Region	Southern Monsoon Region	Mongolia-Xinjiang Plateau	Qinghai-Tibet Plateau
Black Kite	Milvus migrans	●	●	●	●
Upland Buzzard	Buteo hemilasius	●		●	
Steppe Eagle	Aquila rapax			●	
Greater Spotted Eagle	A. clanga	●			
Lammergeier (Bearded Vulture)	Gypaetus barbatus			●	●
Common Quail (Quail)	Coturnix coturnix	●		●	
Blue-breasted Quail	C. chinensis		●		
Common Pheasant	Phasianus colchicus	●	●	●	
Great Bustard	Otis tarda	●			
Pallas's Sandgrouse	Syrrhaptes paradoxus	●			
Tibetan Sandgrouse	S. tibetanus				●
Mongolian Lark	Melanocorypha mongolica			●	
Lesser Short-toed Lark	Calandrella rufescens	●		●	
Skylark (Sky Lark)	Alauda arvensis	●		●	
Horned Lark (Shore Lark)	Eremophila alpestris			●	●
Snow-Finch (White-winged Snow-Finch)	Montifringilla nivalis			●	●
Red-necked Snow-Finch	M. ruficollis				●
Meadow Bunting	Emberiza cioides	●	●	●	
Koslow's Bunting	E. koslowi				●

TYPICAL BIRDS OF THE SEMI-DESERTS

Common name	Latin name	Northern Monsoon Region	Southern Monsoon Region	Mongolia-Xinjiang Plateau	Qinghai-Tibet Plateau
Long-legged Buzzard	Buteo rufinus			●	
Greater Spotted Eagle	Aquila clanga	●		●	
Bonelli's Eagle	A. fasciata (Hieraaetus fasciatus)		●		
Pallas's Sandgrouse	Syrrhaptes paradoxus	●		●	
Tibetan Sandgrouse	S. tibetanus				●
Lesser Short-toed Lark	Calandrella rufescens	●		●	●
Henderson's Ground Jay (Henderson's Desert Chough)	Podoces hendersoni			●	●
Isabelline Wheatear	Oenanthe isabellina			●	
Desert Wheatear	O. deserti			●	●
Trumpeter Finch	Rhodopechys (Bucanetes) githagineus			●	

TYPICAL REPTILES OF THE FORESTS

Common name	Latin name	Northern Monsoon Region	Southern Monsoon Region	Mongolia-Xinjiang Plateau	Qinghai-Tibet Plateau
arboreal agamid lizard ('bloodsucker')	Calotes brevipes		●		
arboreal agamid lizard ('bloodsucker')	C. kingdonwardi				●
arboreal agamid lizard ('bloodsucker')	C. versicolor		●		
flying dragon lizard	Draco blanfordi		●		
flying dragon lizard	D. maculatus		●		●
Butterfly Lizard (Smooth-scaled agamid)	Liolepis belliana		●		
Tokay Gecko	Gekko gecko		●		
Japanese Gecko	G. japonicus			●	●
house (or half-toe) gecko	Hemidactylus frenatus		●		
skink	Eumeces chinensis		●		
skink	E. elegans	●	●		
Long-tailed Mabuya (a skink)	Mabuya longicaudata		●		
racerunner (desert lacertid)	Eremias argus	●	●	●	
Amur Grass Lizard	Takydromus amurensis	●	●		
Six-lined Grass Lizard	T. sexlineatus		●		
dibamid burrowing blind lizard	Dibamus bourreti		●		
Burman Glass Lizard	Ophisaurus gracilis		●		
Hart's Glass Lizard	O. harti		●		
Common Asiatic (Two-banded) Monitor	Varanus salvator		●		
Flowerpot Snake (a blind snake)	Rhamphotyphlops braminus		●		
blind snake	Typhlops diardi		●		
Indian Python	Python molurus		●		
Hainan Sunbeam Snake	Xenopeltis hainanensis		●		
snail-eating snake	Pareas boulengeri		●	●	
snail-eating snake	P. formosensis		●		
snail-eating snake	P. monticola				●
whip snake (or racer)	Coluber spinalis	●	●		
arboreal colubrid snake	Dendrelaphis gorei				●
rat snake	Dinodon rufozonatum	●	●		●
rat snake	Elaphe carinate		●	●	
rat snake	E. davidi		●		

Common name	Latin name	Northern Monsoon Region	Southern Monsoon Region	Mongolia-Xinjiang Plateau	Qinghai-Tibet Plateau
snake	E. dione	•	•	•	
snake	E. schrenckii	•	•	•	
snake	E. taeniura	•	•	•	•
...ngrove snake	Boiga kraepelini		•		
...nded Krait	Bungarus fasciatus		•		
...ny-banded Krait	B. multicinctus		•		
...ental common cobra	Naja naja		•		
...g Cobra	Ophiophagus hannah		•		•
...a's Viper	Azemiops feae		•		•
...rasian Adder	Vipera berus	•		•	
...inese Copperhead	Deinagkistrodon (Agkistrodon) acutus		•		
...ite-lipped Tree ...er	Trimeresurus albolabris		•		
...don's Tree Viper	T. jerdonii		•		
...inese Habu	T. mucrosquamatus		•		
...inese Green Tree ...er	T. stejnegeri		•		

...PICAL REPTILES OF THE RIVERS ...ND WETLANDS

Common name	Latin name	Northern Monsoon Region	Southern Monsoon Region	Mongolia-Xinjiang Plateau	Qinghai-Tibet Plateau
...-headed Turtle (...squed Terrapin)	Platysternon megacephalum		•		
...ellate Pond Turtle	Clemmys (sacalia) bealei		•		
...d turtle	C. (Mauremys) mutica		•		
...inese Terrapin (...inese Pond Turtle)	C. (M.) nigricans		•		
...d turtle	C. (M.) quadriocellata		•		
...ayan pond turtle	Cyclemys mouhotii		•		
...ngler's Terrapin	Geoemyda spengleri		•		
...ond turtle	Chinemys megalocephala		•		
...ve's Turtle (...lden Turtle)	C. reevesii	•	•		
...en-headed Turtle	Ocadia sinensis		•		
...low-headed Box ...tle	Cuora flavomarginata		•		
...nan Box Turtle	C. hainanensis (C.f. hainanensis)		•		
...ree-lined Box ...tle	C. trifasciata		•		
...nan Box Turtle	C. yunanensis		•		
...ressed Tortoise	Testudo (Manouria) impressa		•		
...nt Soft-shelled ...tle	Pelochelys bibroni		•		
...nese Soft-shelled ...tle	Trionyx sinensis	•	•	•	
...th Asia Agamas	Agama tuberculata				•
...nese Xenosaur (...inese Crocodile-...ard)	Shinisaurus crocodilurus		•		
...mmon Asiatic (Two-...ded) Monitor	Varanus salvator		•		
...n wart snake	Acrochordus granulatus		•		
...brid water snake	Enhydris chinensis		•		
...brid water snake	E. bennetti		•		
...nese Alligator	Alligator sinensis		•		

TYPICAL REPTILES OF THE MOUNTAINS

Common name	Latin name	Northern Monsoon Region	Southern Monsoon Region	Mongolia-Xinjiang Plateau	Qinghai-Tibet Plateau
Big-headed Turtle (Casqued Terrapin)	Platysternon megacephalum		•		
agamid lizard	Japalura flaviceps		•		
agamid lizard	J. splendida	•	•	•	•
agamid lizard	J. swinhonis		•		
toad-headed agamid lizard	Phrynocephalus theobaldi			•	•
gecko	Alsophylax tibetanus				•
skink	Eumeces chinensis		•		
skink	E. elegans	•	•		
racerunner	Eremias brenchleyi	•	•		
Viviparous Lizard (Common Lizard)	Lacerta vivipara	•			
Chinese Xenosaur	Shinisaurus crocodilurus		•		
mountain water snake	Opisthotropis latouchii		•		
mountain water snake	O. kuatunensis		•		
Oriental Rat Snake	Zaocys dhumnades	•	•		
pit-viper	Agkistrodon blomhoffii	•	•	•	
pit-viper	A. saxatilis	•			
pit-viper	A. strauchii			•	•

TYPICAL REPTILES OF THE STEPPES

Common name	Latin name	Northern Monsoon Region	Southern Monsoon Region	Mongolia-Xinjiang Plateau	Qinghai-Tibet Plateau
toad-headed agamid lizard	Phrynocephalus frontalis			•	
Chinese Water Dragon	Physignathus concincinus		•		
racerunner	Eremias argus	•	•	•	
Amur grass lizard	Takydromus amurensis	•		•	
pit-viper	Agkistrodon strauchii			•	•
Chinese Copperhead	Deinagkistrodon (Agkistrodon) acutus		•		

TYPICAL REPTILES OF THE SEMI-DESERTS

Common name	Latin name	Northern Monsoon Region	Southern Monsoon Region	Mongolia-Xinjiang Plateau	Qinghai-Tibet Plateau
Horsfield's Tortoise	Testudo (Agrionemys) horsfieldi			•	
Himalayan Agama	Agama himalayana			•	
Xianjiang Agama	A. stoliczkana			•	
Tarimen Agama	A. tarimensis			•	
toad-headed agamid lizard	Phrynocephalus albolineatus			•	
toad-headed agamid lizard	P. axillaris			•	
toad-headed agamid lizard	P. forsythi			•	
toad-headed agamid lizard	P. przewalskii			•	
gecko	Alsophylax przewalskii			•	
gecko	Teratoscincus przewalskii			•	
gecko	T. scincus			•	•
racerunner	Eremias przewalskii			•	
sand boa	Eryx miliaris			•	

INDEX

Publishers' Acknowledgments

Swallow Publishing would like to thank the following people and organizations for supplying the photographs in this book. We apologize to anyone we may have failed to mention.

Heather Angel: 10-11, 13, 17, 18, 19, 24-5, 30, 40, 46t, 46b, 48, 53, 57t, 57c, 63l, 63r, 129, 130bl, 132, 136r, 148b.
Ardea London Limited: 71 (© Masahiro Iijima), 74cl (J L Mason), 124 (Nick Gordon), 164b (Kenneth W. Fink), 167 (© Eric Lindgren), 180 (Hans & Judy Beste, Australia), 187l (John Clagg).
Aspect Picture Library: 42 (Peter Carmichael), 43l (Peter Carmichael).
Bruce Coleman Limited: 68b (John Mackinnon), 76b (Rod Williams), 148t (Norman Tomalin), 151 (© Erwin and Peggy Bauer), 181 (© Erwin & Peggy Bauer), 184 (Rod Williams), 187r (Norman Myers).
Chen Yucan: 69b.
Chinese Glacier, edited by the Institute of Glaciology, Chinese Academy of Sciences: 130tl, 131, 137b, 141, 142bl, 143r.
Deng Heli: 165tr.
Du Zeguan: 174.
Dyan Wenrui: 114tr.
Gao Wei: 77t.
Gao Wu: 125tl, 125tr.
He Shiyao: 137t.
Huabao: 2, 28, 49b, 59, 60, (all Renmin Huabao), 98-9, 100, 101, 103, 126-7, 133, 145, 154-5, 188-9, 199b, 201t, 207, 211.
Huang Lukui: 54.
Hutchison Library: 47t (Trevor Page), 102, 143l (Melanie Friend).
Li Dehao: 163l, 163r, 165br.
Li Desheng: 128.
Lin Xie: 20.
Lu Yaoru: 29, 37, 109r, 142t.
Piao Renzhu: 35tr, 149b, 160b, 186.
People's Pictorial by Renmin Pictorial of the Nationalities: 50-1, 68t.
Renmin Illustrated Magazine: 104bl.
Robert Harding Picture Library: 34, 39 (G&P Corrigan), 47b, 49t, 104tr, 104br (A C Waltham), 103b (G&P Corrigan), 138-9 (G&P Corrigan), 168-9 (G&P Corrigan), 170 (G&P Corrigan), 171b (G&P Corrigan).
Shen Youhui: 97t, 97b.
Shi Zerong: 119b.
Harry Smith: 57b (Horticultural Photographic Society).
Su Hualong: 81tl, 114b, 149c, 152bl, 152tl, 152tr.
The Xinjiang Book: 110, 171t, 179t.
Wang Jiuwen: 52, 130tr, 157br, 158l, 159, 172, 175, 176tr, 176br, 178b, 179br, 191b, 195, 201.
Wang Qishan: 67b.
Wang Xiangting: 77b.
Xhu Zhobin: 78.
Xia Juncheng: 176l.
Xia Xunchung: 106, 191t, 176l.
Xu Jiada: 64.
Xu Jie: 120t.
Zhao Ji: 43r, 61l, 61r, 108, 157cr, 158r.
Zhang Cizu: 1, 4-5, 21r, 21l, 31, 35br, 55, 66, 67tl, 67tr, 69t, 70, 72t, 72bl, 72br, 73, 74tl, 74cr, 75t, 75b, 76t, 79, 80b, 81tr, 81cr, 81br, 82t, 82b, 83, 84, 85, 86, 87br, 87l, 88t, 88b, 89l, 89r, 90l, 90r, 91l, 91r, 92, 93tl, 93tr, 93br, 94, 96l, 105, 107, 109l, 111, 112, 113, 114l, 114c, 115t, 115b, 116l, 116r, 117tl, 117tr, 117b, 118-9, 119t, 120b, 121, 122, 136l, 144, 147t, 147bl, 149t, 150, 153l, 153r, 162, 182, 185b, 193, 196, 197, 198l, 198r, 199t, 199b, 200, 206.
Zhang Weiwei: 27tr, 27cr, 27br.
Zhang Xiaoai: 160tl, 161, 165tl, 185t.
Zheng Guangmei: 80tl, 80tr, 87tr, 96r.

Swallow Publishing would like to thank the following for acting as consultants:

Dr Tom Cope; Graham Drucker; Rob Hume; Charles Jeffrey; Steve Renvoize; Dr Gray Wilson; John Woodward.